PROTEST AND DISSENT

NOMOS

LXII

NOMOS

Harvard University Press
I *Authority* 1958, reissued in 1982 by Greenwood Press

The Liberal Arts Press
II *Community* 1959
III *Responsibility* 1960

Atherton Press
IV *Liberty* 1962
V *The Public Interest* 1962
VI *Justice* 1963, reissued in 1974
VII *Rational Decision* 1964
VIII *Revolution* 1966
IX *Equality* 1967
X *Representation* 1968
XI *Voluntary Associations* 1969
XII *Political and Legal Obligation* 1970
XIII *Privacy* 1971

Aldine-Atherton Press
XIV *Coercion* 1972

Lieber-Atherton Press
XV *The Limits of Law* 1974
XVI *Participation in Politics* 1975

New York University Press
XVII *Human Nature in Politics* 1977
XVIII *Due Process* 1977
XIX *Anarchism* 1978
XX *Constitutionalism* 1979
XXI *Compromise in Ethics, Law, and Politics* 1979
XXII *Property* 1980
XXIII *Human Rights* 1981
XXIV *Ethics, Economics, and the Law* 1982
XXV *Liberal Democracy* 1983

XXVI *Marxism* 1983
XXVII *Criminal Justice* 1985
XXVIII *Justification* 1985
XXIX *Authority Revisited* 1987
XXX *Religion, Morality, and the Law* 1988
XXXI *Markets and Justice* 1989
XXXII *Majorities and Minorities* 1990
XXXIII *Compensatory Justice* 1991
XXXIV *Virtue* 1992
XXXV *Democratic Community* 1993
XXXVI *The Rule of Law* 1994
XXXVII *Theory and Practice* 1995
XXXVIII *Political Order* 1996
XXXIX *Ethnicity and Group Rights* 1997
XL *Integrity and Conscience* 1998
XLI *Global Justice* 1999
XLII *Designing Democratic Institutions* 2000
XLIII *Moral and Political Education* 2001
XLIV *Child, Family, and State* 2002
XLV *Secession and Self-Determination* 2003
XLVI *Political Exclusion and Domination* 2004
XLVII *Humanitarian Intervention* 2005
XLVIII *Toleration and Its Limits* 2008
XLIX *Moral Universalism and Pluralism* 2008
L *Getting to the Rule of Law* 2011
LI *Transitional Justice* 2012
LII *Evolution and Morality* 2012
LIII *Passions and Emotions* 2012
LIV *Loyalty* 2013
LV *Federalism and Subsidiarity* 2014
LVI *American Conservatism* 2016
LVII *Immigration, Emigration, and Migration* 2017
LVIII *Wealth* 2017
LIX *Compromise* 2018
LX *Privatization* 2018
LXI *Political Legitimacy* 2019
LXII *Protest and Dissent* 2020

NOMOS LXII

Yearbook of the American Society for Political and Legal Philosophy

PROTEST AND DISSENT

Edited by

Melissa Schwartzberg

NEW YORK UNIVERSITY PRESS • *New York*

NEW YORK UNIVERSITY PRESS
New York
www.nyupress.org

References to Internet websites (URLs) were accurate at the time of writing. Neither the author nor New York University Press is responsible for URLs that may have expired or changed since the manuscript was prepared.

Library of Congress Cataloging-in-Publication Data
Names: Schwartzberg, Melissa, 1975– editor.
Title: Protest and dissent / [edited by] Melissa Schwartzberg.
Description: New York : NYU Press, 2020. | Series: Nomos ; LXII |
Includes bibliographical references and index.
Identifiers: LCCN 2019012041 | ISBN 9781479810512 (cl : alk. paper)
Subjects: LCSH: Protest movements. | Social movements. | Civil disobedience. |
Democracy. | Political culture.
Classification: LCC HM883 .P758 2020 | DDC 303.48/4–dc23
LC record available at https://lccn.loc.gov/2019012041

New York University Press books are printed on acid-free paper, and their binding materials are chosen for strength and durability. We strive to use environmentally responsible suppliers and materials to the greatest extent possible in publishing our books.

Manufactured in the United States of America

10 9 8 7 6 5 4 3 2 1

Also available as an ebook

CONTENTS

Preface ix
MELISSA SCHWARTZBERG

Contributors xi

Introduction 1
MELISSA SCHWARTZBERG

PART I. JUSTIFYING CIVIL AND UNCIVIL DISOBEDIENCE

1. Uncivil Disobedience 9
CANDICE DELMAS

2. Disobedience *in Black*: On Race and Dissent 45
JULIET HOOKER

3. The Radical Possibilities of Protest 64
AMNA A. AKBAR

PART II. THE STRATEGY OF POLITICAL PROTEST

4. Competing Theories of Nonviolent Politics 83
KARUNA MANTENA

5. *No Justice, No Peace*: Uncivil Protest and the Politics of Confrontation 122
JOSÉ MEDINA

6. Protest Fatigue 161
RICHARD THOMPSON FORD

7. "No Ways Tired": An Antidote for Protest Fatigue in the Trump Era 189
Susan J. Brison

PART III. THE DEMOCRATIC SIGNIFICANCE OF PROTEST AND DISSENT

8. Defining Nonviolence as a Matter of Law and Politics 201
Tabatha Abu El-Haj

9. On the Strike and Democratic Protest 237
John Medearis

10. Are Protests Good or Bad for Democracy? 269
Susan Stokes

Index 285

PREFACE

MELISSA SCHWARTZBERG

This volume of NOMOS—the sixty-second in the series—emerged from papers and commentaries given at the annual meeting of the American Society for Political and Legal Philosophy, held in conjunction with the annual meeting of the American Political Science Association, on August 31, 2017. Our topic, "Protest and Dissent," was selected by the Society's membership.

The ASPLP conference consisted of panels organized around three principal papers and commentaries: (1) "Protest Fatigue: When Mass Demonstrations Become Routine," by Richard Thompson Ford, with commentaries from Susan J. Brison and John Medearis; (2) "In Defense of Uncivil Disobedience," by Candice Delmas, with commentaries from Juliet Hooker and Amna A. Akbar; and (3) "Competing Theories of Nonviolent Politics," Karuna Mantena, with commentaries from Tabatha Abu El-Haj and José Medina. The current volume features revised papers from all of the conference participants, as well as a paper solicited from Susan Stokes. I am grateful to all of these authors for their excellent contributions. Thanks also to Arina Cocoru and Sam Boren Reast of New York University for their valuable assistance during the editorial and production phases of this volume.

I wish to thank the editors and production team at New York University Press, particularly Ilene Kalish, Alexia Traganas, and Sonia Tsuruoka. On behalf of the ASPLP, I express our gratitude to the Press for its ongoing support both for the series and for the tradition of interdisciplinary scholarship that it represents. The ASPLP is also grateful to Brown University, Duke University, New York University, and Stanford University for subventions in support of this and future NOMOS volumes.

Finally, I thank former editor Jack Knight and the members of the ASPLP council—President Stephen Macedo, Vice Presidents

Derrick Darby and Yasmin Dawood, at-large members Michael Blake and Ekow Yankah, Immediate Past President and Secretary-Treasurer James Fleming, as well as former Vice President Michele Moody-Adams, former at-large members David Estlund and Deborah Hellman; former president Debra Satz; and former secretary-treasurer Andrew Valls —for their support and advice.

CONTRIBUTORS

Tabatha Abu El-Haj
Associate Professor of Law, Drexel University, Kline School of Law

Amna A. Akbar
Associate Professor of Law, The Ohio State University, Moritz College of Law

Susan J. Brison
Eunice and Julian Cohen Professor for the Study of Ethics and Human Values and Professor of Philosophy, Dartmouth College

Candice Delmas
Assistant Professor of Philosophy and Political Science, Northeastern University

Richard Thompson Ford
George E. Osborne Professor of Law, Stanford Law School

Juliet Hooker
Professor of Political Science, Brown University

Karuna Mantena
Professor of Political Science, Columbia University

John Medearis
Professor and Chair of Political Science, University of California, Riverside

José Medina
Walter Dill Scott Professor of Philosophy, Northwestern University

Melissa Schwartzberg
Silver Professor of Politics, New York University

Susan Stokes
Tiffany and Margaret Blake Distinguished Service Professor, University of Chicago

INTRODUCTION

MELISSA SCHWARTZBERG

In May 2016, the membership of the American Society for Political and Legal Philosophy selected the topic of "Protest and Dissent" for the 2017 conference. This selection predated Trump's election and Brexit, and the ensuing protests. It occurred before the anti-Erdogan protests in Turkey, before the Iranian economic demonstrations, before the Venezuelan "*La Madre de todas las marchas*," and before the French *gilet jaunes.* Although the selection surely reflected the salience of Occupy Wall Street and the emergence of #BlackLivesMatter, it was hard to imagine then that, by spring 2018, one in five Americans would claim to have participated in a protest or rally during the intervening two years, according to a poll conducted by the *Washington Post* and the Kaiser Family Foundation.[1]

Like all NOMOS volumes, *Protest and Dissent* brings together the work of philosophers, legal scholars, and political scientists to shed light on themes of enduring importance. Rarely, however, are the volumes quite so timely, and the chapters so unified in their sense of what questions matter, while reflecting sharp (if civil) disagreements among the authors. The core themes of the volume include the ethics of civil and uncivil disobedience, asking whether distinguishing between civil and uncivil forms of disobedience is tenable; whether we should distinguish liberal and radical forms and justifications of protest; whether the means of protest can or should be distinguished from its ends; and when we can expect protests to elicit increased engagement in democracy and when it might undermine, or substitute for, other forms of participation. The authors turn repeatedly to African American political thought—from Frederick Douglass to Martin Luther King Jr., to contemporary leaders of the Movement for Black Lives—to challenge received understandings of the Civil Rights Movement, to question the communicative potential of protest under conditions of injustice, and to defend uncivil and radical forms of dissent.

The first section of the volume analyzes the justification of uncivil forms of disobedience and the challenges posed by more radical forms of political dissent, particularly as a means of remedying racialized forms of injustice. It begins with a careful conceptual analysis by Candice Delmas in "Uncivil Disobedience," in which she examines the scope of civil and uncivil disobedience, justifying forms of uncivil disobedience and defending the value of incivility for marginalized or subordinated community members. John Rawls's now-standard account held that, to be justified, principled civil disobedience must be conscientious, nonviolent, public, and respectful; that it should call for the reform of a law or policy; and that the agent must acknowledge legal responsibility for the action. Challenging Rawls, Delmas argues that even paradigmatic cases of civil disobedience do not meet these demanding criteria. Moreover, Delmas argues that there may be good reason to reject civility and, under certain conditions, to embrace the value of constrained forms of incivility for both practical and intrinsic reasons.

In "Disobedience *in Black*: On Race and Dissent," Juliet Hooker argues that African American thinkers have often been skeptical about the value of civil protest. Whereas Delmas highlights the potential communicative and democratic benefits of uncivil disobedience, Hooker suggests that the value of communication presupposes a receptive audience, but receptivity itself may be mediated by injustice. A dominant group may fail to recognize, or seek to justify, profound injustice even when presented with straightforward evidence, as, in Hooker's example, efforts to identify the moral failings of unarmed black child victims of police violence. Indeed, Hooker argues that democratic theory in general overstates the ability of protest and dissent to induce shame or effect any moral suasion among dominant group members. Better, perhaps, to characterize black protest and dissent as beneficial and productive for black citizens themselves—enabling the expression of anger and pain—rather than as a means of communication to an only partially receptive audience. Yet uncivil expressions of disobedience may further redound to the harm of marginalized groups, who may not merely receive further incivility in turn, but whose uncivil behavior may be met with disproportionate and violent responses.

Amna A. Akbar turns to the specific case of the Movement for Black Lives in her chapter, "The Radical Possibilities of Protest," to identify the distinctive value of radical protest movements, which she argues the categorization of disobedience into civil and uncivil forms fails to capture. That is, efforts to limn the boundaries of permissible lawbreaking mischaracterize the radically emancipatory visions of radical racial-justice movements. Akbar challenges Delmas's insistence that uncivil disobedience must reflect respect for people's interests in a stable, secure system of rights, because such rights may reify a status quo that reflects inequalities of resources, in particular racialized inequalities. Moreover, she argues that abolitionist movements, which call for an end to prisons, policing, and criminalization, seek to transform the wider legal structure of a liberal order, rather than to reform individual norms through principled resistance.

The second section of the volume focuses on the strategy of protest: the means, nonviolent or otherwise, by which protests may be most effective in attaining their ends, and the relationship between means and ends in political contestation more broadly. The section begins with Karuna Mantena's chapter, "Competing Theories of Nonviolent Politics," which challenges a sharp dichotomy between *strategic* and *principled* nonviolence. Principled nonviolence, associated with pacifism and with leaders such as Gandhi and King, is typically defined as an ethical practice, whereas strategic nonviolence, associated most centrally with the war resister Gene Sharp, focuses on developing a repertoire of techniques. On a distinctive understanding of the dynamics of political mobilization and protest, Mantena reconceptualizes nonviolence by distinguishing instead between *collective power* and *disciplined action*, each of which constitutes a strategic theory of nonviolent politics. Nonviolence in the form of collective power undermines existing channels of popular consent and establishes and displays new forms of social power through organized mass assembly. Challenging standard accounts of Gandhi and King, Mantena emphasizes that their defense of disciplined action—eschewing coercive displays of collective power—itself constituted a strategy, one that relied on performative practices of self-restraint and self-discipline. The function of discipline, especially in the form of conscious suffering, is to mitigate passions that would exacerbate political conflict: Discipline is a more effective strategy for nonviolent protest, one more likely to persuade opponents, than other forms of mass demonstration.

In "*No Justice, No Peace*: Uncivil Protest and the Politics of Confrontation," José Medina rejects the veneration of the strategic value of purity and disciplined actions, defending a confrontational account of protest. Medina takes the basic strategic question to be: What are the most effective means available to us to resist injustice? The range of responses to that question lie on a continuum between civil and uncivil forms of protest that overlap with a second continuum, between nonviolent and violent forms. Although physical violence must be a last resort, justifiable only to stop or reduce already existing violence, other forms of coercion—psychological, emotional, symbolic—may be required in activist practices. Disciplined protest, avoiding confrontational direct action, may itself become complicit in injustice: Defiant, antagonizing tactics—as in the die-ins of ACT UP activists in the face of the AIDS crisis—may be crucial to halt structural violence.

Richard Thompson Ford's chapter, "Protest Fatigue," argues that the overuse of protest threatens to undermine the efficacy of mass demonstrations when warranted. Paradigmatic protests such as the March on Washington or the Montgomery Bus Boycott, he argues, are politically legitimate, aiming at just causes and warranted, because other formal or informal channels of advocacy were unavailable; effective; and self-sacrificial. In contrast, many contemporary protesters evince "Selma envy," attracted to the experience of social protest. Their protests are primarily self-regarding, preaching to the choir or providing their participants with psychological gratification. They may also serve as an additional means for powerful agents to secure benefits. To address most issues, other forms of dissent—social media campaigns, consumer activism, humorous counter-protest—will be more effective and will enable us to save the use of mass demonstrations for when they are crucially needed.

In a reply to Ford, "'No Ways Tired': An Antidote for Protest Fatigue in the Trump Era," Susan J. Brison argues that Ford wrongly denigrates the experiential value of protest. Valuable protests dignify participants, who may themselves be marginalized; energize those who might otherwise be fatigued by their effacement; make visible invisible injustices; and unify protesters through performance, including singing and dancing.

The third section of the volume addresses the democratic significance of protest: its constitutional history, its most vibrant forms, and its political consequences more generally. In "Defining Nonviolence as a Matter of Law and Politics," Tabatha Abu El-Haj emphasizes the centrality of disruptive protest to American politics since the Founding. Contemporary protests—from Occupy, to Black Lives Matter, to Standing Rock, to the Women's March—have been intentionally disruptive, and in so doing, have joined a distinguished American tradition of "peaceable" assembly. In response to these tactics, state legislatures recently have sought to enhance criminal penalties for blocking traffic and for engaging "economic terrorism" such as obstructing pipelines, and to require disciplinary action against members of university communities who engage in "boisterous" or "loud" conduct, interfering with the free speech of others. Against Richard Ford, Abu El-Haj argues that public protest itself constitutes a form of the normal political process, enshrined by the First Amendment, not an alternative to such procedures. Responding to Karuna Mantena, she worries that to valorize Gandhi's or King's conceptions of nonviolence may contribute, if unintentionally, to political efforts to render certain forms of protest tactics unlawful.

John Medearis defends the distinctive value of the right to strike as an exemplary form of political protest in "On the Strike and Democratic Protest." He argues that the power of the strike consists in *collective action*: not merely the activity of ceasing labor, but in the wider mobilization on which strikes depend, and in the strike's ability to form individual workers into a collective to negotiate with employers. Like Hooker, Brison, Mantena, and other contributors, Medearis emphasizes the value for resisters—here, striking workers—in helping them to achieve consciousness of their own agency: in this context, the centrality of their contribution to their workplaces' enterprise. The strike enables workers to replace the hierarchies of the workplace with horizontal egalitarian ties, as a means of resisting economic domination and achieving a form of collective management of the terms of their labor. Similarly, a democratic protest constitutes a form of *work*: It demands mobilization and constitutes an activity in which ordinary people may come to recognize their capacities. Strikes, as well as other forms of political protests, are not mere means to certain ends, whether in the workplace or in democratic life more generally: In deploying their skills and agency, workers come to recognize their efficacy, their capacity to choose and revise their ends.

In the final chapter, "Are Protests Good or Bad for Democracy?," Susan Stokes examines protest from a comparative perspective, turning to cases from Argentina, the Ukraine, and Turkey, among others, to provide a nuanced account of the benefits and risks of protests, especially in fragile democracies. She argues that protest may enhance democracy by enabling the inclusion of the voices of those excluded from voting and by informing voters and officeholders about especially salient questions. Protests may also destabilize democracy in a variety of ways: Protestors may seek repugnant aims, provoke undemocratic sentiments through what Ford termed "protest fatigue," elicit the types of legislative action described by Abu El-Haj or violent reactions on the part of police, and undermine elections and other key democratic institutions.

As Stokes and other contributors argue, despite the costs of protest, the survival of democracy requires that leaders resist the temptation to suppress mass protests, or to seek to undermine the free press and rights of assembly and dissent. But whether our leaders will find themselves capable of such restraint in the face of persistent resistance, in the United States or elsewhere, is far from clear.

NOTE

1 *Washington Post*/Kaiser Family Foundation Survey on Political Rallygoing and Activism (conducted January 24–February 22, 2018).

PART I

JUSTIFYING CIVIL AND UNCIVIL DISOBEDIENCE

1

UNCIVIL DISOBEDIENCE

CANDICE DELMAS

The suffragettes smashed the windows of London's shopping district, vandalized the Royal Botanic Gardens, cut telephone and telegraph wires, and burned post boxes all over the UK in demand of the franchise.

In the midst of the Arab Spring, "Operation Tunisia" saw the hacktivist collective Anonymous conduct a series of distributed-denial-of-service (DDoS) actions against the Tunisian government's websites in solidarity with pro-democracy activists.

Wearing sleeveless dresses and colorful balaclavas and stockings, members of the Russian feminist band Pussy Riot stormed Moscow's Christ the Savior Cathedral and staged a "Punk Prayer" that called for President Vladimir Putin's removal.

Members of the Sanctuary movement provide unauthorized migrants with food, shelter, and legal aid throughout Europe and North America, and sometimes help them cross borders.

Animal Liberation Front (ALF) activists break into labs, farm factories, and kill shelters to rescue the animals held in these facilities.

Edward Snowden stole 1.7 million classified documents, leaking 200,000 of those to journalists to blow the whistle on the National Security Agency (NSA)'s massive domestic and international surveillance program.

Thousands of protesters poured into the streets of South-Central Los Angeles after a jury acquitted the police officers charged with beating Rodney King. Arsons, lootings, and assaults occurred over the next several days.

The actors involved in these seven vignettes—the suffragettes, Anonymous, Pussy Riot, Sanctuary workers, ALF activists, Snowden, and LA protesters—broke the law on the basis of moral or political principles, determined to take a stand in response to what they perceived as injustice or wrongdoing. Their disobedience took otherwise very different forms, occurred in different societal contexts, and pursued different goals. Actors were seen by officials as "insane," "traitors," "thugs," and even "terrorists."[1] But one thing they have in common—and which motivates my reflection in this chapter—is that their sympathizers have described them as instances of civil disobedience.[2]

There are obvious reasons why those wishing to establish the bona fides of acts of disobedience like those just described call them civil. The label serves to highlight the agent's principled motivations and communicative intentions; to make a disruptive breach of law intelligible as an address to the community; to situate the act in a venerable historical tradition, populated by the likes of Rosa Parks and Martin Luther King Jr.—and thus, given these positive connotations, to begin the work of its justification. Nevertheless, it is easy for opponents to deny that the label applies to activities that are, say, covert, violent, or offensive, since civil disobedience is commonly understood to be public, nonviolent, and respectful, among other essential traits. Opponents usually take it for granted that unlawful resistant activities that fail to satisfy the defining criteria of civil disobedience cannot be morally justified in near-just, legitimate societies (of which ours is one, in their view).

In response, sympathizers adopt one of two strategies. They either operate with the standard understanding of civil disobedience but try to downplay the inconvenient feature in question; or they use a different, broader concept, according to which said feature is not a sine qua non of civil disobedience. Either way, the debates tend to get stuck at the level of definition and classification. Instead I propose to concede—even embrace—the uncivil nature of these activities and defend their potential justification.

On the one hand, I share sympathizers' urge to make room for acts of principled disobedience like the ones above; and I, too, want to articulate an approach that is (a) sympathetic, to wit, open to the justification of the principled breach of law they consider;

and (b) politically useful—able to contribute positively to the public discourse (as sympathizers' two main approaches to civil disobedience purport to be). But I propose to add a third desideratum of accounts of principled disobedience, which sympathizers tend to neglect: (c) phenomenological accuracy, or the capacity to reflect at least to some extent practitioners' own views of their activities.

On the other hand, I agree with opponents that the activities above were not civil; and I think that the most promising route to a sympathetic, politically useful, and phenomenologically accurate account of the activities found in the seven vignettes involves granting their incivility and focusing on their distinct potential justification. What we need is an account of *uncivil disobedience.* It is an important first step toward the justification of types of uncivil disobedience, that is, of particular cross-sections of the dimensions of incivility we'll identify.

The chapter proceeds as follows. The first section explains the problems with the two main approaches to civil disobedience and sketches a basic conceptual account of uncivil disobedience. The rest of the chapter seeks to defend the permissibility of at least some forms of uncivil disobedience even in supposedly legitimate, liberal democratic states like ours: the second section argues that uncivil disobedience can do much of what civil disobedience does, while the third section argues that uncivil disobedience can do and say valuable things that civil disobedience cannot do or say.

Conceptual Issues

Standard Account of Civil Disobedience

Following John Rawls's influential account, civil disobedience is commonly understood as a conscientious, nonviolent, public, respectful breach of law intended to protest and call for the reform of a law or policy, and for which the agent takes full legal responsibility.[3] An act of principled disobedience that fails to be civil in these ways cannot be justified in a near-just society. Some of the theorists and pundits who described Anonymous's DDoS actions, Snowden's leaks, and the suffragettes' destruction of property as instances of civil disobedience did so using this common understanding of civil disobedience. Sympathizers of Snowden, and Snowden himself, even invited the comparison of his whistleblowing with the civil disobedience campaigns organized by Martin Luther King Jr.—the paragon of civil disobedience in the United States. While potentially sympathetic and useful, this approach hasn't been terribly successful, for an obvious reason: the suffragettes, Anonymous, and Snowden clearly violated the defining criteria of civil disobedience just mentioned, since they resorted to violence, sought to conceal their identity, pursued more radical or different goals than reform, and/or evaded arrest and punishment, among other issues.

Consequently, the standard account doesn't align with acts of principled disobedience like the ones above. This is not surprising, since it doesn't align well with its own paradigms, either. Civil rights campaigns such as the Good Friday march in Birmingham (which violated a court order), lunch counter sit-ins, and Freedom Rides shaped the standard account and appeared to satisfy many of Rawls's demanding criteria. They appealed to constitutional principles of political morality and pursued modest goals of reform, not revolution. Activists thoroughly trained in and committed to nonviolence disobeyed the law publicly, often giving authorities advance notice of their plans. They responded to state and mob violence peacefully and willingly submitted to arrest and jail for their lawbreaking.

So why did the Rawlsian account nonetheless fail to adequately describe them? Rawls understood publicity to require that agents give authorities fair notice of their planned disobedient activity, act in public, and appeal to the community's shared conception of justice. He took nonviolence to exclude the use of force and coercion and the direct infliction of harm against persons. (Other theorists explicitly prohibit property destruction.) But Rawls also insisted that agents of civil disobedience, unlike rebels and revolutionaries, accept, and even seek out, the legal consequences of their actions, because doing so would demonstrate their general "fidelity to law"—their endorsement of the system's legitimacy and belief that the state generates a moral duty to obey the law.

As David Lyons has persuasively argued, the standard account wrongly—that is, implausibly and objectionably—ascribed these attitudes and beliefs to civil disobedients whose choices in fact were primarily strategic.[4] King denied that the United States of Jim

Crow deserved respect and called for the complete eradication of the caste system, which he deemed "unjust" and "evil."[5] His famous insistence, in the Letter from a Birmingham City Jail, that civil disobedience expresses the "highest respect for law," has been widely misunderstood. It appears in the context of his discussion of natural law's tenet that "an unjust law is no law at all" and can only be properly understood to enjoin respect for just law, as opposed to deference to any law at all by virtue of its being a law. King also conceived of submission to arrest and punishment in symbolic terms, as a "powerful and just weapon," as in the "Fill the Jails" campaign, and as a matter of prudence, given that civil rights activists were outnumbered and outgunned.[6]

In short, the Civil Rights Movement adopted its particular style of civil disobedience for largely context-dependent, tactical purposes. Yet theorists and pundits turned these tactics into deep moral commitments on the part of agents supposedly eager to demonstrate their endorsement of the state's legitimacy and placed these subjective requirements at the core of their defense of real-world civil disobedience. Theorists' defense of civil disobedience thus contributed to and reinforced an official, idealized narrative of the Civil Rights Movement that largely misrepresents the history of the black freedom struggle post–World War II. Its focus on the nonviolent Civil Rights Movement came at the expense of ignoring other, more radical groups, such as the Black Panther Party, the Deacons for Defense and Justice, black feminist and Marxist groups, with the effect of only recognizing state-legitimizing, nonviolent movements. At stake is not just historical accuracy: The standard conception of civil disobedience continues to be called on as a benchmark by which to assess other disobedient movements. A deeply conservative history of the black freedom struggle is thus intertwined with a theory of civil disobedience that demands respect for authority and deters resistance.[7]

To sum up, it's easy to deny that acts of principled disobedience satisfy the criteria of civil disobedience. Indeed, as I suggested, paradigmatic cases of civil disobedience themselves violate those, making the standard account less than useful. As a result, and despite the intentions of some of its champions, the account doesn't serve well protesters' cause; instead it holds them to narrow and demanding standards that they rarely ever meet.

Inclusive Accounts of Civil Disobedience

Dissatisfied with the standard Rawlsian account, theorists have put forth "inclusive" approaches that broaden the concept of civil disobedience to encompass all sorts of principled lawbreaking. Kimberley Brownlee offers one such account. She problematizes the conceptual distinctions standardly drawn between civil disobedience and other types of dissent, noting that civil disobedients may intend a revolution and that conscientious objectors often seek broad reform and not simply personal exemption. For Brownlee, civil disobedience "must include a deliberate breach of law taken on the basis of steadfast personal commitment in order to communicate our condemnation of a law or policy to a relevantly placed audience."[8] This kind of civil disobedience need not be public or nonviolent. What sets it apart from ordinary crime, radical protests, and private conscientious objection (or "personal disobedience" in her terminology) are its constrained, communicative, and non-evasive properties, which mark the agent's efforts to engage an intended public in dialog (non-evasiveness, for Brownlee, marks a willingness to explain oneself). Thus, Brownlee conceives of the suffragist militant tactics as civil disobedience and she has argued that Snowden's actions were civilly disobedient on her account but not on the standard one.[9]

Robin Celikates, who spearheads the radical democratic approach, has also been a vocal critic of the Rawlsian liberal account of civil disobedience. He challenges the narrowness and ideological underpinnings of the criteria of publicity, nonviolence, willingness to accept punishment, appeal to shared principles of justice, and even conscientiousness.[10] Celikates understands civil disobedience as an intentionally unlawful and principled collective act of protest (in contrast to both legal protest and "ordinary" criminal offenses or "unmotivated" rioting), with which citizens—in the broad sense that goes beyond those recognized as citizens by a particular state—pursue the political aim of changing specific laws, policies, or institutions (in contrast to conscientious objection, which is protected in some states as a fundamental right and does not seek such change) in ways that can be seen as civil (as opposed to military).[11]

This broad conception imposes no requirement on the agent's attitude toward the system, her target, or the principles she appeals to. The civilly disobedient act need not be done publicly. Celikates also questions and ultimately rejects the nonviolence proviso, on the grounds that it reduces civil disobedience to "a purely moral appeal, which sets all hopes on a responsive political system or public sphere," and thereby ignores the "moment of real confrontation" it seeks—and, to be effective, *needs*—to create.[12]

Both Celikates's and Brownlee's inclusive conceptions maintain Rawls's core insight that civil disobedience is essentially a communicative act aimed at political change but leave much else up for grabs. Neither endorses the standardly accepted norms of civility—publicity, nonviolence, non-evasion (or non-avoidance of legal sanctions), and decorum. Both include in the category of civil disobedience controversial acts of resistance performed by suffragists, sanctuary workers, and others.

Brownlee argues in *Conscience and Conviction: The Case for Civil Disobedience* that while liberal societies provide extensive legal protections to conscientious objectors, civil disobedients, who wish to communicate their convictions to their fellow citizens, have stronger claims to these than conscientious objectors, who deem their beliefs a private matter. She also defends a moral right to civil disobedience, which grounds a (defeasible) claim-right against legal sanction. Celikates, meanwhile, offers a radical democratic understanding of disobedience as a dynamic contribution to political processes, contra what he sees as the "overly constrained, domesticated and sanitized" understanding of civil disobedience offered by mainstream liberal accounts.[13] In these ways, Celikates's and Brownlee's accounts of civil disobedience cast a much broader net than the standard account and are sympathetic and useful to emancipatory movements. Other theorists like Howard Zinn and Tony Milligan have offered similarly permissive, inclusive accounts of civil disobedience.[14]

However, first, Brownlee and Celikates stretch the concept of civil disobedience beyond recognition, encompassing in it some features previously deemed to be incompatible with it. For instance, sabotage and violence can be civilly disobedient in Brownlee's view.[15] And Celikates dubs Anonymous civilly disobedient despite the fact that the group members conceal their identity, use coerced botnets to launch distributed-denial-of-service (DDoS) attacks, and admit being motivated by a zeal for pranks—thus exhibiting features that are usually seen as "other" to, or even "opposites" of, civil disobedience.[16] Lumping violence, coercion, covertness (anonymity), evasion, and offensiveness together with their opposites diminishes the account's potential political usefulness, in my view. But even if it were possible and easy to change the public understanding of civil disobedience, I believe it wouldn't be desirable to broaden it so much, insofar as acts of principled disobedience that satisfy the standard norms of civility, and those that don't, exemplify distinct phenomena.

This leads us to the second, more serious problem with inclusive accounts: they miss the point of many disobedient actions, which is to *refuse* to follow the standard script of civil disobedience—partly in reaction to the standard account's counter-resistance strand identified earlier. Emmeline Pankhurst defended suffragists' use of "militant methods" (including heckling, window-smashing, sabotage, and hunger strikes) and characterized herself as a "soldier" in a "civil war" waged against the state. Ukrainian-French radical feminist collective Femen brands its disobedience as radical and provocative, not civil, by calling its tactics—which include "sex attacks, sex diversions and sex sabotage"—*sextremism.*[17] Cultural critic Mark Dery conceives of "culture jammers"—such as billboard bandits, hacktivists, and media hoaxers—as "artistic terrorists" and "communication guerrilla" fighters.[18] And Black Lives Matter hints at the rupture between its self-understanding and the standard account of civil disobedience with the slogan "Not Your Grandfather's Civil Rights Movement." In short, agents may see themselves, and seek to be perceived, as radical and provocative rather than civil.

The next section examines some reasons to reject civility, including the potential efficacy and even necessity of incivility and the fact that some groups may not be in a position to abide by the strictures of civility. Prisoners, for instance, are barred from effective communicative action and cannot take part in civil disobedience even if they wish to. And some activists may explicitly reject civility in order to expose the falseness of the presumption of equal standing embedded within the standard conception of civil disobedience.

As things stand, we are not equipped to analyze and justify these departures from the template of civil disobedience: the public understanding of civil disobedience excludes uncivil disobedience from the realm of justifiable disobedient protest; and inclusive accounts erase the distinctiveness of uncivil means by encompassing them within civil disobedience.

Principled Disobedience

Instead, we should expand our repertoire of potentially acceptable modes of principled disobedience beyond civil disobedience, readily granting the incivility of certain disobedient acts and opening ourselves to the possibility that some types of uncivil disobedience can be justified.

Principled disobedience—which includes civil and uncivil disobedience—is one subset of unlawful resistance.[19] "Resistance" designates a broad range of dissident activities, of varying scope and impact, which express opposition, and perhaps refusal to conform, to a dominant system of values, norms, rules, and practices. Resistors in general and principled disobedients in particular may address private or public actors, at home or abroad. They may seek modest reform or a complete overhaul of a system, or neither (e.g., they may simply wish to express grief or solidarity), and their actions may be communicative or not. ALF activists who rescue animals, for instance, aim to do just that in their rescue operations, independently of their public advocacy work to end animal abuse. The principles that motivate resistors may or may not be worthy of public recognition; and uncivil disobedience undertaken in pursuit of morally abhorrent causes cannot be justified.

Civil disobedience, as one subset of principled disobedience, designates deliberate breach of law intended to protest and amend unjust laws, policies, institutions, or practices and that satisfy the basic norms of civility: publicity (the agent's performance of the act in the open), nonviolence (which rules out the use of force and direct infliction of harm), non-evasion (submission to law enforcement and acceptance of legal sanctions), and decorum (respectful behavior). Accounts of civil disobedience like Rawls's make publicity, nonviolence, and non-evasion necessary to the disobedient act's communicativeness—its nature as a speech-act—and civility. But there is more to it.

For one, civil disobedients themselves sometimes highlight the self-discipline, love, and respect necessarily displayed by their lawbreaking—beyond the criteria of publicity, nonviolence, and non-evasion. Mahatma Gandhi described civil disobedience as "gentle, truthful, humble, knowing, willful yet loving, never criminal and hateful."[20] King likewise contrasted the loving disobedience of his followers with segregationists' hateful defiance of the law.[21]

In addition, some critics of contemporary protest movements also hint at another important mark of civility. Though public, non-evasive, and nonviolent, Pussy Riot's "Punk Prayer" was denied the label of civil disobedience because, detractors argued, it desecrated a religious place and defiled the state. Members of the group were convicted of "premeditated hooliganism," which is defined as "the flagrant violation of public order expressed by a clear disrespect for society." Today, some veterans of the Civil Rights Movement worry that Black Lives Matter activists lack the self-discipline and respectable appearance that are necessary to distinguish their disobedience from that of criminals.[22] Gandhi, King, and these critics of BLM and Pussy Riot point us to a fourth norm of civility, which I included above: decorum, which demands behaving in a dignified, courteous manner and treating one's audience respectfully, as people one seeks to persuade.[23]

While I favor readily granting the incivility of acts denied the label of civility, I do not mean to suggest that any novel act of principled disobedience that does not closely resemble our preconceived notions of civil disobedience is necessarily uncivil or that any denial of civility should always be taken at face value. San Francisco 49ers' quarterback Colin Kaepernick's silent protest in 2016, as he sat during the national anthem to protest racial oppression, provoked widespread outrage. Kaepernick was condemned as a "traitor," disrespectful to the flag.[24] But his protest, and the take-a-knee campaign that followed the next year, had been lawful and respectful.[25] Construing it as a breach of civility seems exaggerated and disingenuous. Those in power often unjustly wield accusations of incivility to silence and stigmatize protesters—especially when these are black.[26]

The definition of civil disobedience as a public, nonviolent, nonevasive, respectful principled breach of law intended to persuade the majority captures well the public's rather narrow understanding of the boundaries of acceptable political protest. It constitutes a pared-down version of the standard Rawlsian account, as it keeps the marks of civility and communicative nature of the action but does not include any subjective requirements such as the agent's endorsement of the state's legitimacy or belief that the state generates a moral duty to obey the law (although civil disobedience may well be perceived as communicating these). Conscientious objection, which is usually distinguished from civil disobedience, may count as civil or uncivil disobedience on my view, depending on its characteristics; it may also fall in the category of lawful resistance if it is legally protected.

The other subset of principled disobedience—uncivil disobedience—designates a principled breach of law in response to perceived wrongs (injustice or wrongdoing) and that fails to satisfy the basic norms of civility by being either: covert/anonymous, evasive, violent, or offensive/disrespectful. Uncivil disobedience should not be conceived as a distinct kind or a single, neat category. It is rather a cluster concept, for whose application we might treat displays of any one of the four features—covertness, evasion, violence, and offensiveness—as sufficient.

The category of uncivil disobedience is thus much broader than that of civil disobedience, since it includes acts in pursuit of any of a variety of goals (e.g., status quo, reform, system overhaul, education, aid, harm prevention, retaliation, expression of discontent etc.). The activities described at the outset of this chapter, as well as coercive and violent strikes, guerrilla street art, ecosabotage, black bloc tactics, and vigilantism, are aptly described as uncivil disobedience. At the edge of uncivil disobedience lie terrorism and guerrilla warfare (whose scale of violence and revolutionary goals render inadequate the more limited lens of principled disobedience) and acts of unlawful resistance that are not primarily principled but can be interpretively construed as (thinly) principled, such as digital piracy and unauthorized immigration.[27]

Many acts of uncivil disobedience are impermissible because they pursue illegitimate ends and undermine people's fundamental interests in the process. The types of uncivil disobedience I am interested in defending are constrained in various ways: resistors must act with respect for other people's interests, including their basic interests in life and bodily integrity, their interests in choosing the values that shape their lives, and their interest in a stable, secure system of rights. These basic human interests constrain both the legitimate goals of resistance and the appropriate means to achieve one's goals; and one must accept and seek to protect them when engaging in principled disobedience. So, the defense of uncivil disobedience I outline below is both partial and general. It sketches several rationales that can be put forth in favor of certain types of uncivil disobedience. But it does not provide the necessary and sufficient conditions for the justification of particular acts of uncivil disobedience within each type. It offers instead a sort of kaleidoscopic picture of the ethics of uncivil disobedience.

In Defense of (Un)civil Disobedience

Disobedience—even principled and civil—is generally conceived as wrongful for at least four reasons. First, disobedients violate the moral duty to obey the law, which binds citizens in legitimate states; second, like vigilantes or free riders, disobedients wrongfully take the law into their own hands; third, disobedience undermines law and order and thereby destabilizes society; fourth, disobedients flout democratic processes. Champions of civil disobedience have responded to each objection successfully: today, few deny that civil disobedience can be justified and has a role to play in liberal democracy. But their justifications apply beyond the boundaries of civility and point to arguments which can support some types of uncivil disobedience. I'll try to show, in short, that uncivil disobedience can be justified on the same grounds that commonly support civil disobedience.

The Duty to Obey the Law

Many philosophers believe that people have a moral duty to obey the law *because it is the law*, which disobedience, principled or not, violates. While they disagree about what grounds this duty, they agree as to its shape: it binds everyone within the jurisdiction and applies to all laws, independently of their merit. According to this first argument, it is essential that citizens recognize this duty, especially in pluralist societies, where people disagree about matters of justice (otherwise they might destabilize society, erode the rule of law, and threaten democracy, as we'll see next). Whereas Socrates in Plato's *Crito* believed this duty to be absolute even in the face of injustice, philosophers now agree that the duty to obey the law does not arise or can be defeated where injustice is severe and persistent. This makes room for civil disobedience in societies that successfully generate the duty to obey the law, and full-fledged rebellion where the state wholly fails to generate this duty by exercising arbitrary and tyrannical power, as per John Locke's social contract theory.[28] So: Civil disobedience can sometimes be justified even in otherwise legitimate states.

But this is not all: Some theorists further argue that civil disobedience is compatible with the moral duty to obey. For instance, David Lefkowitz has articulated a disjunctive account of political obligation according to which citizens of legitimate liberal democracies have a moral duty either to obey the law or to disobey it civilly.[29] The moral right to civil disobedience embedded in this account rests on citizens' basic right to political participation.

Importantly, in some cases, citizens might better respond to the normative principles that support the duty to obey the law by engaging in principled disobedience, civil or uncivil, rather than by complying with the law. Or so I argue in my book, *A Duty to Resist: When Disobedience Should Be Uncivil.*[30] I contend that we should expand the concept of political obligation to include duties to resist injustice and disobey the law, even in liberal democracies like ours; and I defend these duties on the basis of four of the grounds commonly used to support the moral duty to obey the law, namely, the duty of justice, the principle of fairness, the Samaritan duty, and political membership. To take just one example, the Samaritan duty, used by Christopher Wellman to ground the duty to obey the law, can ground duties to disobey the law covertly where assisting undocumented migrants is legally prohibited. The result of the book is by no means the wholesale justification of uncivil disobedience but instead a patchwork of arguments defending different kinds of constrained uncivil disobedience in pursuit of goals that align with the grounds of political obligation considered.

Free Riding

A second objection to disobedience is that it is a form of moral self-indulgence akin to free riding: Disobedients accord themselves a larger say in public matters, objectionably taking the law into their own hands and making themselves an exception to prevailing rules.[31] They claim, in effect, to better understand what the public good requires than do their fellow citizens, whose compliance with the law they exploit. Their apparent disregard for laws may seem like an assertion of moral superiority, a way to say, "I know better than everyone else what is right and wrong." Asserting such privilege amounts to a wrongful kind of exploitation, an impermissible form of vigilantism, and, at its core, a failure to treat others as equals.[32]

Civil disobedience has been adequately defended against the claims above: The agent does not profit from her lawbreaking and indeed bears significant burdens and risks, including social sanctions, arrest, and punishment. King describes the planning of the Birmingham desegregation campaign:

> We had no alternative except to prepare for direct action, whereby we would present our very bodies as a means of laying our case before the conscience of the local and the national community. Mindful of the difficulties involved, we decided to undertake a process of self-purification. We began a series of workshops on nonviolence, and we repeatedly asked ourselves: "Are you able to accept blows without retaliating?" "Are you able to endure the ordeal of jail?"[33]

And, indeed, they accepted blows without retaliating and endured the ordeal of jail. It seems incongruous if not disingenuous to describe civil disobedients as free riders, given their sacrifices and conscientiousness.

The same can be said about some uncivil disobedients, including some who evade law enforcement and punishment such as

Sanctuary workers and government whistle-blowers, given the sacrifices and risks involved in their activities. In fact, under unjust sociopolitical conditions, citizens' compliance with the law, not disobedience, is akin to free riding (I argue in my book that citizens' willful compliance with a system of laws that wrongfully benefits them while exploiting others involves the same deontic wrongs that free riding does and is thus prohibited by fairness).[34]

The objection that principled disobedience involves making oneself an exception or free riding on others' compliance and thereby failing to treat others as equals further falters when applied to a range of disobedient actions undertaken by, in solidarity with, or on behalf of those whom the polity wrongly treats as less than equals. Agents often resort to disobedience because they, or those with whom they stand in solidarity, or on whose behalf they act, are marginalized and excluded, deprived of a say in the decisions that affect them. Disobedience—civil or uncivil—intended to protest this inferior treatment cannot reasonably be thought of as violating mutual reciprocity.

However, a range of uncivil disobedience does resemble or actually consist in vigilantism. Anonymous and the Minuteman Project (a collective of armed vigilante groups that patrol the US border) are aptly described as vigilantes; and elsewhere I have conceived of government whistle-blowing as a kind of "political vigilantism," which involves transgressing the boundaries around state secrets to contest the allocation or use of the executive power to determine secrecy.[35] Government whistle-blowers unilaterally and irreversibly undo state secrets, imposing serious national security risks in the process. In contrast, civil disobedients protest laws without being able to change them: They only ever offer a "plea for reconsideration," in Peter Singer's words.[36] Government whistle-blowers' disclosure may nonetheless be justified, and it can only be justified according to different standards than those that apply to civil disobedience.[37]

The Rule of Law

Another objection is that any disobedience—be it criminal or principled; civil or uncivil—sows anarchy and invites violence. If one violates the law each time one thinks it is unjust, one destabilizes society, undermines law and order, erodes the rule of law, and prevents the legal system from performing its essential function of protecting rights. States cannot tolerate such exercise of discretionary judgment on the part of individuals without risking falling in a state-of-nature-like condition.[38] This general objection can take at least two slightly different forms: a law-and-order concern, according to which political stability requires universal compliance with the law and is effectively undermined by disobedience, and a rule-of-law concern that views disobedience as an impermissible and dangerous expression of contempt for the legitimacy of the legal order.

Some champions of civil disobedience have questioned both concerns. Howard Zinn, for instance, stressed that the stability of oppressive legal orders is a bad thing, that the latter don't deserve any respect, and that mass civil disobedience to unjust law (contra the worry with proliferation) is a valuable tool to help close the gap between legality and justice.[39] However, many theorists take both law-and-order and rule-of-law concerns seriously. Rawls addressed the first one in his account of the justificatory conditions of civil disobedience, which purport to minimize the disruptive effects of civil disobedience by requiring that the act (i) target a serious violation of the first principle of justice ("the principle of equal basic liberties" in Rawls's theory), (ii) be undertaken as a last resort, and (iii) be coordinated with other groups with similar grievances. For Rawls, then, agents must carefully weigh their resort to (even civil) disobedience, choosing it reluctantly, as it were, and taking great precaution to defuse its destabilizing potential and avoid its proliferation.

Particular accounts of the conditions necessary to justify specific types of uncivil disobedience can likewise heed the law-and-order concern in some ways. For instance, my own justificatory account of government whistle-blowing requires unauthorized leaks to be undertaken as a last resort (counting previous employees' attempts to blow the whistle internally) and with due care so as to minimize the harms that could result from the disclosure.[40]

In response to the rule-of-law concern in particular, republican and liberal theorists have argued that, far from undermining the stable system of rights, civil disobedience can instead strengthen it. For Hannah Arendt, mass civil disobedience always occurs under unstable political circumstances and ultimately stabilizes society by reenacting the horizontal social contract and strengthening civic bonds (she articulated her argument in 1970 in response to American student activism).[41] Ronald Dworkin conceived of pro-civil rights and anti-Vietnam War civil disobedients as engaged in constitutional disputes over the law and contributing in that way to law's integrity.[42] And following Rawls, William Scheuerman argues that, far from undermining the rule of law, civil disobedience buttresses it. In his view, fidelity to the law—the paradigmatic feature of civil disobedience—pushes actors not only to denounce government's lapses but also to prefigure a legitimate legal order.[43] Beyond the particulars of these arguments, the potential of civil disobedience to protect rather than undermine the rule of law is now widely accepted in the literature and (to a lesser extent) in public discourse.

What about uncivil disobedience, though? Can it also exemplify respect for the rule of law and serve to bolster law's integrity? I believe some of it can. Government whistle-blowing, again, is one type of uncivil (covert and often evasive) principled disobedience that purports to preserve the rule of law. Among the plausible candidates for unauthorized whistle-blowing that strengthened the rule of law are: Daniel Ellsberg's leaks of the Pentagon Papers, which uncovered the state's commission of war crimes in Vietnam, Cambodia, and Laos, as well as deception at home; Deep Throat's leaks about the Watergate scandal, which resulted in punishment for White House officials' lawbreaking; and Snowden's whistle-blowing on the NSA's massive, unconstitutional domestic and international surveillance program.

Leaks of this nature, which expose serious wrongdoing and abuses, promote the rule of law. While many people describe instances of government whistle-blowing they approve of as civil disobedience, in part because of their common potential to support the rule of law, it is important not to confuse the two, as I just explained in response to the free riding and vigilantism objection.

Democracy

A fourth objection to disobedience is that it erodes democratic authority. By flouting democratic lawmaking processes, and refusing to comply with their outcomes, disobedients make themselves enemies of democratic ideals and undermine the conditions for democratic concord in pluralist societies.

Liberal philosophers such as Rawls generally concede this objection: They view civil disobedience as essentially antidemocratic but highlight its potential to enhance justice, against flawed democratic majoritarian decisions. But, these theorists stress, by disobeying civilly, the agent communicates that she is neither disobeying lightly nor taking advantage of others' compliance with the law.

Republican and democratic theorists have articulated their alternative accounts of disobedience largely in response to this objection concerning democracy. They have shown that, far from threatening democracy, much civil disobedience purports to invigorate democratic institutions, for instance by combatting the rigidifying tendencies of state institutions and highlighting democratic deficits.[44] These theorists often use alter-globalization, anti-nuclear, and Occupy activism to illustrate this potential of civil disobedience. They make two important points. First, civil disobedients often protest precisely a lack of democracy, such as their exclusion from collective decision-making processes, and thus promote democratic causes. Second, civil disobedience should be conceived as an exercise in political participation to which citizens are morally entitled, not as an extra-institutional form of action that is only appropriate when normal political processes fail.[45]

The first point about the democratic potential of civil disobedience clearly extends to uncivil disobedience. A look at historical and current practices of resistance indeed suggests that agents may choose uncivil forms of disobedience to the same democratic effects that theorists attribute to civil disobedience. The suffragists escalated from words to deeds—first lawful attempts, then civil and uncivil disobedience—to demand the democratic franchise. Some of their uncivil acts, such as storming legislative assemblies and electoral precincts, or going on hunger strikes while in prison, were clearly intended to assert political agency and protest exclusion. More recently, hacktivists have used digital disobedient tactics—mostly uncivil—to protest the illegitimacy of online governance and invite fellow citizens to understand, care about, and participate in the effort to democratize the Internet. Some guerrilla communication tactics such as those of ACT UP (the AIDS

Coalition to Unleash Power), which included spectacular flash mobs, storming, and heckling, may also be framed as uncivil protests against government apathy and indifference to the fate of the LGBT population amidst the AIDS crisis (basically a democratic failure of equal concern). In short, there may be uncivil pursuits of democratic inclusiveness, agenda-setting, and other measures to improve democratic legitimacy.

Does the second point about citizens' moral entitlement to civil disobedience also extend to uncivil disobedience? Not quite. Champions of the right to civil disobedience insist that civil disobedients have a presumptive claim-right against punishment, even if they act in pursuit of an illiberal or morally abhorrent cause such as white nationalism. The moral right to civil disobedience is thus understood as a right to do wrong, which protects unjustified civil disobedience, too. There can be no moral right to violent and harmful uncivil disobedience (even if some of it is justified). However, a case could be made that the right to political participation protects some communicative and nonviolent acts of uncivil disobedience, whether they are justified or not, such as guerrilla protests, hunger strikes, labor strikes, and assembly storming. Other types of (constrained) uncivil disobedience may also be found presumptively permissible, on different bases than political participation rights. For instance, humanitarian assistance could protect Sanctuary work; and the public good can justify some "civic" acts of uncivil disobedience that are undertaken in pursuit of government accountability (e.g., leaks and "cop-watching," which I'll discuss shortly).[46]

To recap, none of the four objections—from the duty to obey, free riding, the rule of law, and democracy—set a viable moral prohibition against principled disobedience. Meanwhile, the arguments offered in response by champions of civil disobedience can be extended to justify some uncivil types of principled lawbreaking. However, one will object that I could only extend the arguments in favor of the former to the latter at the cost of ignoring the moral significance of civility. Even if uncivil disobedience can do what civil disobedience does, one will insist that the latter is always to be preferred. I deny this in the next section, where I respond to arguments for preferring civil over uncivil disobedience and identify some valuable uses of incivility.

THE USES OF (IN)CIVILITY

There are (at least) three main arguments for preferring civil over uncivil disobedience: (a) an empirical argument stressing the superior effectiveness of nonviolent civil resistance; (b) a forward-looking argument according to which the means should prefigure the ends; and (c) an argument based on the need to preserve the ties of civic friendship in pluralist liberal societies marked by reasonable disagreements. Here again, my strategy will be to upend these arguments, showing in the process that uncivil disobedience can serve to do and say valuable things that civil disobedience cannot do or say.

Effectiveness

It is almost an article of faith that incivility is counterproductive. This is especially clear in the demand for nonviolence in resistance movements. Some empirical evidence from the social sciences supports this point. Analyzing 323 twentieth-century violent and nonviolent civil resistance campaigns, Erica Chenoweth and Maria Stephan find that nonviolent campaigns that have reached a significant size are twice as likely to succeed as violent campaigns. While many violent decolonization movements were successful in the 1970s and 1980s, the success of violent resistance campaigns has since declined. For their part, nonviolent campaigns have become increasingly successful since the 1950s, and especially since the end of the Cold War.[47]

While this statistical argument for nonviolence holds across sociopolitical contexts, political scientists argue that violence is especially counterproductive in liberal and democratic societies, and some believe that the violent edges of civil disobedience campaigns undermine their efforts.[48] For this reason, Chenoweth has recently warned the anti-Trump resistance movement, which she supports, not to resort to uncivil means, including black bloc tactics, "Nazi punching," street fighting, and rioting, which risk turning off the public.[49]

These are important findings. But note that the argument only applies to violent acts of uncivil disobedience. Nonviolent yet uncivil acts of principled disobedience—such as leaks, which proliferate in Trump's White House, and guerrilla communication—are not singled out as problematic and may be useful to civil protests. In addition, not all principled disobedience is communicative, and that which is nonviolent and covert, such as illegal assistance to unauthorized migrants, is unlikely to be detected by the public. Even if it were, Chenoweth and Stephan's analysis does not give any reason to believe that it would have on the broader pro-immigrant movement the negative effects supposedly associated with failures of civility. So, the empirical argument for the superior effectiveness of nonviolent resistance and civil disobedience in the context of large movements does not suffice to establish uncivil disobedience's ineffectiveness or counterproductivity.

Uncivil disobedience may in fact be effective for other purposes. Indeed, effectiveness should not be measured solely in terms of contribution to a campaign's success. Other important goals of principled disobedience include, but are not limited to, aid (e.g., to victims of war), protection (viz. self-defense, defense of others, or environmental protection), rescue (e.g., of captive animals), halting ongoing wrongs (such as war crimes), and communication without intent to persuade (e.g., expression of solidarity or distrust). Civility in the form of publicity, non-evasion, nonviolence, and decorum could significantly hinder the realization of some of these goals.

For instance, covertness is key to members of the Sanctuary movement who have created an "underground railroad" to move immigrants from dangerous areas to safer ones and help them get to Canada.[50] Civil, that is public and open, disobedience would doom the enterprise to failure and further put in jeopardy the immigration prospects of those it purports to help. It is therefore not to be preferred, at least not for the purpose of directly helping unauthorized migrants (though of course it may be for other purposes).

Or again, consider the Deacons for Defense and Justice, which formed under Jim Crow as an armed group to protect members of the Congress for Racial Equality (CORE) from Ku Klux Klan (KKK) violence (they soon extended their activities to civil rights work such as organizing and voter registration). Self-defensive force against immediate threats to one's life is lawful, but the Deacons made a point of publicly displaying their force, sometimes in violation of local gun laws.[51] Similarly, the Black Panthers (originally called the Black Panther Party for Self-Defense) publicly carried loaded firearms, first legally then illegally after the 1967 Mulford Act, which was crafted in response to Black Panthers' armed patrolling of Oakland, California.[52] These groups' uncivil threats of violence were essential to their mission—collective self-defense against white supremacist violence. They could of course have registered their grievances through lawful and civil ways (and did, also), calling for better protection of their communities and denouncing systematic police brutality. But doing so did not in itself amount to armed collective self-defense. The latter required the threat or use of force.

The efficacy of incivility, of course, is not sufficient to justify its use by disobedients: One must also show that they pursue worthy ends through proportionate means. Context, ends, and means must be taken into account to draw the line between, say, the vigilantism of the Deacons for Defense and that of the KKK, or between the Sanctuary movement and the anti-abortion Christian terrorist group Army of God. The KKK deployed efficacious but disproportionate and excessive violence in pursuit of morally horrendous ends. The Deacons resorted to violence in a context where authorities failed to protect (and directly violated) the basic rights of African Americans and where dissidents risked their lives, even when they were contesting the established order through lawful channels. The Deacons' violence was proportionate as they only ever harmed those who sought to harm them. The Sanctuary movement conducts covert, nonviolent activities to assist migrants, without threatening others' interests. And though liberal societies tolerate "pro-life" activism, Army of God clearly deployed disproportionate and excessive violence, committing bombing attacks, acts of kidnapping, attempted murder, and murder.[53]

Champions of civil disobedience recognize that violence and incivility are generally permissible and may even be necessary in unjust states. But as I tried to show here, uncivil disobedience may sometimes (*often*) be preferred to civil disobedience, depending on the goals pursued, even in states widely deemed nearly just and legitimate.

Forward-Looking Concerns

Another pragmatic rationale for preferring civil over uncivil disobedience points to the socially beneficial consequences of civil disobedience as compared with uncivil disobedience. It comes in two versions, which are both grounded in forward-looking concerns, and boil down to the notion that resistors should choose courses of action that enact and foster the just society they aspire to.

One version of this pragmatic argument is encapsulated in the principle "the means should prefigure the end." According to this principle, which is generally attributed to some political anarchists, the values guiding resistance in liberation struggles should be those animating the ideal world. The "should" here is pragmatic or prudential: One simply cannot achieve a just, egalitarian society free from oppression and state violence through a movement that is hierarchically organized and that uses violence to dominate others. In the words of James Guillaume, a friend and collaborator of Mikhail Bakunin, "How could one want an equalitarian and free society to issue from an authoritarian organization? It is impossible."[54] From this perspective, prefiguration is a necessary condition for liberation movements' success (at least where ideals of justice, freedom, and equality are concerned). More basically, a struggle whose participants routinely violate its expressed ideals falls prey to charges of inconsistency and hypocrisy, which are likely to diminish public support and to affect the movement's legitimacy. This prefiguration argument can thus support the superiority of civil over uncivil disobedience, presuming that one seeks a civil future characterized by democratic concord.

On the other version of the pragmatic argument, even if the ruling group's mistreatment of a subordinated group warrants revolutionary activity, and even if revolution could succeed (contrary to the prefiguration argument), there are still good forward-looking reasons for resistors to exercise restraint and disobey civilly. Andrew Sabl develops this argument for civil disobedience in the context of the "piecewise-just society," which involves "fair treatment, mutual cooperation, and a sense of justice by a ruling group with respect to its own members, simultaneous with a cruel and near-absolute tyranny towards people outside its own membership."[55] Powerful members of society, by dominating and brutalizing other groups in society, may well have made themselves liable to violent resistance. But the fact that they have shown themselves capable of governing on fair terms of cooperation within their own group offers reasons (a) to believe in their capacity "to extend this habit to their relations to other groups," and thus (b) to disobey civilly, in a way that treats current oppressors as future equals.[56] According to Sabl, "a regard for future possibilities," especially "the desire not to foreclose future cooperation," underpinned King's Civil Rights Movement, for instance.[57] In short, civil disobedience offers the best (perhaps the only) chance of fostering the prospects for post-struggle democratic concord, by displaying equal concern for all and a commitment to fair cooperation in the struggle. I address this second point in the next section, where I argue that sometimes powerful members have shown themselves capable of governing fairly among equals, but not willing to extend this capacity beyond their own group.

In response to the prefiguration argument for civil disobedience, it is not clear that activists disposed to use some uncivil, including violent, methods in the struggle for emancipation are thereby exhibiting inconsistency or betraying their ends. For instance, did female suffragists who burned golf course turfs with acid and engaged in other acts of sabotage and destruction reveal their unfitness to cooperate with men in the gender-just society they envisioned? Opponents thought so, calling the suffragists "unladylike" and "unnatural" and committing some of them involuntarily to insane asylums. These opponents claimed that women's uncivil disobedience was a living refutation of their feminist ideal of gender equality. Yet nothing supported these judgments. Uncivil disobedience neither necessarily reflects problematic ideals and goals nor necessarily thwarts the possibility for future cooperation with fellow citizens.

Some theorists have put the prefiguration argument on its head, arguing that the means ought to reflect not their ends but their beginnings. Frantz Fanon thus defended (without valorizing it, as Lewis Gordon insists[58]) the necessary role that violence had to play in decolonization struggles, in response to the brutal violence systematically visited upon native subjects to maintain colonial oppression. Fanon's defense rests on two grounds: a pragmatic argument, according to which politics (in the form of negotiations with the colonizers and/or the work of nationalist parties) would not end but might instead facilitate the persistence of colonial violence; and an existentialist argument, according to which the natives would only reach subjecthood (agency) when they "refuse to occupy the position of violence-absorbing passive victim," as Tracey Nicholls puts it.[59] Insurrectional violence is thus a matter of eradicating colonial violence.

In response, objectors usually point to Gandhi's nonviolent decolonization struggle against the British Raj. Yet inferring from Gandhi's success in India the adequacy of a categorical prohibition of violence in anti-oppression movements the world over is naïve and dangerous. Hannah Arendt astutely observed that "If Gandhi's enormously powerful and successful strategy of nonviolent resistance had met with a different enemy—Stalin's Russia, Hitler's Germany, even pre-war Japan, instead of England—the outcome would not have been decolonization but massacre and submission."[60] Arendt's anti-absolutist point about violence is limited to extreme cases. But activists and critics have denounced the categorical prohibition of violence in emancipatory struggles in the United States, too.

Angela Davis problematized this demand in a 1972 interview, describing "the violence that exists on the surface everywhere" for blacks, which she experienced first-hand in Los Angeles: being eyed with suspicion, constantly stopped and frisked by police, treated as criminals or agitators. She goes on:

> And then you ask me whether I approve of violence . . . That just doesn't make any sense at all. Whether I approve of guns? I grew up in Birmingham, Alabama. Some very, very good friends of mine were killed by bombs—bombs that were planted by racists. From the time I was very small I remember the sound of bombs exploding across the street, our house shaking. I remember my father having to have guns at his disposal at all times because of the fact that at any moment we might expect to be attacked. The man who was at that time in complete control of the city government—his name was Bull Connor—would often get on the radio and make statements like "Niggers have moved into a White neighborhood. We'd better expect some bloodshed tonight!" And sure enough there would be bloodshed.[61]

Davis's answer suggests that those who absolutely oppose violence tend to do so in a vacuum, viewing it as aggressive instead of defensive, and in ways that obfuscate the regime of terror that blacks lived under.

So the point is not to justify any and all kinds of violence, but at a minimum, to challenge its universal condemnation. To the extent that displays of force and the use of self-defensive violence may be effective to protect the oppressed from the brutal violence visited upon them, there is no reason to reject these from a forward-looking standpoint. They may further be critical to expose the regime of state-sanctioned violence that agents seek to replace with just, democratic institutions. The Black Panthers practiced and invited "cop-watching" in response to police brutality (though the watching was lawful, members were arrested and charged with assault on police officers whenever they intervened)—a tactic still advocated today by some local chapters of Black Lives Matter (e.g., Sacramento) and the People's Justice for Community Control and Police Accountability, among others.[62] Incivility as violence and incivility as vigilant distrust may thus be critical steps on the path to a more just society.

(In)civility and Civic Friendship

A final argument for civil disobedience and against uncivil disobedience in societies like ours is that civility is a moral duty. Citizens of liberal democracies have a special duty to comport themselves in ways that nurture and preserve civic bonds. Aristotle talked about "civic friendship" to describe citizens' bonds in just polities, their concern for each other's flourishing (they "wish their fellow citizens well"), and their shared values and sense of justice.[63] The modern, liberal version of civic friendship is thinner but still important: It consists in citizens' common endorsement of mutual reciprocity—their willingness to live together despite their differences.[64]

Lawbreaking, on this view, dissolves the ties of civic friendship. But as we saw earlier, champions of civil disobedience have persuasively shown that, by acting civilly, disobedients still demonstrate their commitment to mutual reciprocity. The civility of civil disobedience thus defuses its tendency to erode civic bonds and destabilize society. Theorists carved a special niche for civil disobedience as the only form of unlawful resistance compatible with the demands of life in a liberal democracy.[65] But they insist that no such place can exist for uncivil disobedience, which seriously threatens civic friendship.

One might respond by examining types of uncivil disobedience that are unlikely to undermine civic friendship, such as government whistle-blowing (which, I noted, is problematic in other ways). But let us grant that some types of communicative uncivil disobedience—urban uprisings, coercive strikes, roadblocks, black bloc tactics, DDoS, guerrilla street art, and sex attacks, for example—are in fact likely to undermine civic friendship.

My contention is that this may be a virtue rather than a problem: In some circumstances, uncivil disobedience may appropriately highlight—and, yes, undermine—all-too-flimsy or illusory ties of civic friendship. It can do so better than civil disobedience ever could. Examining why further enables us to identify the potential intrinsic (non-instrumental) value of incivility, as an expression of warranted distrust.[66]

There is a place for civic friendship-threatening uncivil disobedience in liberal democratic societies when the following conditions apply: The public is assured of the state's commitment to respecting everyone's full and equal status, a commitment typically embedded in a constitution or other basic law that guides institutional design and lawmaking; some citizens are effectively (de facto and possibly also de jure) denied full and equal status; and the injustice of this denial is not publicly recognized, perhaps because that injustice is not deliberate but results from the interplay of social practices and institutional structures, as in cases of structural injustice, or because it simply doesn't seem like an injustice at all (think of felon disenfranchisement or immigration enforcement). Under these circumstances, the majority may be bound by civic friendship, but for oppressed minorities, it is an illusion.

In this case, the oppressed minority might fruitfully resort to civil disobedience, and no doubt observers will counsel that doing so provides the best chance of winning over the majority, based on the forward-looking concerns previously articulated. But uncivil disobedience might be even more apt to radically disrupt the status quo and grip the public's attention. Where civil disobedients typically seek to coax and persuade, uncivil disobedients can shock and shame—they can force the community to confront the disconnect between its reality and its professed ideals and cast doubt on the authenticity of its commitment to civic friendship.

Importantly, by disobeying uncivilly rather than civilly, agents refuse to play by the strictures of civility. The latter presuppose an equal standing among all members of the polity that is missing, and whose absence they seek to highlight. They question the rules of public engagement and their exclusionary effects: Who gets to speak, where, when, and how. Their incivility helps to isolate the deceptions of civic friendship. It calls civility's bluff. ACT UP, Femen, and Black Lives Matter, among other groups, model this powerfully as they denounce through sensational, often uncivil, acts the supposed near-absence of anti-gay prejudice, sexism, and racism in liberal democracies. They contest and disrupt the moral and political consensus.

This kind of uncivil disruption can advance justice and democracy. But it may also set back activists' cause by reducing popular support. However, the potential value of this kind of uncivil disobedience does not hinge on its ability to garner public support, nor even on its potential to shock and shame the community. Indeed, the public may not be moved by, or may miss entirely, the "message" of certain acts of uncivil disobedience. Americans' reaction to the riots that erupted in Ferguson, Baltimore, Charlotte, and Milwaukee in the aftermath of fatal instances of police brutality against blacks, typifies this problem: The issue is not that uncivil protests repel the public, thereby causing civic friendship to further dissolve, but rather that the community is morally and epistemically deaf to unruly dissent, in a way that itself signals the lie of civic friendship. We could say, a bit dramatically, that civic friendship is dead long before rioters come to bury it.

Even where there is neither hope of moral suasion nor chance of inducing shame, then, uncivil disobedience may still have intrinsic value as an expression of warranted frustration and distrust. These latter attitudes are especially worth communicating to fellow oppressed, further enabling expressions of in-group solidarity. Finally, the expressions of disrespect and anger that are characteristic of urban uprisings, for instance, may be seen as assertions of agency and dignity in the face of threats to both.

Certain kinds of uncivil disobedience are thus non-instrumentally, intrinsically valuable—as warranted judgments about society's failures, as expressions of solidarity, and as affirmations of agency, to the extent that they threaten a concord that wrongly excludes some people. The harms inflicted in the course of the uncivil activity or its negative impact on the movement's overall goals may well outweigh this value; but it ought to register in the assessment of uncivil disobedience.

In conclusion, agents engaged in uncivil disobedience are sometimes doing the right thing. What does this defense imply for how the state should treat them? Some scholars argue that the government has a responsibility to engage in dialog with civil disobedients and accommodate their activities insofar as possible.[67] Others have defended, minimally, the government's responsibility of leniency in prosecution and sentencing.[68] Their arguments could extend to some (and only some) types of uncivil disobedience, in ways I will not attempt to develop here. At the very least, liberal democratic societies must provide all principled disobedients with the opportunity to defend their actions in trial. The rationales for civil and uncivil disobedience identified in this chapter could ground legal defenses on the basis of the public interest, democratic inclusion, necessity, collective self-defense, dignity, and more. Today, principled disobedients rarely have the opportunity to defend their actions. Should Snowden return to the United States to face justice for his leaks of classified information, for instance, the terms of the Espionage Act would bar him from attempting to justify his actions. Even where agents have this opportunity, the chances of succeeding are slim given that the injustice agents were responding to in the first place probably infects the courtroom, too. Still, it seems important for liberal states to listen to principled disobedients, at least when their actions brought about minimal harms, and however unpopular the cause they pursue.

Fyodor Dostoyevsky said that one can judge a society by how well it treats its prisoners. I venture that a society's treatment of its civil and uncivil disobedients would be a good yardstick, too. According to the standard dichotomy between liberal and illiberal societies, the latter arrest, jail, beat, torture, and even murder dissidents, while the former welcomes and protects dissent. In reality, few societies are liberal when it comes to *unlawful* dissent, including civil and uncivil disobedience: they choose condemnation, retribution, and deterrence, not dialog or leniency. For now, the costs of legal noncompliance remain high in supposedly liberal democracies, and extremely high everywhere else.

Acknowledgments

I began this chapter while visiting the New York University School of Law's Center for Law and Philosophy as a Dworkin-Balzan Fellow in 2016–2017. Versions of this chapter were presented at the University of Richmond's Political Philosophy Learning Community, the New York University School of Law Global Fellows Forum, the American Society for Political and Legal Philosophy Conference at the American Political Science Association (APSA) meeting, the Northeastern University Faculty Work-in-Progress Series, Boston University's Ethics Seminar, the Workshop in Social & Political Philosophy at Fordham University, the Safra Center at Harvard University, the McMaster University Philosophy Department Speaker Series, the University of New Hampshire Philosophy Department, the Union College Philosophy Speakers Series, and the International Conference on Injustice and Resistance (held at the London School of Economics and jointly organized by LSE and Georgia State University). I thank the organizers, participants, and audiences at these events for engaging discussions and useful suggestions. I am especially grateful to Guy Aitchison, Amna Akbar, Emanuela Ceva, Chiara Cordelli, Jeff Flynn, Alex Gourevitch, Samir Haddad, Javier Hidalgo, Juliet Hooker, Rob Jubb, Jeff Lenowitz, David Lyons, Liam Murphy, Avia Pasternak, Melissa Schwartzberg, and Daniel Viehoff.

Notes

1 The suffragettes were deemed "insane," LA protesters mere "thugs," Snowden a spy or "traitor," and the FBI considers Anonymous and ALF activists "terrorist threats."

2 See, e.g., Linda Ford, "Alice Paul and the Politics of Nonviolent Protest," in *Votes for Women: The Struggle for Suffrage Revisited*, edited by Jean H. Baker (New York: Oxford University Press, 2002), 176; Tom Watson, "Why #PussyRiot Is the Future of Civil Disobedience (and Not Just in Pu-

tin's Russia)," *Forbes.com* (August 17, 2012); Peter Ludlow, "Hacktivists on Trial," *The Nation* (December 4, 2013); Molly Sauter, *The Coming Swarm: DDOS Actions, Hacktivism, and Civil Disobedience on the Internet* (London: Bloomsbury Academic, 2014); William Scheuerman, "Whistleblowing as Civil Disobedience: The Case of Edward Snowden," *Philosophy and Social Criticism* 40, 7 (2014): 609–628; Tony Milligan, *Civil Disobedience: Protest, Justification and the Law* (New York and London: Bloomsbury Press, 2013), ch. 11–12 (on animal rescue); Barbara B. LaBossiere, "When the Law Is Not One's Own: A Case for Violent Civil Disobedience," *Public Affairs Quarterly* 19, 4 (2005): 317–330 (on the 1992 LA riots).

3 John Rawls, *A Theory of Justice* (Cambridge, MA: Harvard University Press), 320. I examine in detail the requirement to accept legal sanctions in Candice Delmas, "Civil Disobedience, Injustice, and Punishment," in *Palgrave Handbook on Applied Ethics and the Criminal Law*, edited by Kimberley Ferzan and Larry Alexander (Palgrave, forthcoming).

4 David Lyons, "Moral Judgment, Historical Reality, and Civil Disobedience," *Philosophy and Public Affairs* 27, 1 (1998): 31–49.

5 Martin Luther King Jr., *A Testament of Hope: The Essential Writings and Speeches*, edited by James M. Washington (New York: HarperCollins, 2003), 47, 360, 429.

6 King, *Testament of Hope*, 348. See also Erin Pineda, "Civil Disobedience and Punishment: (Mis)reading Justification and Strategy from SNCC to Snowden," *History of the Present: A Journal of Critical History* 5, 1 (2015): 1–30.

7 See Candice Delmas, *A Duty to Resist: When Disobedience Should Be Uncivil* (New York: Oxford University Press, 2018), ch. 1.

8 Kimberley Brownlee, *Conscience and Conviction: The Case for Civil Disobedience* (Oxford: Oxford University Press, 2012), ch. 1.

9 Kimberley Brownlee, "Civil Disobedience," in *The Stanford Encyclopedia of Philosophy*, edited by Edward N. Zalta (Fall 2017 edition), https://plato.stanford.edu; "The Civil Disobedience of Edward Snowden: A Reply to William Scheuerman," *Philosophy and Social Criticism* 42, 10 (2016): 965–970.

10 Robin Celikates, "Civil Disobedience as Practice of Civic Freedom," in *On Global Citizenship James Tully in Dialogue*, edited by David Owen (London: Bloomsbury Press, 2014), 207–228.

11 Robin Celikates, "Democratizing Civil Disobedience," *Philosophy and Social Criticism* 42, 10 (2016): 982–994, 985.

12 See Robin Celikates, "Rethinking Civil Disobedience as a Practice of Contestation—Beyond the Liberal Paradigm," *Constellations* 23, 1 (2016): 37–45, 41–42; "La désobéissance civile: entre nonviolence et violence," *Rue Descartes* 77, 1 (2013): 35–51.

13 Brownlee, *Conscience and Conviction*; Celikates, "Democratizing Disobedience."

14 Howard Zinn, *Disobedience and Democracy: Nine Fallacies on Law and Order* (New York: Vintage Books, [1968] 2002); Milligan, *Civil Disobedience*. But Tony Milligan also examines some movements that refuse to describe their methods as "civil disobedience" because of their deliberate departure from the standard conception.

15 Brownlee, *Conscience and Conviction*, 20.

16 Robin Celikates and Daniel De Zeeuw, "Botnet Politics, Algorithmic Resistance and Hacking Society," *Hacking Habitat* (Rotterdam: nai010, 2016): 209–217, 213. I examine some other arguments for conceiving of DDoS actions and related hacktivist acts as electronic civil disobedience in Candice Delmas, "Is Hacktivism the New Civil Disobedience?" *Raisons Politiques* 69, 1 (2018): 63–81.

17 Femen, "About Us," Femen blog: http://femen.org.

18 Mark Dery, "Culture Jamming: Hacking, Slashing and Sniping in the Empire of Signs," *Open Magazine Pamphlet Series* (Unknown, 1993).

19 Unlawful resistance includes other subsets, such as, on one end of the spectrum, terrorism (though some terrorist activities may fall in the category of uncivil disobedience), armed guerrilla warfare, and revolution, and, on the other end, some types of unlawful activities undertaken by agents who don't necessarily see themselves as engaged in resistance (among other types of unlawful resistance). For instance, Tommie Shelby conceives of welfare fraud and drug trafficking as permissible resistance under unjust conditions, in chapters 6 and 7, respectively, of *Dark Ghettos: Injustice, Dissent, and Reform* (Cambridge, MA: Harvard University Press, 2016).

20 Mahatma Gandhi, *The Essential Gandhi: An Anthology of His Writings on His Life, Work, and Ideas*, edited by Louis Fischer (New York: Vintage, 2002), 148.

21 King, *Testament of Hope*, 294.

22 See, e.g., Barbara Reynolds, "I Was a Civil Rights Activist in the 1960s. But It's Hard for Me to Get Behind Black Lives Matter," *Washington Post* (August 24, 2015), www.washingtonpost.com.

23 For King and especially for Gandhi, civil disobedience involves more than decorum and the other marks of civility, given its connections to truth, love, and self-rule. See, e.g., Tony Milligan, "Civility and Politicized Love in Gandhi," *Religions of South Asia* 8, 3 (2014): 285–300; Alexander Livingston, "Fidelity to Truth: Gandhi and the Genealogy of Civil Disobedience," *Political Theory* 46, 4 (2018): 511–536.

24 See, e.g., "Colin Kaepernick Branded a 'Traitor' by NFL Executives over Anthem Protest," *The Guardian* (August 31, 2016), www.theguardian.com.

25 In May 2018, the National Football League approved a new policy that mandates players on the field to either stand during the national anthem or remain in the locker room, thus making take-a-knee protests clearly against the rules. The policy states, "the Commissioner will impose discipline on league personnel who do not stand and show respect for the flag and the Anthem." See *Statement from NFL Commissioner Roger Goodell*, https://nflcommunications.com.

26 See, e.g., Bernard Harcourt, "The Politics of Incivility," *Arizona Law Review* 54, 2 (2012): 345–373.

27 See, e.g., Luis Cabrera, *The Practice of Global Citizenship* (Cambridge, UK: Cambridge University Press, 2010) on illegal border crossing as global civil disobedience; and Michael Strangelove, *The Empire of Mind: Digital Piracy and the Anti-Capitalist Movement* (Toronto: University of Toronto Press, 2005). Some types of economic crimes could also fall in that category. See also note 19.

28 John Locke, *Second Treatise of Government*, edited by Jonathan Bennett (2017 [1690]), ch. 19.

29 David Lefkowitz, "On a Moral Right to Civil Disobedience," *Ethics* 117, 2 (2007): 202–233.

30 Delmas, *A Duty to Resist*, ch. 3–6.

31 Carl Cohen presents and rebuts these objections in: Carl Cohen, *Civil Disobedience: Conscience, Tactics, and the Law* (New York: Columbia University Press, 1971), 138–145. See also Daniel Weinstock, "How Democratic Is Civil Disobedience?" *Criminal Law and Philosophy* 10, 4 (2016): 707–720.

32 Jonny Thakkar has recently offered another way of putting it, centered on character and relying on Aaron James's conception of the asshole, as someone who "allows himself to enjoy special advantages in social relations out of an entrenched sense of entitlement that immunizes him against the complaints of other people." See Aaron James, *Assholes: A Theory* (New York: Random House, 2012). Thakkar suggests that disobedients like King "run the risk of not only being perceived as, but actually being, self-aggrandizing arseholes." The "self-aggrandizing" asshole in particular is someone who invokes moral causes in order to enhance his own power. The opposite of the asshole is the fully cooperative person who recognizes others as equals and treats them respectfully. See Jonny Thakkar, "On Being an Arsehole: A Defense," *The Point* 16 (2018), https://thepointmag.com.

33 King, *A Testament of Hope*, 291.

34 Delmas, *A Duty to Resist*, ch. 4.

35 Candice Delmas, "The Ethics of Government Whistleblowing," *Social Theory and Practice* 41, 1 (2015): 77–105.

36 Peter Singer, *Democracy and Disobedience* (Oxford: Clarendon Press, 1973), 84.

37 In my view, government whistle-blowing can be justified when (1) agents seek to expose serious government wrongdoing or programs and policies that ought to be known and deliberated about; (2) they undertake lawful, internal attempts to alert the public; and (3) they take serious precautions in the disclosure so as to minimize the harms that could potentially ensue, including by carefully choosing the leaks' recipients and editing the information disclosed. See "The Ethics of Government Whistleblowing," 94–105.

38 See Jeremy Waldron, *The Dignity of Legislation* (Cambridge, UK: Cambridge University Press, 1999), 59ff.

39 Zinn, *Disobedience and Democracy.*

40 See explanation in note 37.

41 Hannah Arendt, "Reflections on Civil Disobedience," *The New Yorker* (September 12, 1970): 70–105.

42 Ronald Dworkin, "A Theory of Civil Disobedience," in *Ethics and Social Justice*, edited by Howard Evans Kiefer and Milton Karl Munitz (Albany: State University of New York Press, 1970), 225–239.

43 William E. Scheuerman, *Civil Disobedience* (Cambridge, UK and Malden, MA: Polity Press, 2018).

44 See Daniel Markovits, "Democratic Disobedience," *Yale Law Journal* 114 (2005): 1897–1952; Celikates, "Civil Disobedience as Practice of Civic Freedom"; William Smith, *Civil Disobedience and Deliberative Democracy* (Abingdon: Routledge, 2013), ch. 3.

45 See Lefkowitz, "On a Moral Right to Civil Disobedience"; Brownlee, *Conscience and Conviction*, ch. 4; Smith, *Civil Disobedience and Deliberative Democracy*, ch. 4.

46 This is an admittedly very sketchy argument, the full elaboration of which I leave for another time.

47 Erica Chenoweth and Maria Stephan, *Why Civil Resistance Works: The Strategic Logic of Nonviolent Conflict* (New York: Columbia University Press, 2011).

48 See, e.g., Omar Wasow, "Do Protests Matter? Evidence from the 1960s Black Insurgency" (unpublished manuscript, February 2, 2017), www.omarwasow.com (arguing that proximity to black-led violent protests in the United States likely tipped the 1968 presidential election from Hubert Humphrey, the Democratic candidate, to Richard Nixon); Eline de Rooij, Mark Pickup, and Matthew J. Goodwin, "Threat, Prejudice and the Impact of the Riots in England," *Social Science Research* 51 (October 2014), DOI: 10.1016/j.ssresearch.2014.09.003 (finding that the 2011 riots in England increased individuals' perception of threats

to society's security and culture and their prejudice toward black British and East European minorities). Research on the detrimental and/or beneficial effects of radical flanks on nonviolent protest movements has so far been inconclusive. See Elizabeth Tompkins, "A Quantitative Reevaluation of Radical Flank Effects within Nonviolent Campaigns," *Research in Social Movements, Conflicts and Change* 38 (2015): 103–135 (finding that radical flanks increase both the likelihood and degree of repression by the state and are most significantly linked with decreased mobilization post-repression, without being necessarily detrimental to overall campaign progress).

49 Erica Chenoweth, "Violence Will Only Hurt the Trump Resistance," *New Republic* (February 7, 2017); Erica Chenoweth and Kurt Shock, "Do Contemporaneous Armed Challenges Affect the Outcomes of Mass Nonviolent Campaigns?" *Mobilization: An International Quarterly* 2, 4 (2015): 427–451.

50 See Jake Halpern, "The Underground Railroad for Refugees," *The New Yorker*, March 13, 2017, www.newyorker.com.

51 See Lance Hill, *The Deacons for Defense: Armed Resistance and the Civil Rights Movement* (Chapel Hill: University of North Carolina Press, 2004).

52 See Adam Winkler, Gunfight: The Battle over the Right to Bear Arms in America (New York: Norton, 2011).

53 See Jennifer Jefferis, *Armed for Life: The Army of God and Anti-Abortion Terror in the United States* (Santa Barbara, CA: ABC-CLIO, 2011).

54 Quoted in K. J. Kenafick's 1950 "Foreword" to Mikhail Bakunin, *Marxism, Freedom, and The State* (London: Kessinger Publishing, 2010 [1950]), 4.

55 Sabl conceives of the piecewise-just society as the best way to understand Rawls's "nearly just" society. Andrew Sabl, "Looking Forward to Justice: Rawlsian Civil Disobedience and its Non-Rawlsian Lessons," *Journal of Political Philosophy* 9, 3 (2001): 307–330, 311.

56 Ibid., 310.

57 Ibid. Sabl talks about American blacks in general, not the narrower subset of King's Civil Rights Movement. I changed this in my reconstruction of his argument, since many black activists in fact favored revolution.

58 Lewis R. Gordon, *What Fanon Said* (New York: Fordham University Press, 2015), ch. 4.

59 Tracey Nicholls, "Frantz Fanon," *Internet Encyclopedia of Philosophy*, www.iep.utm.edu.

60 Hannah Arendt, *Crises of the Republic* (New York: Harcourt Brace, 1972), 152.

61 Interview featured in *The Black Power Mixtape 1967–1975*, DVD, directed by Göran Olsson (Sweden: Louverture Films, 2011).

62 See Nashelly Chavez, "Volunteers May Soon Film Cops on Sacramento Streets. Will It Curb Use of Force?" *Sacramento Bee* (March 17, 2018), www.sacbee.com; Cop Watch Alliance, http://peoplesjustice.org.

63 Aristotle, *Nicomachean Ethics*, trans. Terrence Irwin (Hackett, 1999), Book IX.

64 Rawls, *Theory of Justice*, 5; and *Political Liberalism* (New York: Columbia University Press, 1993), xlix and 253.

65 Conscientious objection might be viewed as another form, but, as I mentioned earlier, to the extent that it is to be not simply tolerated but also legally protected in liberal societies, it should not count as unlawful resistance.

66 This last section greatly benefited from Amna A. Akbar's and Juliet Hooker's responses to my paper, which they gave at the annual APSA meeting's American Society for Political and Legal Philosophy 2017 Conference in San Francisco.

67 See Lefkowitz, "On a Moral Right to Civil Disobedience"; Brownlee, *Conscience and Conviction*, ch. 4; Smith, *Civil Disobedience and Deliberative Democracy*, ch. 4.

68 See, e.g., Ronald Dworkin, "On Not Prosecuting Civil Disobedience," *New York Review of Books* (June 6, 1968).

2

DISOBEDIENCE *IN BLACK*

ON RACE AND DISSENT

JULIET HOOKER

In the Trump era, civility is very much a topic of debate. For those who see the US presidency of Donald Trump as a dangerous exacerbation of authoritarianism, sexism, racism, xenophobia, homophobia, etc., the question of how to resist is a pressing one. Should those who oppose Trump fight fire with fire? This debate encompasses questions of both efficacy and ethics. Will the kind of shaming and social condemnation that opponents believe is warranted end up being counterproductive because it will alienate persuadable Trump supporters? When is it permissible for owners of private establishments to refuse to serve those whose conduct they find morally objectionable? It is of course highly ironic that Trump opponents are being castigated (or indulging in self-flagellation) for incivility, when what powered his victory was precisely his pandering to the fury of angry white voters who viewed him as the embodiment of the norm-transgressing masculinist avatar of their dreams. Yet it has been protests or calls to protest (of both the civil and uncivil kind) by black public figures that have generated the greatest outrage on both the right and left, such as the NFL athlete protests against police violence initiated by Colin Kaepernick, which involved peaceful kneeling during the performance of the US National Anthem, and Congresswoman Maxine Waters's suggestion that "if you see anybody from that Cabinet in a restaurant, in a department store, at a gasoline station, you get out and you create a crowd and you push back on them and you tell them they're not welcome anymore, anywhere."[1] This is not coincidental. Black anger is hardly ever accepted as a legitimate response to political, social, and economic grievances. How to contain or channel black anger has been a core preoccupation of the United States since its founding, and of the settler colonies that preceded it.[2] Waters herself recognized this dynamic in 1992 when she refused to condemn those who took to the streets of Los Angeles to protest, sometimes violently, the acquittal of the white police officers that had brutally beaten Rodney King. Waters described the events as an insurrection rather than a riot. She refused "to tell people to go inside, to be peaceful, that they have to accept the verdict . . . I accept the responsibility of asking people not to endanger their lives. I am not asking people not to be angry . . . I am angry and I have a right to that anger and the people out there have a right to that anger."[3] I read Waters's refusal to acquiesce to the demand that she condemn expressions of black anger at injustice as a recognition of the fact that black politics has been uniquely constrained by expectations of democratic civility in the face of deadly racial injustice. As a result, philosophical and political questions about the legitimacy of uncivil disobedience have been a core preoccupation of African American thinkers, and indeed of non-US black thinkers and other marginalized peoples. Thus, one important thread throughout Candice Delmas's nuanced and rigorous defense of uncivil disobedience is the extent to which philosophical and public understandings of civil disobedience have been shaped by (a systematic misreading of) black protest movements. In what follows I use Delmas's defense of uncivil disobedience as a point of departure to reflect on how African American political thought challenges dominant liberal understandings of civil (and uncivil) disobedience, and to consider the conceptions of political obligation that should accompany defenses of principled lawbreaking.

In her thought-provoking defense of uncivil principled lawbreaking, Delmas offers a compelling critique of both philosophical justifications and popular understandings of the concept of civil disobedience. Delmas wants to expand our understanding of what constitutes principled lawbreaking to include uncivil acts of dissent and protest. She argues that it is a mistake to seek to broaden the concept of civil disobedience to include a wide range of acts of dissent, some public and some covert, some involving violence and others not, such as the disruptive and sometimes violent tactics of twentieth-century suffragettes, distributed-denial-of-service (DDoS) hacking attacks by the digital collective Anonymous, Pussy Riot's blasphemous "Punk Prayer," the covert provision of food, shelter, and legal aid to unauthorized migrants by members of the Sanctuary movement, the break-ins of Animal Liberation Front activists to rescue animals, Edward Snowden's leaking of classified national security documents to the media, and the violent protests that erupted in Los Angeles after the Rodney King verdict. Delmas understands the appeal of wanting to label an act of dissent as falling within the category of civil disobedience, since it "serves to highlight the agent's principled motivations and communicative intentions; to make a disruptive breach of law intelligible as an address to the community; to situate the act in a venerable historical tradition, populated by the likes of Rosa Parks and Martin Luther King Jr.—and thus, given these positive connotations, to begin the work of its justification." Yet this approach is misguided in her view because actions that are "covert, violent, or offensive" inevitably fail to meet the standard of civil disobedience, which "is commonly understood to be public, nonviolent, and respectful, among other essential traits."[4] The deeper problem in Delmas's view, however, is the assumption that acts of dissent that do not meet the exacting criteria of civil disobedience cannot be morally justified, when they might in fact be just as, if not more, effective as those that do fall within the accepted norm of civility. On the one hand, she thus believes that it is preferable to preserve a fairly narrow account of civil disobedience and to maintain the distinction between civil and uncivil acts of dissent, while, on the other hand, she believes it is also possible to make a case for why certain kinds of uncivil disobedience can be justified. She contends that "we should expand our repertoire of potentially acceptable modes of principled disobedience beyond civil disobedience, readily granting the incivility of certain disobedient acts and opening ourselves to the possibility that some types of uncivil disobedience can be justified."[5]

Delmas distinguishes between two subsets of principled disobedience: civil and uncivil. Civil disobedience is generally understood to refer to a deliberate breach of the law whose aim is to protest and lead to the amendment of unjust laws, policies, institutions, or practices and that adheres to various norms of civility: publicity (it must be performed openly rather than covertly), nonviolence (which excludes the use of force and coercion, the direct infliction of harm against persons, and the destruction of property), non-evasion (acceptance of punishment), and decorum (respectful behavior). In contrast, uncivil disobedience also refers to a principled breach of the law in response to injustice that does not meet the standard of civility because it is covert or anonymous, evades punishment, involves violence, or is offensive/disrespectful. According to Delmas, uncivil disobedience should not be conceived as a single category, but rather as a cluster concept, such that the presence of either covertness, evasion, violence, or offensiveness would be sufficient to merit this designation. Moreover, uncivil disobedience is not solely concerned with reforming unjust laws, it can also include acts aimed at dismantling existing systems, self-defense, retaliation, expressing anger, etc. Thus, in addition to digital hacking, leaking, providing sanctuary, rioting, "coercive and violent strikes, guerrilla street art, eco-sabotage, black bloc tactics, and vigilantism" are also examples of uncivil acts of dissent, in her view.[6] Yet Delmas's defense of uncivil disobedience is not unqualified, it is subject to the following constraint: that dissenters' goals and the means they use to achieve them reflect "respect for other people's interests, including their basic interests in life and bodily integrity, their interests in choosing the values that shape their lives, and their interest in a stable, secure system of rights."[7]

Delmas's aim is thus to provide an "ethics of uncivil disobedience" that is politically useful and phenomenologically accurate, i.e., one that at least partially reflects dissenters' own understanding of their actions.[8] The latter is an important criterion because, as Delmas persuasively demonstrates, the dominant liberal account of civil disobedience derived from Rawls (as well as contemporary accounts that seek to broaden the definition of civil disobedience to encompass uncivil forms of dissent) generally fail to meet this standard. As she observes, inclusive accounts of civil disobedience that seek to include controversial acts of resistance "miss the point of many disobedient actions, which is to *refuse* to follow the standard script of civil disobedience . . . agents may see themselves, and seek to be perceived, as radical and provocative rather than civil."[9]

This is an important point, as it speaks to a pervasive problem in the literature on civil disobedience: the way in which dominant philosophical justifications of civil disobedience depend on a significant *misreading* of the empirical/historical examples underlying its theoretical justification. With respect to civil disobedience in particular, Alexander Livingston has suggested that a mythology "developed around civil disobedience as it migrated from an insurgent political practice in the streets to a problem of moral philosophy studied in university seminars" that illustrates how "received theories and narratives in political theory that began their career as liberating ideas can become debilitating traps when we lose sight of the interpretive work of translation, transmission, and conscription that theories accrue in their travels."[10] Indeed, as other scholars have noted, what proponents take to be hallowed examples of civil disobedience were in practice much more uncivil than is reflected in both philosophical defenses of civil disobedience and public understandings of the concept.[11] One of the important strengths of Delmas's defense of uncivil disobedience is thus its insistence on phenomenological accuracy. Beyond that, however, I want to suggest that what is required to fully do justice to the profound imbrication of race and resistance is an examination of the sophisticated and theoretically rich debates within African American political thought on the meanings and aims of dissent.

African American Political Thought on Dissent

Since the earliest moments of the tradition, African American thinkers have grappled with many of the key questions posed in twentieth-century debates in philosophy and political theory about civil/uncivil disobedience and principled lawbreaking. For example, as Bernard Boxill has argued, disobedient and defiant "philosopher slaves" inaugurated a tradition that "in the middle of the twentieth century Martin Luther King Jr. . . . recovered and formed into his theory of civil disobedience or nonviolent direct action."[12] In spite of this, the rich, complex, and sustained debates in African American political thought about the meaning and goals of civil/uncivil disobedience have been comparatively underutilized as a resource for understanding and theorizing dissent. This is especially striking given the centrality to orthodox accounts of civil disobedience of both a certain flattened misreading of King's political ideas and a romantic narrative of the praxis of the US Civil Rights Movement of the 1960s.

At the same time, however, this omission is not surprising, as it reflects certain interpretative obstacles that continue to shape how African American political thought is viewed in political theory/ philosophy. Brandon Terry and Tommie Shelby identify a dynamic in relation to King that is indicative of the problem faced by the tradition as a whole:

> In other words, the defining meaning of the civil rights movement is understood as derivative of long-standing American ideals, enshrined within the founding documents, and thus most crucially realized via the impassioned insistence that America simply live up to its creed. From this vantage, what *appears* most innovative and valuable about the civil rights movement and the intellectual contributions of leaders like King is essentially *tactical* and *rhetorical*. . . . [This results in] the deeply misguided notion that black politics and political thought can be reduced largely to *strategic* thinking concerning how best to advance black interests by exploiting convictions and sentiments widely held among whites, and the *rhetorical* identification of black interests with the most deeply cherished American ideals and practices.[13]

Flattened readings of African American political thought and black politics thus obscure the fact that thinkers within this tradition have developed capacious accounts of the meaning and forms of dissent that depart substantially from standard liberal accounts of civil disobedience.

If one takes African American political thought rather than orthodox liberal accounts of civil disobedience as the point of departure for thinking about dissent, what becomes immediately clear is that, for African American thinkers, the distinction between civil and uncivil disobedience has never been as strict as the sharp separation that liberal thinkers who came to embrace the idea of a right to civil disobedience sought to create. Even King, for example, the tradition's most famous proponent of nonviolent civil disobedience, "conceded that a 'pure nonviolence' that abjures even self-defense cannot be the foundation of black protest politics because it requires forms of discipline and courage that are implausibly 'extraordinary' and cannot attract mass support."[14] At the other end of the spectrum, as Brandon Terry has argued, Black Power intellectuals of the same era grappled with subtle political and philosophical disagreements about the use of various forms of violence: "(1) armed self-defense, (2) rioting, and (3) revolutionary violence (including terrorism and other asymmetric violence such as guerrilla warfare."[15] Thus, African American thinkers have already formulated multiple accounts of uncivil disobedience, and there has been a sophisticated and robust debate within African American political thought about the goals and aims of dissent. Moreover, African American thinkers have rejected many of the key assumptions underlying the liberal defense of civil disobedience, particularly the necessity of fidelity to the law and the commitment to civility. Most fundamentally, many African American thinkers have rejected the central assumption shared by liberal accounts of principled disobedience (civil or uncivil) that the United States is a well-ordered democracy. This has had at least two important implications. First, many of these thinkers have challenged standards of permissible forms of dissent that rest on shared democratic commitments. And second, because many thinkers in this tradition have been pessimistic about the possibility of overcoming white intransigence to racial justice, disobedience has often been understood as an assertion of human dignity on the part of individual black persons and the group as a whole. Dissent and disobedience *in black* on this reading are therefore not necessarily about repairing a democratic project that encompasses the broader political community.

Long before the 1960s, African American thinkers fiercely debated the necessity of engaging in principled lawbreaking in order to achieve racial justice. Civil disobedience, and debates about its effectiveness vis-à-vis other forms of dissent, have been a central problematic for African American thinkers dating back to the earliest moments of the tradition. For example, in his famous "What to the Slave is the Fourth of July" speech, Frederick Douglass argued in favor of breaking the law in the name of higher moral and political principles. Douglass also makes a case for the value of incivility in the speech. In response to those who suggested that abolitionists would garner more support if they used less confrontational tactics, he replied: "But I fancy I hear some of my audience say . . . Would you argue more and denounce less, would you persuade more, and rebuke less, your cause would be much more likely to succeed."[16] It is bracing to read Douglass's vigorous defense of the value of incivility in 2019, when debates about civility are also used to suggest that moral outrage is unhelpful in the face of legal actions that are nevertheless judged by many to be inhumane, such as the separation from their parents of children who have been apprehended trying to enter the United States illegally and the "Muslim ban" on legal immigration from several Muslim-majority countries. In contrast to those who argued during the era of slavery that it was reasoned argument not moral outrage that would convert whites to abolitionism, Douglass made a powerful case for incivility: "At a time like this scorching irony, not convincing argument, is needed. O! had I the ability, and could I reach the nation's ear, I would, today, pour out a biting stream of *fiery ridicule, blasting reproach, withering sarcasm, and stern rebuke. For it is not light that is needed, but fire; it is not the gentle shower, but thunder. We need the storm, the whirlwind, and the earthquake.*"[17]

Beyond dismissing arguments that supporters of slavery should be engaged in civil forms of political dialogue, Douglass also argued against the idea of fidelity to the law. In a context in which slavery was legal and enslaved persons had little to no legal standing, and certainly were not citizens, it would of course have been difficult to argue that they had a duty to obey the law. Nevertheless, abolitionists and fugitive slaves were accused of undermining the rule of law. In his Fourth of July speech Douglass disputed this argument by comparing fugitivity, abolitionism, and sanctuary politics to the revolutionary activities of the Founding Fathers. He went even further in his autobiographies, arguing that unjust laws called into question the idea of fidelity to law. According to Douglass: "Slaveholders made it almost impossible for the slave to commit any crime, known either to the laws of God or the laws of man. If he stole, he but took his own; if he killed his master, he only imitated the heroes of the revolution."[18] Douglass's argument here reflects a long-standing tradition in African American political thought questioning whether the oppressed can be said to have an obligation to obey the law. Beyond raising the question of how to conceive the meaning of fidelity to the law, however, Douglass's arguments suggest that he believed there was a political obligation to dissent. Indeed, throughout his career Douglass extolled the political virtues of violent resistance to slavery, from his description of the pivotal fight with Covey in his first autobiography published in 1845, to a speech delivered toward the end of his life commemorating the anniversary of Haitian independence in 1893. Douglass's endorsement of the use of revolutionary violence to abolish slavery reflects an important debate among African American thinkers about the possibility of moral suasion—i.e., whether the powerful can be persuaded to act justly—that has significant implications for liberal defenses of civil (and uncivil) disobedience that privilege the communicative character and persuasive capacity of dissent.[19]

Indeed, while many African American thinkers have formulated theoretically sophisticated defenses of civil and uncivil disobedience, one of the paradoxical insights that emerges from engaging with African American political thought on dissent is the extent to which key arguments in the tradition are at odds with liberal defenses of both civil and uncivil disobedience. African American thinkers are not alone in this regard. According to Livingston, for example, there is a similar dynamic at work with Gandhi's political thought. He argues that it is "something of a historical irony that both Gandhi and his exemplars would find themselves today conscripted as models of the very civilizational liberalism he sought to escape."[20] Delmas recognizes one aspect of this problem when she observes that the understanding of the Civil Rights Movement in liberal accounts of civil disobedience exemplified by Rawls and his successors

> distorted political reality. For activists' outward submission to law did not in fact reflect their endorsement of the system's legitimacy or their acceptance of a moral duty to obey the law . . . the civil rights movement adopted its particular style of civil disobedience for context-dependent, tactical purposes. Yet theorists and pundits turned these tactics into deep moral commitments on the part of agents supposedly eager to demonstrate their endorsement of the state's legitimacy, and placed these subjective requirements at the core of their defense of real-world civil disobedience.[21]

Creative misreadings of Civil Rights Movement praxis thus served as the basis for the formulation of philosophical standards of civil disobedience that in practice function to inhibit dissent. As Delmas observes, "A deeply conservative history of the black freedom struggle is thus intertwined with a theory of civil disobedience underpinned by a counter-resistance bias."[22] There have thus been significant *political* impacts to Rawls's liberal philosophical defense of civil disobedience.

Scholars working within African American political thought have also critiqued Rawls's flawed understanding of the Civil Rights Movement and taken issue with how an idealized account of civil disobedience functions to constrain contemporary black protest movements. Brandon Terry, for example, has argued that romantic narratives of the Civil Rights Movement perpetuate deeply misguided assumptions about how progress toward racial justice has historically occurred in the United States. Because romantic narratives of the Civil Rights Movement situate it as a story of national unity emerging from racial strife and as the "victory" of equality over racial oppression in the United States, racism is understood as epiphenomenal to US democracy, and progress toward racial justice is viewed as inevitable and teleological. In other words, the fact that in US history eras of racial progress have been immediately followed by backlash is ignored, and momentary discontinuities in white supremacy are read as decisive breaks.[23] In a related critique, I have argued elsewhere that romantic historical narratives of black activism that recast peaceful acquiescence to loss as a form of democratic exemplarity function to delegitimize contemporary black protest movements, such as Black Lives Matter, that resist the template of civil disobedience derived from sanitized portrayals of the Civil Rights Movement of the 1960s. While African American political thought as a whole has historically been broad and varied on questions of dissent, the idealization of the Civil Rights Movement as emblematic of a certain kind of democratic civility has narrowed the legible terrain of black politics.

> This narrow conception of the civil rights movement functions to foreclose other (possibly more radical) forms of black politics, and pre-emptively delegitimizes them. It results in the assumption that non-violent protest aimed at inclusion into the existing legal and

> political order is the most effective political strategy that black citizens can and should pursue. Black politics that doesn't follow the script of the romantic narrative of the civil rights movement, with its implicit expectation of democratic sacrifice, then comes to be viewed as both illegitimate and ineffective.[24]

A distorted account of the Civil Rights Movement thus continues to shape expectations of what constitute permissible forms of protest in negative ways that tend to promote compliance or acquiescence. And while this dynamic applies to dissent in general, it is particularly acute in the case of black politics.

One of the most important areas of disagreement between African American thinkers and liberal defenders of civil/uncivil disobedience, however, is regarding the possibility of moral suasion, or how to understand the communicative character of dissent. This issue comes up at various points in Delmas's argument. For example, in her response to social scientific studies that purportedly demonstrate that nonviolent campaigns are more successful and that incivility is thus counterproductive, Delmas rightly observes that this depends in large part on how success and effectiveness are defined, and in particular on whether the success of dissenters should be judged solely on their ability to "persuade" their fellow citizens or to bring about short-term legal reform. The issue reappears in her discussion of whether uncivil disobedience strains the ties of civic friendship. She argues that this might indeed be the case, but that it might also "be a virtue rather than a problem: in some circumstances, uncivil disobedience may appropriately highlight—and, yes, undermine—all-too-flimsy or illusory ties of civic friendship. It can do so better than civil disobedience ever could."[25] According to Delmas, in societies with a professed commitment to equal treatment where this commitment is routinely violated in the case of certain groups, i.e., where civic friendship only exists for the majority, uncivil disobedience is a more effective method for making injustice visible. Uncivil disobedience is "more effective because of its ability to radically disrupt the status quo and *grip the public's attention.* Uncivil disobedients can *force the community to confront the disconnect between its reality and its professed ideals* and cast doubt on the authenticity of its commitment to civic friendship. Instead, civil disobedients typically seek to coax and persuade, not shock and shame."[26] Delmas thus simultaneously dispenses with the requirement that the aim of disobedience should be persuasion, while also claiming that uncivil disobedience can be more effective on the dimension of democratic communicativeness than civil disobedience.

African American political thought has generally been much less sanguine about the communicative possibilities of dissent, as a result of an account of how white supremacy functions to distort white moral psychology in ways that cast doubt on the possibility that commitments to racial transformation will be enduring. Charles Mills's work on white ignorance is instructive in this regard. Mills defines white ignorance as "an ignorance, a nonknowing, that is not contingent, but in which race—white racism and/or white racial domination and their ramifications—plays a crucial causal role." In his view, white ignorance encompasses both "straightforward racist motivation and more impersonal social-structural causation, which may be operative even if the cognizer in question is not racist . . . Racialized causality can give rise to . . . white ignorance, straightforwardly for a racist cognizer, but also indirectly for a nonracist cognizer who may form mistaken beliefs (e.g., that after the abolition of slavery in the United States, blacks generally had opportunities equal to whites) because of the social suppression of the pertinent knowledge, though without prejudice himself."[27] The problem is thus that arguments about the communicative effects of dissent assume a straightforward context of reception that ignores the fact that the act of reception is itself mediated by the very unjust conditions that dissent is supposed to make visible. An example that illustrates this dynamic are the numerous viral videos of police killings of unarmed black persons that galvanized the Black Lives Matter protests. It is not the case that those watching the videos were unanimously persuaded that the police were at fault. Instead, the dissection of the actions and pasts of unarmed black victims of police violence for evidence of criminality or bad judgment—including even children, as in the case of seven-year-old Aiyana Stanley-Jones and twelve-year-old Tamir Rice—in order to justify the deadly actions of police officers point to the need to complicate assumptions about the communicative properties of dissent. Indeed, in my view there is a general tendency in democratic theory to overstate the ability of protest/

dissent to induce shame and thereby produce a moral reorientation among members of the dominant group. It reflects a mistaken theoretical account of white moral psychology that overlooks the effects of racialized solidarity on the ethical-political orientations of citizens in racially hierarchical societies.[28]

As a result of this skepticism about the likelihood of moral suasion, African American thinkers have long argued that it is necessary to question the standard whereby the legitimacy of acts of dissent by oppressed groups is assessed by how they contribute to perfecting a democratic project in which these groups are not fully included. In 1968, for example, shortly after King's assassination and the uprisings that followed in various cities across the country, *Esquire* magazine published an interview with James Baldwin in which he repeatedly refused to engage the interviewer's framing of black anger and violence in terms of the issue of how to repair US democracy.

> ESQ: How can we get the black people to cool it?
> JAMES BALDWIN: It is not for us to cool it.
> ESQ: But aren't you the ones who are getting hurt the most?
> JAMES BALDWIN: No, we are only the ones who are dying fastest. . . .
> [ESQ] So that when we come to you with the question, How do we cool it? All we're asking is that same old question, What does the Negro want?
> [JAMES BALDWIN] Yes. You're asking me to help you save it.
> [ESQ] Save ourselves?
> [JAMES BALDWIN] Yes. But you have to do that.

Baldwin's repeated refusal to entertain the interviewer's implication that black citizens should express their demands in less violent ways reflects the refusal of African American thinkers to disavow incivility and black anger. When asked what he would say to "an angry black man ready to tear up the town," Baldwin replied:

> I'll tell you what I *can't* tell him. I can't tell him to submit and let himself be slaughtered. I can't tell him that he should not arm, because the white people are armed. I can't tell him that he should not let anybody rape his sister, or his wife, or his mother. Because

> that's where it's at. And what I try to tell him, too, is if you're ready to blow the cat's head off—because it could come to that—try not to hate him, for the sake of your soul's salvation and for no other reason. But let's try to be better, let's try—no matter what it costs us—to be better than they are. You haven't got to hate them, though we do have to be free.[29]

Notably, Baldwin's insistence on "not hating them" is not motivated by a concern with the demands of civic friendship, but rather with the effect of (justified) racial hatred on the moral and spiritual capacities of blacks. His simultaneous insistence that blacks "have to be free" and that it is whites who have to "save it" likewise reflects an understanding that struggles for black freedom should not be equated with projects of democratic repair.

In light of the more recent "riots" or uprisings in Ferguson and Baltimore associated with the Black Lives Matter protests against police violence, contemporary scholars have followed Baldwin and other African American thinkers in arguing that we need to reconsider the political utility of anger for black citizens. For example, I have suggested that a more useful way of thinking about uprisings or riots is in terms of their effects on participants, i.e., in terms of the civic work they perform for citizens who are already unduly shouldering the burden of racism. In a context in which deviations from the sanitized template of the Civil Rights Movement enshrined by liberal theorists of civil disobedience renders other forms of black dissent illegitimate, "perhaps we should instead consider instances of 'rioting' as a form of democratic redress for black citizens, even if in and of themselves they cannot transform the prevailing racial order. These instances of violence, which are often viewed as self-destructive, might be productive for black citizens because they allow for the expression of black anger and pain, which is otherwise precluded."[30] The expression of black rage, and of political emotions that are deemed uncivil, might thus be productive in ways that are not necessarily compatible with the aim of shoring up liberal democracy. As Debra Thompson suggests:

> Anger is *productive* in that it can serve as a unifying discourse that seeks liberation rather than liberal democratic incorporation and is *disruptive* to the hegemony of powerful national narratives such

> as the belief in the forthcoming postracial era, which is premised on the inevitability of racial progress but which actually hides and enshrines mechanisms of white supremacy. Thus liberal democracy's failure to understand black rage as a legitimate response to white supremacy reveals the limits of the liberal imagination as a means of challenging America's white democracy.[31]

Delmas recognizes this non-instrumental value of dissent when she argues that: "Even where there is neither hope of moral suasion nor chance of inducing shame, then, uncivil disobedience may still have intrinsic value as an expression of warranted frustration and distrust."[32] African American political thought has long recognized that the value of dissent exceeds its communicative potential, i.e., its effect on spectators.

In sum, accounts of dissent from within African American political thought push us to consider important questions obscured in accounts of civil and uncivil disobedience that draw on the dominant liberal framework initiated by Rawls. African American thinkers by and large eschew a strict separation between civil and uncivil disobedience. Many African American thinkers have also formulated conceptions of dissent that reject the imperative to subsume it to questions of democratic repair. Indeed, for many African American thinkers even the language of "disobedience" is problematic, as was the notion of lawbreaking for the fugitive slaves that inaugurated the tradition, as it affords an unwarranted legitimacy to political communities constituted by racial injustice. African American political thought thus provides alternative theoretical resources for the kind of expanded account of justifiable lawbreaking that Delmas would like us to embrace.

Uncivil Disobedience and Political Obligation

Finally, I want to briefly turn my attention to the question of what follows from a defense of uncivil disobedience, and specifically to the question of how we should think about the currently very unequal distribution of the burden of dissent. Delmas, whose larger project seeks to argue that "the concept of political obligation should be expanded to include duties to resist injustice and disobey the law," limits her discussion of our obligations to dissenters in this piece to the suggestion that "conscientious individuals (including police, prosecutors, judges, and jurors) should show leniency toward agents engaged in justified uncivil disobedience."[33] I want to move beyond the question of penalties for uncivil disobedience to consider whether the burden of dissent falls disproportionately on those already most vulnerable.

Recent examples of both civil and uncivil dissent highlight the vulnerability of those who are already marginalized. During the "Unite the Right" rally in Charlottesville, Virginia in August 2017, for example, white supremacists, white nationalists, neo-Confederates, Klansmen, neo-Nazis, and various white militias, marched through the University of Virginia campus and the city chanting racist slogans and carrying swastikas, Confederate battle flags, anti-Muslim and anti-Semitic banners. They were in turn met by counter-protesters, whose vulnerability was starkly illustrated by images of young students surrounded by angry, racist mobs on campus, and by the violent attacks on citizens protesting the rally the following day on the streets of Charlottesville, including the beating of Deandre Harris and the killing of Heather Heyer. Orthodox accounts of civil disobedience do not seem especially helpful in making sense of the events in Charlottesville, as the idea of a moral right to dissent treats all civil disobedience as equally permissible, and would thus appear to endorse President Trump's claim that there was "blame on both sides."[34] Meanwhile, Delmas's ethics of uncivil disobedience would presumably find the actions of the Unite the Right rally participants and their supporters morally impermissible given the substance of their political beliefs. Yet this question points to a concern that it is groups who do *not* meet Delmas's criteria for justified uncivil disobedience, i.e., whose aims and means do not respect other people's interests, which have often resorted to violence in the course of US history, such as Southern lynch mobs, the contemporary white militia movement, and border vigilantes.[35] There is thus a risk that uncivil disobedience rather than being a weapon of the marginalized is more often used against those already vulnerable.

In addition to the issue of how to protect the already vulnerable from the consequences of incivility, there is also the question of who has an obligation to resist. How should existing power relations within a society be taken into account when considering who has a duty to resist unjust laws? For example, should it be trans persons, who already suffer from hyper-visibility and its attendant vulnerability, who take the lead in violating gender restrictions in public restrooms to protest against discriminatory bathroom bills, or should the burden fall on cisgender allies? Similar questions can be asked about the duties of citizens versus noncitizens to resist racist or inhumane immigration policies. Considering the question of the political obligations of the already marginalized, for example, Tommie Shelby has argued that citizens of the ghetto do not have the same political obligations as other citizens.[36] This suggests that civility should be a political obligation of the powerful but not necessarily of the marginalized, and that those already vulnerable should not bear the burden of dissent alone, and certainly not its consequences. One example of how to incorporate concerns with vulnerability into accounts of uncivil disobedience can be derived from the aftermath of the events in Charlottesville. Two days after the Unite the Right rally, activists engaged in the unauthorized removal of a confederate statue in Durham, which led to the arrest of one of the organizers, Takiya Thompson, a North Carolina Central University student, on charges of felony offenses such as "participation in a riot with property damage" and "inciting others to riot." In this instance an act of uncivil disobedience led to punitive actions by the state against those least able to withstand them. In subsequent days, however, in a show of solidarity, supporters and allies flooded the sheriff's office asking to also be arrested.[37] This example points to the obligations of the more privileged toward those who take up the task of dissent, as they too benefit from their actions. Delmas's thought-provoking defense of uncivil forms of dissent thus raises important questions about how to incorporate concerns with vulnerability into an account of uncivil disobedience that expands our repertoire of political resistance.

Notes

1 Rebecca Traister, "The Summer of Rage: White Men Are the Minority in the United States, No Wonder They Get Uncomfortable When Their Power Is Challenged," *The Cut*, June 29, 2018. www.thecut.com. Notably, while Waters was attacked by conservatives, she was also rebuked by congressional leaders and fellow Democrats.

2 See Debra Thompson, "An Exoneration of Black Rage," *South Atlantic Quarterly* 116, no. 3 (2017): 457–481.

3 Cited in Traister, "Summer of Rage."

4 See Candice Delmas, "Uncivil Disobedience," in this volume.

5 Ibid.

6 Ibid.

7 Ibid.

8 Ibid.

9 Ibid.

10 Alexander Livingston, "Fidelity to Truth: Gandhi and the Genealogy of Civil Disobedience," *Political Theory* 46, no. 4 (2018): 511–536, quote on 512–513.

11 On Gandhi, see Livingston, "Fidelity to Truth." On the debates about tactics, such as "jail no bail," within the US Civil Rights Movement of the 1960s, see Erin Pineda, "Civil Disobedience and Punishment: (Mis) Reading Justification and Strategy from SNCC to Snowden," *History of the Present* 5, no. 1 (2015): 1–30.

12 Bernard Boxill, "The Roots of Civil Disobedience in Republicanism and Slavery," in *To Shape a New World: Essays on the Political Philosophy of Martin Luther King, Jr.*, edited by Tommie Shelby and Brandon M. Terry (Cambridge, MA: The Belknap Press of Harvard University Press, 2018), pp. 59, 73.

13 Brandon M. Terry and Tommie Shelby, "Martin Luther King, Jr., and Political Philosophy," in *To Shape a New World*, pp. 3–4.

14 Brandon M. Terry, "Requiem for a Dream: The Problem-Space of Black Power," in *To Shape a New World*, p. 296.

15 Ibid., p. 295.

16 Frederick Douglass, "What to the Slave Is the Fourth of July," in *The Oxford Frederick Douglass Reader* (New York: Oxford University Press, 1996), p. 117.

17 Ibid., p. 118. Emphasis added.

18 Frederick Douglass, *The Life and Times of Frederick Douglass* (Mineola, NY: Dover Publications, 2003), p. 69.

19 Derrick Bell, for example, has argued that progress toward racial justice in the United States has occurred, not as a result of moral suasion, but because at certain moments, supporting equality coincided with white material interests. See Derrick Bell, "*Brown v. Board of Education* and the Interest Convergence Dilemma," in *Critical Race Theory: The Key Writings That Formed the Movement*, edited by Kimberlé Crenshaw, Gary Peller, and Kendall Thomas (New York: New Press, 1995), pp. 20–29.

20 Livingston, "Fidelity to Truth," pp. 529–530.

21 Delmas, "Uncivil Disobedience."

22 Ibid.

23 See Brandon M. Terry, Which Way to Memphis? Political Theory, Narrative, and the Politics of Historical Imagination in the Civil Rights Movement (PhD dissertation, Yale University, 2012).

24 Juliet Hooker, "Black Lives Matter and the Paradoxes of U.S. Black Politics: From Democratic Sacrifice to Democratic Repair," *Political Theory* 44, no. 4 (2016): 457–458.

25 Delmas, "Uncivil Disobedience."

26 Ibid. Emphasis added.

27 Charles Mills, "White Ignorance," in *Race and Epistemologies of Ignorance*, edited by N. Tuana and S. Sullivan (Albany: State University of New York Press, 2007), p. 21.

28 See Juliet Hooker, *Race and the Politics of Solidarity* (New York: Oxford University Press, 2009), and Hooker, "Black Lives Matter and the Paradoxes of U.S. Black Politics."

29 "James Baldwin: How to Cool It. Read the Landmark 1968 Q&A on Race in America," *Esquire*, August 2, 2017, www.esquire.com.

30 Hooker, "Black Lives Matter and the Paradoxes of U.S. Black Politics," p. 464.

31 Thompson, "An Exoneration of Black Rage," p. 460.

32 Delmas, "Uncivil Disobedience."

33 Ibid.

34 Michael D. Shear and Maggie Haberman, "Trump Defends Initial Remarks on Charlottesville; Again Blames 'Both Sides,'" *New York Times*, August 15, 2017.

35 See Jennet Kirkpatrick, *Uncivil Disobedience: Studies in Violence and Democratic Politics* (Princeton, NJ: Princeton University Press, 2008).

36 See Tommie Shelby, *Dark Ghettos: Injustice, Dissent and Reform* (Cambridge, MA: Harvard University Press, 2016).

37 Beatrice Hazlehurst, "Durham Activists Who Toppled Confederate Statue Are Turning Themselves in for Arrest," *Paper Magazine*, August 17, 2017, www.papermag.com.

3

THE RADICAL POSSIBILITIES OF PROTEST

AMNA A. AKBAR

In the fall of 2014—shortly after the people of Ferguson first took to the streets in response to police officer Darren Wilson's killing of eighteen-year-old Michael Brown—I walked alongside a hundred protesters for 12 miles in Ohio.[1] We marched from the Walmart where police officer Sean Williams killed twenty-two-year-old John Crawford to the courthouse where the grand jury deliberated over whether to criminally charge Williams. The Ohio Student Association, a youth-led racial and economic justice organization, organized the march. Among the protesters were people young and old, straight and queer, black, white, and brown, labor and community organizers, academics, and religious leaders from all over the state and across the country.

The sun was bright, the fields separating the suburban Walmart to the Dayton courthouse sprawling and verdant. The protesters sang songs like this adaptation of an old labor song:

> Ella Baker was a freedom fighter
> And she taught us how to fight
> [Say what?]
> We go'n' fight all day and night
> Until we get it right
> Which side are you on, my people, which side are you on?
> [We're on the freedom side!]

We marched for hours, occasionally taking breaks to rest our feet. A church sheltered us for bathroom breaks and snacks. But space and time changed in quality. I felt connected to the freedom struggles of black and brown people in the United States. I remembered what I knew of the Civil Rights, Black Power, Chicano, and antiwar movements' tactics: marches, sit-ins, occupations, and more. Walking through the fields—the honks of the passing pickup trucks and the stalled traffic in turns menacing and supportive—we felt connected to each other, to those who came before, to histories we weren't taught in school. Our coming together felt transgressive, constitutive, and soaked in alternative possibilities. Another tomorrow felt within reach, as we marched in resistance to the prevailing political and social norms that had empowered Williams to take Crawford's life, and the grand jury to find no probable cause that Williams committed a crime.

At the courthouse, we were greeted by organizers and community members who had camped out on the courthouse lawn since morning. There was a schedule of workshops and activities in motion on the lawn and in a makeshift office across the street. People were building with each other, creating spaces to learn and to teach, to heal and to organize. The march and courthouse encampment were part of a national movement for transformation, rather than a singular act of disobedience. It was an attempt at conjuring a different world, more committed to racial, economic, and social justice. As with any movement and movement activity, our vision and purpose were not singular, and contradictions and tensions presented themselves on all manner of strategy and tactic, big and small.

In her chapter "Uncivil Disobedience" in this volume, Candice Delmas critiques the Rawlsian account of civil disobedience for its whitewashing of the black freedom struggle. The Rawlsian account attributes to civil disobedience an "endorsement of the system's legitimacy," misunderstanding that an "outward submission to law" may instead reflect a strategy of resistance. To allow for a broader range of politically motivated lawbreaking, Delmas makes the case for uncivil disobedience: "a principled breach of law in response to perceived wrongs . . . that fails to satisfy the basic norms of civility by being either: covert/anonymous, evasive, violent, or offensive/disrespectful" and that pursues any number of goals including "status quo, reform, system overhaul, education, aid, harm prevention, retaliation, expression of discontent, etc." She argues that justifications for civil disobedience can be extended to uncivil disobedience "even in supposedly legitimate, liberal democratic states like ours."

In advancing an argument that uncivil disobedience may be justified, Delmas evaluates the strategic dimensions of incivility and asks us to examine our commitments to civility in lawbreaking for social change. I share her concerns with Rawlsian civil disobedience, in part because her underlying diagnosis—that our common understanding of social change serves up an all-too-convenient account of history—is exactly right. But a civil disobedience–oriented account, even one that focuses on points of departure, remains ill-equipped to evaluate social movements with more radical projects in mind.

In this chapter, I consider Delmas's argument through the lens of the Movement for Black Lives and the waves of protest and rebellion accompanying it.[2] I raise four questions about the capacity of a (un)civil disobedience framework to understand the more radical possibilities of protest. First, protest is important not simply for its capacity to communicate with the broader public, but for its expressive and constitutive functions. Second, individual acts of protest cannot be divorced from the larger organizing and social movements in which they operate. Third, a civil disobedience framework may not be compatible with movements that seek more structural political, economic, and social transformation. Fourth, elevating a particular form of explicitly politicized lawbreaking over the sort of lawbreaking that these movements seek to denaturalize poses tensions worth grappling with, in particular because Delmas aims for "phenomenological accuracy."

Throughout the chapter, unless referring to the discursive construct, I use the term protest rather than (un)civil disobedience because it covers a larger array of lawbreaking and does not resort to civility as a primary index of value.

Expressive, Constitutive Protest

Scholarly accounts of protest often focus on its utility or efficacy in terms of its capacity to engage "the public" and to improve state and society, most often through court decisions or congressional lawmaking. The tacit question is whether the protest will appeal to an audience with greater power than those protesting. Protest is often evaluated for its capacity to engage with elites—whites, wealthy people, judges, lawmakers—to work on their sympathies. Undoubtedly, protest is important for what it can communicate to those outside of the rebellious community that engages in it. But focusing on the receptiveness of elites misses the expressive and constitutive aspects of protest. Protest is an expression of feeling, a tool of constituting a political community alternative to the mainstream and communicating to other similarly situated people. It cannot simply be evaluated for what it communicates to those outside of the protest community in itself and other similarly situated people.

Juliet Hooker and Jackie Wang write powerfully about the expressive dimensions of protest. Hooker deconstructs the "demonization" of the Ferguson and Baltimore uprisings as tantamount to demands on black citizens to forego protest despite a long history of racialized violence and inequality.[3] Expectations of civility "create a trap whereby any deviation from submission, respectability, and non-violence serves to render black grievances illegitimate."[4] Hooker suggests "rioting" is "a form of democratic redress for black citizens" that is "productive" in how it "allow[s] for the expression of black anger and pain, which is otherwise precluded by expectations of black sacrifice and forgiveness."[5] Wang contrasts the mainstream media's depictions of such riots as "social disruptions as apolitical, criminal, and devoid of meaning" with leftist recharacterizations of them as "politically reasoned."[6] While the media representations erase the social, economic, and political context for these "social disruptions," leftists erase the political and demographic heterogeneity of rebelling people. Leftists create a "[m]orally ennobled victimization" as "the necessary precondition for determining which grievances we are willing to acknowledge and authorize."[7] Together, Hooker and Wang move us away from the problematic terrain of evaluating protest—and black protest in particular—for the benefits it accrues the broader polity, and ask that we pay attention to its expressive functions.

In Ferguson, Missouri, people took to the streets in multiple waves from August to December 2014, provoked by Wilson's killing of Brown, the police and prosecutor's handling of Brown's death and Wilson's actions, the grand jury's refusal to indict Wilson. In Baltimore, people took to the streets in April 2015, from the point at which Baltimore police caused Freddie Gray's death through Gray's funeral. In both places, local rebellions took on a national significance, with people from all over the country joining the street actions in Ferguson and Baltimore, and then creating their own solidarity actions nationwide. These multitudinous protests cannot be properly understood as reflecting one set of political opinions, strategies, or tactics, or even one discrete set of grievances. Organizers and movement builders may have provided strategic, tactical, and/or legal support during the uprisings. But localized and widespread disobedience simultaneously reflected an outpouring of grief, rage, frustration, and even a sense of futility in response to a deeper and wider terrain of anti-black state violence, democratic exclusion, and material inequality.

Scholarly accounts focused on the legitimacy and utility of protest also overlook its distinct constitutive function: how protest movements seek to reach other similarly situated people, and to constitute alternative modes of political engagement and possibility. Such accounts of black protest in particular placed utmost importance on an imagined white and upper-/middle-class audience. These accounts ignore the reality that other black people, as opposed to whites, are a key constituency for the black freedom struggle. From the Black Panther Party to the Movement for Black Lives, black social movement organizations often seek to speak to and validate black experience, to demonstrate the power of protest and the importance of resistance, to mobilize and build with more black people, and to radicalize each other in service of self-determination connected to the long tradition of black freedom struggles. Indeed, a primary measure of success for many movements is whether they speak to and grow their identity-sharing base.

Moreover, convening in protest forms an alternative political community, where people come together to break the rules of engagement and forge different possibilities of democratic engagement beyond the formal channels of participation like voting. The community born of protest and struggle is connected in different ways, to different histories, and to different possible futures. It is about building power in communities in order to create lasting change over the long haul. Sometimes, protest is less about winning over elites than convincing other black and marginalized people to join in the struggle and to build toward different political possibility. In that moment of protesting with others, movement actors develop a sense of agency, self-determination, and collective recognition that elites cannot provide.

Delmas argues that efficacy can be measured by more than its "contribution to reform," including its capacity for "communication without intent to persuade (e.g., expression of solidarity or distrust)." But alongside efficacy, Delmas advocates for an evaluation of the worthiness of the ends and the proportionality of the means. Even as she resists a narrow efficacy frame, she cannot entirely escape it. Take the Ferguson and Baltimore rebellions, or even the LA riots, which Delmas mentions as disobedience of the sort she hopes to justify. It is unclear how one would identify the ends of these uprisings or evaluate whether the means were proportionate. But this should not take away our ability to understand or appreciate the immense power of these rebellions, for those who participated in them, and far beyond.

Moreover, utility and efficacy are dangerous benchmarks for movements that have in their sights structural inequality. The perverse outcome of acceding to such metrics is this: The longer the odds, the more structural and complete the violence and inequality that protesters target, the less likely any particular action will accomplish its ends, and the less likely we will see it as justified. While social movements often seek to express a point of view, the focus on elites as the audience misses these movements' focus on shifting power through community organizing and building mass movements.

Social Movements and Organizing

Civil rights history has been criticized for its focus on individual heroes (Martin Luther King Jr.) or one-time acts of courage (Rosa Parks's refusal to give up her seat on a racially segregated bus), and for how it obscures the grueling collective work of social movements and community organizing (including those collective efforts in which King and Parks participated).[8] In its implicit focus on individualized acts, the (un)civil disobedience frame risks similar obscuring. Indeed, Delmas features a number of individual actions for public good, like Edward Snowden's whistle-blowing or

Pussy Riot's Moscow church performance. While we may celebrate individual protest actions, individual actions mean little without the mass movements and community organizing that lend them momentum, meaning, and force. Conversely, mass movements and community organizing are constituted and sustained by many, small acts of protest. There is a daily grind to movements and organizing that is essential to their success.

A focus on individual acts of protest obscures the role of community organizing and social movements in social change. Community organizing is the other side of disruptive direct actions and large-scale street mobilizations. Mass mobilizations create important disruptions, provoke "moments of the whirlwind," and contain immense power to change the public conversation.[9] Community organizing creates the infrastructure through which people can join organizations and work toward substantive change through waging campaigns and engaging in other forms of sustained political struggle. While protest brings more people into the fold, community organizing allows for articulating demands, building sustainable power, and absorbing those who have been radicalized by protest.[10]

Furthermore, focusing the scale of inquiry to individual acts suggests that an act that draws attention to the contradictions between the promises and realities of a society might actually lead to meaningful change. But individual acts of disobedience that take place without larger mobilizations or social movements cannot mount a serious challenge to the social order. While an individual act of disobedience may shock or jar, it does not itself build sustainable power in black or otherwise marginalized communities to meaningfully shift the social, political, or economic structures of inequality.

Delmas mentions Black Lives Matter multiple times in passing. That movement was launched by the rebellions in Ferguson and Baltimore and fueled by community organizing, protests, and mobilizations around the country: law reform campaigns; die-ins, sit-ins, protests, and funeral processions at courthouses, police stations, universities, and mayoral residences; marches small and large ending in blockages of bridges, streets, and highways. While each action was significant for its disruptive and remedial potential, its power borrowed from the national social movement and organizing ecosystem in which it participated. Moreover, the movement's target was not simply police killing, but the larger histories and structures that constitute and propel anti-black racism in the United States.[11]

Radical Projects

Delmas demarcates her interest in disobedience in service of particular emancipatory projects. She opens her chapter with examples of disobedience that motivate her inquiry, including that of suffragettes, sanctuary workers, the Animal Liberation Front, and "LA protesters" in the context of the LAPD's brutalization of Rodney King. She sets a limit on her interest, too. She explains that some uncivil disobedience is "impermissible" because it seeks "illegitimate ends" like white supremacy. "The types of uncivil disobedience I am interested in defending are constrained in various ways: Resistors must act with respect for other people's interests, including their basic interests in life and bodily integrity, their interests in choosing the values that shape their lives, and their interest in a stable, secure system of rights." While the edges of her interest are fuzzy, Delmas makes it clear that she does not intend her framework to justify acts of the Klan and neo-Nazis.[12]

But what about radical protest movements? Two aspects of her argument suggest less space for understanding more radical disobedience.

First, in her limit-setting paragraph, Delmas centralizes an "interest in a stable, secure system of rights." In so doing, Delmas sidesteps the established critique of rights as status-quo preserving and enhancing.[13] Even putting aside questions about revolutionary means of social change, it is unclear how a social movement committed to a major redistribution of land and resources would fare. Such a movement would likely challenge, reconfigure, and possibly even reject current rights arrangements—away from a model that emphasizes individual entitlements and negative rights, toward the collective and positive entitlements, for example, to housing or health care. There is a long-standing critique of how our current rights regime gives cover for unequal distributions of resources, land, and life chances, and how an emphasis on civil and political rights undermines social, economic, and cultural rights.[14] The rights-bearing individual is central to liberal modernity borne of capitalism, colonialism, and enslavement.[15] The current rights arrangements in the United States are a roadblock to even minor redistributions. Consider, for example, how poorly affirmative action has fared in the face of the US Supreme Court's color-blind race jurisprudence.

Second, Delmas's discussion of the rule of law elides the conflict between redistributive or restructuring projects with law's stability. In examining the argument that civil disobedience is illegitimate for the way it undermines law, order, and democracy, Delmas argues that uncivil disobedience can "exemplify respect for the rule of law and serve to bolster law's integrity." As examples, she points to Daniel Ellsberg's and Edward Snowden's leaks, which "expose serious wrongdoing and abuses" and thereby "promote the rule of law." Delmas includes no real accounting of how these disruptions promote law's stability. Complicating any potential account, the law was brought down to bear on both men—who were charged with serious federal crimes—as punishment for their dissidence.

Racial justice movements often run up against the rule of law, which is central to the architecture of racial injustice. Chattel slavery and Jim Crow, for example, were legal—as is mass incarceration or widespread immigrant detention and family separation (stemming from both incarceration and detention) now. Movements that challenge these regimes often seek to disrupt and challenge the law. From the Civil Rights and Black Power movements to antiwar mobilizations to labor strikes, the state often works quickly and brutally to reestablish the rule of law through arrests, brutality, infiltration, curfews, and more. Recall Bull Connor's dogs and hoses in Birmingham; the Ferguson Police Department and National Guard's tanks and tear gas in Ferguson; the Morton County Sheriff's Department's use of rubber bullets and pepper spray against the water protectors at Standing Rock, North Dakota; and the NYPD's raids of the Occupy Wall Street encampment in Zuccotti Park. The rule of law is reestablished through repressive tactics and, at times, with legal change. Often, this is a process of "preservation-through-transformation,"[16] whereby the state changes its policies and practices just enough to absorb movement critique without disrupting the fundamental distribution of resources and life chances.[17] More often than not, the reestablishment of the rule of law is not pretty and represents the defeat of social movements.

In defending principled lawbreaking by drawing on defenses of civil disobedience—a framework that Delmas herself observes is awash in "counter-resistance bias"—Delmas limits her ability to grapple with movements for radical social change. The most radical movement organizations are not fighting for more representation or better democracy, rights or traditional law reform. They are seeking a radical shift in governance and a redistribution of resources.

Consider the Movement for Black Lives—the larger movement configuration made up of 60+ black-led organizations, including Black Lives Matter. The Movement released a policy platform in August 2016, dubbed "A Vision for Black Lives: Policy Demands for Black Power, Freedom, and Justice" (the Vision).[18] The Vision announces as its goal "a complete transformation of the current systems, which place profit over people and make it impossible for many of us to breathe." The Vision's six major demands are: an end to the war on black people; reparations; invest-divest; economic justice; community control; and political power. The Vision is focused on shifting power into black and other marginalized communities; shrinking the space of governance now reserved for policing, surveillance, and mass incarceration; and fundamentally transforming the relationship among government, market, and society.[19]

The Vision is radical in significant ways. The Vision situates the problem of police violence as a tool and product of white supremacy and capitalism, produced and tolerated by law. Police violence is not exceptional or occasional, it is fundamental, normal, and persistent. Moreover, the Vision advances an abolitionist-inspired agenda. The platform demands "investments in the education, health and safety of Black people" and divestments from "criminalizing, caging, and harming of Black people." Stated another way, it demands that money spent on prisons, police, surveillance, and corporations be directed instead toward reparations and reinvestments in restorative services.

Thus, while the Vision makes a few mentions of rights, it cannot be described simply as a project aimed at strengthening rights or the rule of law.[20] The Movement for Black Lives is not alone in rejecting traditional legal equality and rights campaigns: Feminist, antiracist, and penal abolitionist organizations have been running such campaigns for some time.[21] Instead, these campaigns focused on redistribution of resources and shrinking the role of the carceral state in communities of color.

The Vision reflects an experimental project of reimagining possibilities of governance, rooted in black intellectual traditions and political projects. The contemporary call for abolition—reflected in key aspects of the Vision—for example, has its roots in W.E.B. Du Bois's writings on the abolition of slavery, and the need for a political project that would not simply end slavery, but would reconstitute the economic, political, and social structure of the country.[22] Significantly, the abolitionist framework rejects the idea that the United States, now or before, is a just or near just society. To the contrary, the Vision posits that ours is a fundamentally unjust society. It does this by centering the experiences of black people—chattel slavery, mass incarceration, devastating economic inequality, and regular police brutality and lethality—in its reading of US history. The law and the state are deeply implicated in, and significantly responsible for, historic and present violence and inequality. Wins have been hard fought, incremental, and curtailed—while the underlying systems have remained intact.

This underlying analysis of the United States as fundamentally unjust is not unique to contemporary abolitionist organizing or the Vision for Black Lives. The Vision calls up earlier platforms of the Black Panther Party and the Young Lords, embodying the unfinished work of the radical movements that came before. Radical movement actors in the 1960s and 1970s analogized the struggle for black liberation in the United States with that of the anti-colonial struggles being waged all over the world: Black communities were a colony within.

Political Lawbreaking

From racial to immigrant justice movements, penal abolitionist politics are resurgent. As a result, contemporary movements question the very metric of criminality. But the civil disobedience framework elevates the propriety of lawbreaking in service of political change over lawbreaking for survival—say, theft to feed your family, selling drugs because you are locked out of the legal economy, or crossing the border without proper legal authorization. Delmas writes: "At the edge of uncivil disobedience lie terrorism and guerrilla warfare . . . and acts of unlawful resistance that are self-interested and not primarily principled but can be interpretively construed as (thinly) principled, such as digital piracy and unauthorized immigration." In characterizing "unauthorized immigration" as "self-interested" but "[a]t the edge of uncivil disobedience," Delmas gestures at the political content to this form of lawbreaking. But nowhere does she meaningfully explore the possible legitimacy of unauthorized migration or other acts that contemporary movement actors consider criminalized acts of survival. Given her commitment to phenomenological accuracy, this tension is worth exploring. A sharp distinction between lawbreaking that seeks to change the status quo and lawbreaking that in itself is a sign of the brokenness of the status quo is problematic for her account.

Contemporary abolitionist movements call for the end of prisons, policing, and criminalization as primary modes for governing black and brown people in the United States. Abolitionist organizing situates criminal law enforcement and policing as central to the long history of enslavement, racial capitalism, and settler colonialism. Through the lens of abolitionist movements, prisons, policing, and criminalization are not neutral unbiased law enforcement, but represent fundamentally racialized, gendered, and capitalist instruments that are central to the racialized, gendered, and classed distribution of resources and life chances more broadly. Criminalization serves to move responsibility for fundamentally social, political, and economic problems of collective life onto the individual. In this way the criminal legal system punishes the individual for problems the state itself had a major hand in creating. Rather than aiming to improve criminal law enforcement through better regulation and more resources (e.g., training, oversight, body cameras), abolitionist approaches to reform aim to shrink the role and space of prisons, policing, and criminalization in the world, with the ultimate goal of eliminating our reliance on criminal law enforcement altogether, and shifting toward non-penal modes of collective governance. So, abolition is more than a call to tear down—it is a call to transform our political, economic, and social order, to build alternate systems for collective self-governance, to work toward, in the words of W.E.B. Du Bois and Angela Y. Davis, "abolition democracy."[23]

Abolitionists aim to denaturalize crime and criminalization. With the entanglement of immigration, criminalization, policing, and incarceration, immigration is of growing concern for abolitionist organizations. In its organizing toolkit, *A World "Without" Walls*, the abolitionist organization Critical Resistance repeatedly brings attention to the contradiction between criminalization and people's needs. In the section on immigration, the toolkit explains:

> Immigration policies are based on force, punishment, and racism. They don't take into account the real social and economic needs of people who enter, live, and work in the US. People are punished and locked up just for trying to live in the same country as their family members, to find a better-paying job, or to escape from political, race, gender, or heterosexist discrimination in another country. Military and police make it more dangerous than ever for people to move across national borders.[24]

Throughout the toolkit, Critical Resistance problematizes the state's investments in prisons, police, and criminalization as the primary mode of responding to the needs of people, creating a vicious cycle between insecurity and imprisonment. Posing the contradiction between prison and basic needs also gestures toward a radically different world where those needs would be addressed. "By not using punishment as a response to human insecurity, we can begin truly to prioritize basic needs like health care."[25]

In the abolitionist account, then, criminalization is itself a structural problem at the center of racial justice struggle. As a result, contesting the vectors of criminalization is a central terrain of social movement activity. Consider the 2018 policy platform of the important immigrant justice organization Mijente. Mijente's platform is focused on two core objectives: to abolish US Immigration and Customs Enforcement (ICE) and other immigration enforcement agencies, and the "full-scale decriminalization of immigration."[26] Mijente explains that the criminalization of border crossing has its roots "in a 1929 law explicitly designed to deter immigration from Mexico," and "a long legacy of white supremacist legislation denying citizenship, immigration and free movement to black, Native, Asian, and Latinx people."[27] Jeff Sessions has taken up this mantle, Mijente argues, using language that "dehumanizes the mostly brown immigrants crossing the border and exposes Sessions' racist criminalization project."[28]

Critical Resistance and Mijente contest the very legitimacy of criminalizing "unauthorized migration." I suspect they would be suspicious of an argument that deconstructs the criminality of protest while leaving in place the criminality of migration, all in service of a framework that takes as its starting point that we live in a "supposedly legitimate, liberal democratic state." While Delmas's commitment to the legitimacy of our liberal democratic order is qualified, she holds onto it as necessary to her framework, and thereby muddles the potential of her account for understanding radical protest movements that contest the logics of our political, economic, and social order.

Conclusion

In her thought-provoking chapter, Delmas asks us to reexamine our commitments to civility in lawbreaking for social change in our unequal world. In this response, I have raised four questions about the capacity of a (un)civil disobedience frame for understanding more radical currents within contemporary social justice movements. In radical social movements, protest can be an exercise of imagination and memory, rooting in histories of resistance, and calling up the possibility of a different political, economic, and social order. Radical protest does not simply refuse the politics of the day or aim to improve it, it gestures at and constitutes new futures and dissident modes of engagement. It does this in part by modeling sprawling and collective forms of embodied dissent—from direct action and mass mobilization to community organizing and more. We should aim to better understand the radical protest of today and the past, before we decide we are in any position to judge it.

Notes

1 I was there as a National Lawyers Guild legal observer.

2 Amna A. Akbar, "Law's Exposure: The Movement and the Legal Academy," *Journal of Legal Education* 65, no. 2 (2015): 352–373; Amna A.

Akbar, "Toward a Radical Imagination of Law," *New York University Law Review* 93, no. 3 (2018): 405–479.

3 Juliet Hooker, "Black Lives Matter and the Paradoxes of U.S. Black Politics: From Democratic Sacrifice to Democratic Repair," *Political Theory* 44, no. 4 (2016): 449.

4 Hooker, "Black Lives Matter," 464.

5 Hooker, "Black Lives Matter," 464.

6 Jackie Wang, *Carceral Capitalism,* Semiotext(e) Intervention Series 21 (Cambridge, MA: MIT Press, 2018), 277.

7 Wang, *Carceral Capitalism,* 277–278.

8 Jeanne Theoharis, *The Rebellious Life of Mrs. Rosa Parks* (Boston: Beacon Press, 2015); Jeanne Theoharis, *A More Beautiful and Terrible History: The Uses and Misuses of Civil Rights History* (Boston: Beacon Press, 2018).

9 Mark Engler and Paul Engler, *This Is an Uprising: How Nonviolent Revolt Is Shaping the Twenty-First Century* (New York: Nation Books, 2016), 185–188.

10 Saul D. Alinsky, *Rules for Radicals: A Practical Primer for Realistic Radicals* (New York: Vintage Books, 1989); Mark Engler and Paul Engler, *This Is an Uprising: How Nonviolent Revolt Is Shaping the Twenty-First Century* (New York: Nation Books, 2016); Frances Fox Piven and Richard A. Cloward, *Poor People's Movements: Why They Succeed, How They Fail* (New York: Pantheon Books, 1977).

11 Akbar, "Law's Exposure," 357–360.

12 Later, she compares the Jim Crow era Deacons for Defense and Justice with the Ku Klux Klan, and the immigrant Sanctuary movement with "the anti-abortion Christian terrorist group Army of God." The Deacons and Sanctuary movement pursued proportionate means to their justified ends, while the KKK and Army of God "deployed efficacious but disproportionate and excessive violence." She distinguishes between the "morally horrendous ends" of the KKK with the Army of God, noting briefly that "'pro-life' activism must of course be tolerated in liberal societies."

13 David Kairys, ed., *The Politics of Law: A Progressive Critique* (New York: Pantheon Books, 1982); Duncan Kennedy, "The Critique of Rights in Critical Legal Studies," in *Left Legalism/Left Critique,* edited by Wendy Brown and Janet Halley (Durham, NC: Duke University Press, 2002).

14 Alan D. Freeman, "Race and Class: The Dilemma of Liberal Reform," *Yale Law Journal* 90, no. 8 (1981): 1880–1895; Mark Tushnet, "An Essay on Rights," *Texas Law Review* 62, no. 8 (1984): 1363–1403.

15 Walter Johnson, "To Remake the World: Slavery, Racial Capitalism, and Justice," *Boston Review,* https://bostonreview.net; Aziz Rana, *Two Faces of American Freedom* (Cambridge, MA: Harvard University Press, 2010).

16 Reva Siegel, "Why Equal Protection No Longer Protects: The Evolving Forms of Status-Enforcing State Action," *Stanford Law Review* 49, no. 5 (1997): 1111–1148.

17 Ruth Wilson Gilmore, *The Golden Gulag: Prisons, Surplus, Crisis, and Opposition in Globalizing California* (Berkeley: University of California Press, 2007), 28.

18 Movement for Black Lives, "A Vision for Black Lives: Policy Demands for Black Power, Freedom, and Justice," 2016, https://policy.m4bl.org.

19 Akbar, "Toward a Radical Imagination of Law," 426–434.

20 The Vision calls for "anti-discrimination civil rights protections" for "trans, queer and gender nonconforming people"; a "constitutional right at the state and federal level to a fully-funded education"; a "right for workers to organize in public and private sectors"; and "full access, guarantees, and protections of the right to vote for all people" (Movement for Black Lives 2016).

21 Dean Spade, "Intersectional Resistance and Law Reform," *Signs* 38, no. 4 (2013): 1031–1055.

22 W.E.B. Du Bois, *Black Reconstruction in America 1860–1880* (New York: Free Press, 1998).

23 Du Bois, *Black Reconstruction*; Angela Y. Davis, *Abolition Democracy: Beyond Empire, Prisons, and Torture: Interviews with Angela Davis* (New York: Seven Stories Press, 2005).

24 Critical Resistance, *A World "Without" Walls: The CR Abolition Organizing Toolkit*, www.journals.uchicago.edu, 13.

25 Critical Resistance, *A World "Without" Walls*, 5.

26 Mijente, "Free Our Future: An Immigration Policy Platform for Beyond the Trump Era," https://mijente.net.

27 Mijente, "Free Our Future," 9.

28 Mijente, "Free Our Future," 9.

PART II

THE STRATEGY OF POLITICAL PROTEST

4

COMPETING THEORIES OF NONVIOLENT POLITICS

KARUNA MANTENA

Nonviolent political action is a distinctive genre of political protest identified most closely with mass disobedience and radical acts of non-cooperation. As a self-conscious form of political action, it is primarily a twentieth-century invention. While instances and ideas of conscientious dissent and disobedience, non-resistance and passive resistance, as well as contentious politics in the form of boycotts, strikes, and work stoppages have longer histories and genealogies, it was M. K. Gandhi's innovations that originated the modern theory and practice of nonviolent politics.[1] The name Gandhi designated to signal the novelty on nonviolent politics was the neologism *satyagraha,* which in the midcentury came to be translated as nonviolent direct action. Today, it is commonly referred to as nonviolent resistance or civil resistance.

In the century that has passed since Gandhi's first mass *satyagraha* campaigns, activists have emulated and adapted nonviolent protest in various global settings, most prominently in the midcentury US Civil Rights Movement and in anti-authoritarian struggles from the 1980s to the Arab Spring.[2] In its globalization, however, the meaning and practice of nonviolence has significantly changed. One especially notable development has been the rise to prominence of the school of *strategic nonviolence.* A key feature of classical nonviolence, associated most prominently with Gandhi and Martin Luther King, was the claim that nonviolent direct action was both morally *and* practically superior to violence in waging political conflict, overcoming oppression and injustice, and advancing social change. In the last half-century, however, among theorists, advocates, and practitioners of nonviolence, the balance has definitively shifted toward endorsing nonviolence on purely strategic or pragmatic grounds.[3]

Gene Sharp is credited, and rightly so, with inaugurating and consolidating the turn toward strategic nonviolence.[4] Sharp was a committed war resister and self-styled disciple of Gandhi, who, from the 1960s onward, began to systemize what he termed *nonviolent technique.* Developing technique involved documenting case studies of successful nonviolent struggles and, from this archive, building explanatory theory and a repertoire of effective nonviolent strategies and tactics. For Sharp, the advantage of focusing on strategic or pragmatic technique over moral or principled arguments for nonviolence was threefold. First, it was more descriptively true to the way nonviolence worked in practice; he argued that the overwhelming majority of participants in nonviolent movements were neither pacifists nor absolutist defenders of nonviolence. Second, learning successful strategy from past political experience rather than abstract debates on tactics would better equip activists in the throes of political struggle. Finally, demonstrating pragmatic success would be the most persuasive argument for nonviolence against skeptics of all stripes. For Sharp, the last two aspects were crucial for realizing the long-term goal of replacing violent methods of political struggle.

Sharp's innovations were profoundly influential both for the global dissemination of nonviolent tactics as well as in defining the academic field of study of nonviolent resistance, so much so that in the last decades he has become the international icon and standard-bearer for nonviolence.[5] In this respect, the model of strategic nonviolence has made possible some truly impressive practical and theoretical achievements. And yet with this consolidation and celebration there is a danger of losing sight of the diversity of ways that nonviolence has and can be practiced. More specifically, strategic theories tend to ignore or underestimate the political valence of some key elements of classical nonviolence—such as the dynamics of discipline, suffering, and conversion—which are often dismissed as outworn ethical and religious ideas.

Strategic nonviolence is premised upon a sharp contrast with *principled nonviolence.* Most often associated with pacifism and figures like Gandhi and King, principled nonviolence is characterized as a religious, spiritual commitment that its critics view as unnecessary for the successful practice of nonviolence.[6] Principled nonviolence is most often defined as an ethical practice and choice—a creed or way of life. As a result, it is also often devoid of political content. Especially in the work of its critics, principled nonviolence has become something of a straw man, a placeholder for a variety naïve, apolitical convictions such as a belief in harmony and an aversion to conflict, a focus on moral purity and the intrinsic value of action, and an ethical objection to all forms of coercion.[7]

This chapter is framed by a fundamental doubt about the cogency of this distinction between strategic and principled nonviolence and the work it does in obscuring the theoretical underpinnings of nonviolent politics. Neither strategic nor principled models as currently conceived capture the most innovative and distinctive features of classical nonviolent politics, namely how the moral-ethical and political were creatively imbricated. Consider, for example, the myriad ways in which Gandhi and King staged dissent in nonviolent protest via displays of self-discipline or self-suffering. Crucially, they did so because they understood these ethical practices to be an essential part of the strategic logic and tactical dynamic of nonviolence. That is, ethical practice and moral orientation associated with nonviolence were valued not only for intrinsic but also for instrumental reasons; they were thought to be uniquely efficacious in conditions of deep conflict.

Many critics have questioned the strategic-principled distinction on normative, political, and analytical grounds. In abandoning nonviolence's creedal vision, critics argue that Sharp's focus on pure technique strips nonviolence of any ethical grounding; nonviolent methods themselves appear neutral and readily adaptable by any political movement, even those seeking "evil" ends. For others, strategic and pragmatic nonviolence amounts to a "moderate Machiavellianism," aimed simply at short-term political gains and victories rather than more radical, revisionary, and transformative politics.[8] Critics have questioned the sharpness of the distinction itself, and contend that the two forms of nonviolence involve elements of their supposed opposite, and therefore are better understood as lying on a "continuum" rather than a strict binary.[9] In this, they rightly point out that the main architects of principled nonviolence such as Gandhi and King "also grounded their nonviolent actions on pragmatic and strategic excellence."[10] All of these critical positions aim to reunite strategic and principled nonviolence, either by enclosing strategic technique within a principled framework[11] or by blurring the line between the two.[12]

I want to turn the discussion in the opposite direction and think more capaciously about the diversity of strategic theories and orientations. My contention is that there is more than one way to understand, conceptualize, and theorize the strategic logic of nonviolence. Rather than collapse the distinction between the so-called pragmatic and the principled, instead, I offer an alternative classification of competing strategic theories of nonviolent politics. These I characterize as nonviolence as *collective power* versus nonviolence as *disciplined action*. This classification will sometimes overlap with the existing strategic-principled distinction. But I especially want to resist equating disciplined action with principled nonviolence, for the reasons outlined above. Principled nonviolence implies the privileging of ethical commitment and orientation *over* political objectives and is thereby shorn of any strategic dimension. By contrast, I take both collective power and disciplined action to be strategic theories of nonviolent politics, albeit premised on different theories of politics and, hence, offering different accounts of how the dynamics of political mobilization and protest work.

The chapter begins with a discussion of nonviolence as collective power and the theory of politics that underpins it. I foreground and analyze two key elements: the social theory of power as elaborated most influentially by Gene Sharp, and nonviolence as a technique of mass mobilization. For a discussion of the latter, I turn to Krishnalal Shridharani's *War without Violence*, an important early interpretation of nonviolence as an insurgent form of mass power. I then analyze nonviolence as disciplined action and delineate more precisely its conceptual logic. The two aspects I focus on are its ontology of action and its account of the persuasive logic of nonviolent discipline. I begin by placing Gandhian *satyagraha* alongside skeptical theories of action that highlight the psychological burdens and frustrations of action. I then explore the ways in which disciplined action and its orientation toward persuasion navigate the inherent dilemmas of action and transform the affective dynamics of political conflict. I conclude with some thoughts on what is theoretically and politically at stake in diversifying theoretical models of nonviolent politics.

Defining Collective Power: Waging War without Violence

Regularly dismissed as naïve pacifism, impractical, and akin to weakness and compromise, nonviolence has always faced severe skepticism. This in part compels the recourse to a categorical distinction between moral and political accounts of nonviolence. Combating such skepticism has been one of the salutary contributions of the paradigm of strategic nonviolence. What has been especially cogent is its insistence that nonviolence be viewed as a theory of action rather than a restrictive political morality or ethics (defined, for instance, by severe injunctions against war and violence). Characterizing nonviolence as a theory of action rebuts implications of passivity, inaction, or a turning away from politics. Rather than the avoidance of conflict, Sharp, for instance, dubs it "an active technique of struggle"; it is a special type of action that aims to show "how to wield power effectively" and wage "conflict without violence."[13] Gandhi pursued a similar form of polemic when he sharply differentiated *satyagraha* from passive resistance. In his terms, *satyagraha* was "pure soul-force," a "power" that "calls for intense activity."[14]

Understood as a political technique, nonviolent action would also differ from a purely aspirational, exemplary, or "prefigurative" politics, as implied, for example, in the bumper-sticker slogan, "be the change."[15] Here, nonviolent action is often conceived as a form of embodied ethical practice. This view posits a tight unity of means and ends such that action's primary function is to express intrinsic values or principles. In contrast to ethical practice, the idea of *strategic* action at its core implies a field of iterative social interaction. Nonviolent action emerges then as a method of political contestation, conflict, and struggle, aimed at overcoming opposition to achieve specific goals and change structures of power. In Weberian terms, it is not just value-rational, but also instrumentally rational. I take all of these features to be definitionally true of both disciplined action and nonviolence as collective power.

A theory of action also implies a theory of politics, a set of background assumptions about the nature and sources of political conflict, where the main practical impediments to political change lay, and how they manifest themselves. It then posits forms of action that would be most successful at overcoming them to effect progressive change. It is here that we can begin to meaningfully distinguish collective power and disciplined action. I hope to show that they stem from disparate theories of politics, and hence emphasize different political strategies and tactics, which, ultimately, issue in divergent forms of nonviolent protest.

The picture of politics implied by the strategic perspective emphasizes the contestation of power, of generating and wielding power to confront and disrupt existing structures of power. I term this view nonviolence as *collective power*, because its two central theoretical elements are a distinct theory of power—what Gene Sharp terms the social view of power—and an account of how mass mobilization can be used to challenge and remake power relations.

The social view of power posits a strong empirical theory of consent or obedience.[16] It extends a broadly Humean intuition that, following the eighteenth-century formulation, "all government is founded on opinion."[17] That is, government is premised on the actual and voluntary as opposed to the hypothetical or formal consent of the people as the fundamental root of authority, legitimacy, and power. For Sharp, consent to authority has a psychological component—obedience—as well as a material one, namely, cooperation or collaboration. These two features—popular consent and cooperation—have been foundational to nonviolent politics since its invention. In one of his earliest formulations Gandhi argued that "in politics, it [*satyagraha*] is based on the immutable maxim, that government of the people is possible only so long as they consent either consciously or unconsciously to be governed."[18] In a similar vein, in *Hind Swaraj*, Gandhi provocatively claimed that "the English have not taken India; we have given it to them. They are not in India because of their strength, but because we keep them."[19] In more material terms, he contended that without Indian lawyers, judges, civil servants, policemen, and soldiers, the English could not maintain their rule over India. For Gandhi, all regimes—even the most authoritarian—were based on the acquiescence and collaboration of the many and could never be sustained by pure force. The implication was that all regimes could also be disrupted by the withdrawal of that consent on a mass scale. This logic was famously enacted in the theory and practice of mass non-cooperation, a nonviolent strategy to dramatize disaffection, disrupt the machinery of government, and dilute sources of governmental support to undermine state authority.

For Sharp, this theory of power/consent is the great innovation and conceptual heart of Gandhian nonviolence.[20] It foregrounded what he calls "the social roots of political power." A ruler's power is neither intrinsic nor self-sustaining but dependent on the ability to command obedience and mobilize resources that have their roots in a plurality of social relationships and institutions.[21] Hence, this view of power is also often referred to as a "pluralistic" theory of power that stresses the bottom-up, popular basis of power.[22] Building on this account of consent and power, studies of strategic nonviolence have tried to delineate with precision the process of breaking the material and ideological infrastructure of state legitimacy. In Sharp's account, this involves a three-pronged process, each utilizing a different method of nonviolent action. The first are forms of symbolic protest, publicity, and persuasion that through mass assembly—such as marches, demonstrations, and collective vigils—expose injustice and express dissent. The second method implements strategies of non-cooperation and boycott. These are a material indication of noncompliance and the withdrawal of consent that, when effective, can also threaten the regime's resource base. Finally, nonviolent "interventions" and civil disobedience represent the most active and intense methods of contestation. These include sit-ins, occupations, blockades, and strikes that aim to obstruct and disrupt the machinery of government. Taken together, these tactics undermine the existing regime's ideological apparatus as well as its resource base, its "pillars of support," and eventually its ability to implement and benefit from the use of repressive power.[23]

The theory of strategic nonviolence came into its own in the aftermath of the successful wave of democratic transitions of the 1980s and 1990s, which were driven by movements that conspicuously deployed mass-based nonviolent resistance. The success stories of Poland, the Philippines, South Africa, Argentina, and Chile, as well as the more precarious achievements of the first Intifada and Tiananmen Square, were analyzed and incorporated into a broad explanatory theory of strategic nonviolent conflict. These movements were also coupled with earlier historical examples—from the Indian independence movement and the Civil Rights Movement to revisionary accounts of earlier revolutions and wartime resistance—to give shape to a sweeping historical narrative that tracked and celebrated the rise of "people power," with the twentieth century singled out as "the century of nonviolence."[24] In addition to an array of important empirical studies of civil resistance, unarmed insurrections, and nonviolent revolutions, scholars also began to elaborate more nuanced and expansive theories of nonviolent power, drawing connections, for example, between nonviolent power, democracy, and Arendtian theories of power and revolution.[25]

All of these accounts commend nonviolence as providing a uniquely effective form of mass mobilization by which ordinary people can organize and act outside of conventional political institutions and structures.[26] The attention to mass mobilization is the direct analogue of the theory of popular consent, and likewise had genuine roots in Gandhian politics. To analyze this second, key theoretical element of nonviolence as collective power, I want to turn to an older text, Krishnalal Shridharani's *War without Violence* (1939), which was the first to conceptualize nonviolent action as an insurgent form of organized mass power.[27] Returning to Shridharani reveals how theories of strategic nonviolence—and what I am redefining as collective power—did not emerge as wholescale rejections of Gandhian nonviolence. Rather, they are part of a longer history of interpretation of Gandhian politics that accentuated one particular dimension of *satyagraha,* namely as a mode of power and mass struggle. In tracking this development, we can also see how collective power models came to transform, downplay, and eventually jettison other prominent elements of classical nonviolence such as the strategic role of suffering and discipline.

In the wake of the Salt *Satyagraha* of 1930, the campaign that garnered Gandhi and nonviolence unprecedented global notoriety, a number of seminal texts appeared which theorized *satyagraha* as a novel form of political action that could be adapted to political settings outside of India. Shridharani's *War without Violence* was one such effort to publicize Gandhian politics in the

United States, which, alongside Richard Gregg's *The Power of Nonviolence,* became influential in the Civil Rights Movement and the wider dissemination of nonviolent methods.[28] Selections from *War without Violence* were republished in pamphlet form by the Fellowship of Reconciliation, a major pacifist organization, and became the handbook of its offshoot, Congress of Racial Equality (CORE), and through them other campaigns against segregation. Indeed, we can trace some of Shridharani's ideas and language at work in Martin Luther King's seminal text "Letter from Birmingham Jail."[29]

Of these early works, *War without Violence* was also the text most admired by Sharp because it prefigured his own view of nonviolent action as "a technique of concerted social action."[30] Shridharani was keen to show that *satyagraha* was not premised on "Oriental mysticism" or pacifism but "a very matter-of-fact pragmatism" whose purpose was "securing effective action . . . for achieving realistic and needed ends."[31] Shridharani was harshly critical of pacifism and argued that *satyagraha* was better understood as a species of war.[32] He therefore very purposefully analogized the logic of nonviolent direct action to that of warfare. Politics as such is pictured as social warfare, and nonviolent resistance mimicked the strategic logic of armed rebellion. Like war, nonviolence was relevant to situations in which parliamentary procedures were absent or so broken that justice required the resort to "extra-legal and extra-constitutional" measures. This was akin to a revolutionary situation in which "the people take the law into their own hand."[33] And, like war, concerted mass action required an army, trained in "organization, discipline and strategy."[34] In this respect, Gandhi's institution-building and strategic orientation made him, according to Shridharani, "the greatest general in the field of 'non-violent direct action.'"[35]

War without Violence offered the first generation of Gandhian activists a step-by-step playbook of how to engage in this novel form of social combat. The steps included preparatory stages of negotiation, agitation, demonstration, and self-purification followed by progressively more combative forms of direct action.[36] An inventory of the various forms of direct action utilized by the Indian nationalist movement—such as strikes, pickets, fasts, boycotts, non-payment of taxes, hizrat (emigration), non-cooperation, ostracism, civil disobedience—was presented and each tactic defined in turn.[37] Shridharani argued that these techniques used on a mass scale would "dramatize" grievances and "arouse mass interest and mass enthusiasm." Like the process of war, they worked to precipitate "an emotional crisis in the life of the community," they shook people out of normal politics and habitual modes of thinking and behavior.[38]

Shridharani celebrated nonviolent direct action as the first real innovation of the theory of popular revolution, one that, like its violent counterpart, required intense collective consciousness secured by organized and concerted mass action.[39] Through its emphasis on suffering, courage, and sacrifice, *satyagraha* entailed all the romance, heroism, risk, and adventure of war.[40] As the scene for the display of the "higher virtues" traditionally associated with war, *satyagraha* fulfilled William James's hope and demand for a "moral equivalent of war."[41] Crucially, in Shridharani, the "moral" aspects of *satyagraha*—like self-purification, suffering, and sacrifice—became techniques for building solidarity and collective cohesion. To be sure, Shridharani also noted their unusual efficacy, following Richard Gregg, in surprising and throwing the opposition "off balance." The prime examples were of soldiers and policemen who refused to attack unarmed *satyagrahis* (practitioners of *satyagraha*). Here, nonviolent suffering served to "neutralize" and "paralyze" the "coercive agencies of the state."[42] At the same time, Shridharani was careful to insist that this was not a scene of "mere moral suasion." Indeed, it is worth noting that Shridharani never uses the language of conversion to describe the efficacy of "organized sacrificial suffering." Rather, "conscious suffering" was understood as a "generator of power," a "source of social power which compels and coerces."[43]

In Shridharani's account of nonviolent technique, its overriding purpose is collective mobilization and solidarity, which itself generates and displays social power. A further implication of the directness of the analogy to war was that Shridhrani was willing to accept a "compelling" element as a necessary feature of the power of nonviolent suffering.[44] To be sure, this was not equivalent to the outright coercion of warfare, which inflicted suffering on others, often in an unbridled spirit of vengeance and punishment. Nonviolent suffering was directed "inward," its strategic purpose and effect was to "compel" the opponent to realize their errors, change behavior, and come to a settlement or accommodation. The acceptance of the necessity of compulsion also allowed Shridharani to recommend a more extensive array of tactics, including some that Gandhi had explicitly rejected as coercive (such as social ostracism and hunger strikes).[45] Here "nonviolence" is understood in an almost literal sense—anything short of coordinated armed struggle or direct physical harm seemingly falls under its rubric.

The question of coercion, of its necessity and its definition, has always been a source of controversy in the theory and practice of nonviolent politics. Many accounts of nonviolence, from Clarence Case's *Non-violent Coercion* (1923), Reinhold Niebuhr's *Moral Man and Immoral Society* (1932), through to Joan Bondurant's *Conquest of Violence* (1959), expressed varying degrees of skepticism of Gandhi's strict insistence that *satyagraha* ruled out all forms of coercion.[46] For advocates of strategic nonviolence, especially, accepting the necessity of coercion is what renders their version of nonviolence more pragmatic and realistic than principled alternatives. They are right to note that Gandhi did not endorse tactics he deemed coercive, such as sabotage, the hunger strike, and ostracism. And, more generally, Gandhi worried that almost all ostensibly nonviolent techniques could come to function coercively, especially in the contexts of mass action, i.e., when their purpose and effect was the display of collective power.[47] But what is misleading is the assumption that the eschewal of coercion was made on purely principled rather than strategic grounds. For Gandhi and King, coercive tactics that relied on intimidation or veiled force were a problem because they could, like violence itself, intensify cleavages, undermine public support, and thereby threaten the coherence and success of the movement. The point here is that while it might be analytically true that nonviolent direct action necessarily works via the compelling force of mass action, Gandhi and King argued that it was tactically important to mitigate as much as possible the *appearance* of brute coercion via performative practices of self-restraint and self-discipline.

The alternative model of nonviolence as discipline action shares with collective power an underlying theory of consent and power that celebrates the transformative effects of disruptive mass action. Both Gandhi and King utilized, advocated, and praised nonviolence for its ability to organize and mobilize oppressed people on a mass scale. At the same time, for mass disruption to do its transformative work, it had to be organized and performed in a definite way. Gandhi and King were especially attuned to the distinctive *forms* nonviolent action ought to take, beyond simply the size and scale of protest. For both, mass disruption and disobedience are most potent when *disciplined*, or more precisely when enacted through forms of protest that display and dramatize discipline. The performative dynamics of discipline distinguish the logic of nonviolence from *both* the pure violence of armed rebellion and the "nonviolent coercion" at work in collective power.

DISCIPLINED ACTION: NAVIGATING THE HAZARDS OF ACTION

If collective power emphasizes power and mass struggle, the theory of politics underlying disciplined action foregrounds the affective dynamics of political conflict. Here, the problem of entrenched domination is not only material, requiring the generation of alternative force and displays of mass power, but also moral-psychological. For Gandhi and King, the burdens of political action are heightened or made more dangerous because political contestation unearths and intensifies negative passions and egoistic dispositions. These ideas can be usefully linked to a broadly skeptical or realist view of politics as a realm of recurring violence and of political action as a peculiarly hazard-bound activity.[48] When left unchecked, the escalating logic of political contestation leads to polarization and entrenchment and inflames feelings of indignation and resentment which, in turn, feed the temptation toward retaliation and violence. I will explore this account—one might even call it an ontology—of political action by reading Gandhi alongside other skeptical theorists of action such as Max Weber and Hannah Arendt.

The animating worry of this competing understanding of nonviolence is that traditional forms of political action and contestation—i.e., enacting politics as a form of combat, even ostensibly nonviolent combat—may exacerbate the given tendencies of politics toward conflict, coercion, and violence. The function of discipline is to navigate these inherent dilemmas of political action, especially the psychological burdens and frustrations of action. The distinctive innovation of nonviolence as disciplined action is to build into its modes of dissent and disruption, forms of self-limitation and restraint. The aim is not to simply overwhelm or defeat opposition but to undermine and transform it through a complex politics of persuasion. Persuasion involves more than making the better argument or displaying more power; rather, it works via forms of direct action that mitigate the passions that aggravate political conflict. The display and dramatization of discipline weakens, undermines, or otherwise disorients psychological resistance. Discipline thus renders nonviolent protest more effective than either physical violence or other kinds of overt coercion and intimidation involved in traditional forms of mass action.

In what follows I try to specify the theoretical underpinning of aspects of nonviolence—such as the dynamics of discipline, suffering, and persuasion—that have been misunderstood and sidelined in the development of theories of strategic nonviolence that focus on nonviolence as a form of collective power. This section will focus on the dilemmas and hazards of action, while the next will turn to what persuasion means in the context of mass nonviolent protest.

Gandhi and King placed great emphasis on how nonviolent mass disruption was organized and enacted. This is where the real novelty of nonviolence lay—not just in the avoidance of violence, but in the innovation of forms of protest that would expose injustice and unsettle affective resistance to radical change. Such close attention to the style and structure of nonviolent protest was the direct analogue of the extraordinary emphasis they placed on the means of political action.

Gandhi would go so far as to suggest that the determination of means might matter more than specifying the final goal or end pursued. In a 1933 exchange with Jawaharlal Nehru, Gandhi elaborated his position this way:

> [Y]ou have emphasized the necessity of a clear statement of the goal, but having once determined it, I have never attached importance to the repetition. The clearest possible definition of the goal and its appreciation would fail to take us there if we do not know and utilize the means of achieving it. I have, therefore, concerned myself principally with the conservation of the means and their

> progressive use. I know that if we can take care of them, attainment of the goal is assured. I feel too that our progress towards the goal will be in exact proportion to the purity of our means.[49]

Typically, Gandhi's use of terms like "purity" has been interpreted as a plea for the ethical purity of the actor or act in question—and hence a prime example of a principled or moral constraint on action. I want to suggest that purity can also be understood as a category of efficacy. In what follows, I uncover the underlying assumptions about the nature of action such that it demands the constant vigilance and scrutiny implied in Gandhi's emphasis on the "conservation," "purity," and "progressive use" of nonviolent means.[50]

Disciplined action resonates with broadly skeptical theories of action that foreground the contingency and unmasterable character of action. They emphasize action's imbrication in a political field characterized by necessary conflict and hostage to the play of unintended consequences. This lends action if not a wholly tragic character at least an inherent fragility. For Weber, political action works in a field of interaction in which no individual actor or agent can know or fully control all the effects of action. This unmasterability is an essential part of what he termed the tragedy of action. In his words, "it is a fundamental fact of history . . . that the eventual outcome of political action frequently, if not regularly, stands in a quite inadequate, even paradoxical relation to the original, intended meaning and purpose."[51] In "Politics as a Vocation," Weber suggested that this was a hard fact of history, one that neither the power politician nor the moral absolutist can truly understand or accept. The power politician believes in the easy efficacy of force. This is as much a fantasy as the conviction politician's belief that demonstrating passion for a cause is the same as realizing it. Neither display enough humility before the brute fact of contingency or can bear what Weber termed "the ethical irrationality of world."[52]

Arendt similarly focuses on the "boundlessness" of action, how action "inserts itself into an already existing web of human relationship, with its innumerable, conflicting wills and intentions."[53] Every action sets off a "chain reaction" of new actions and reactions. For Arendt, action's unpredictable endlessness is part and parcel of its generative capacity, its ability to initiate radical newness into the world. From the viewpoint of the actor, however, this capacity is more often felt as a deep burden. Action seems to never achieve its purpose. It discloses an agent who is at once both doer and sufferer, not an author or producer, a reversal that drives an ongoing frustration with the frailty of action.[54]

Gandhi held to a similar view of action as enmeshed in irreversible, unmasterable, and unknowable chains of cause and effect. This understanding bears the imprint of an underlying theory of karma, an account of ethical causation in which the chains of intentionality and responsibility reverberate in unforeseen and extreme ways. In a karmic worldview, action leads to an irreducible entanglement in and with an irreducible violence; indeed, it imposes on all a fundamental culpability in violence. This extreme sense of culpability underlay the traditional suspicion of action in the Indian tradition and its cultivation of ideals of non-acting and non-attachment. But Gandhi—alongside a number of key Indian thinkers such as Bankimchandra Chatterjee, Vivekananda, and Bal Gangandhar Tilak—rejected the renunciation of action as the appropriate response to the problem of ethical entanglement. In place of renunciation, these thinkers reinterpreted the Gita to instantiate a new model of detached, worldly action—a revisionist understanding of karma yoga—that could meet the demands of political awakening.[55]

Gandhi was suspicious of the choice of "non-acting," of removing oneself from the chains of action, *himsa* (violence or injury), and destruction, and instead held to a notion of renunciation that "should be sought for in and through action."[56] To admit indeterminacy was not to foreswear attempts at facing violence or actively seeking political change. Rather, Gandhi tried to reconfigure the inward orientations of non-attachment and discipline to promote the outward efficacy of action.

Crucially, what makes action dangerous is not the mere fact of action's contingency or unmasterability or boundlessness but the psychological response to these dilemmas and especially reckless attempts to master or subdue them. Arendt, Weber, and Gandhi all worry about two kinds of insufficient reactions to the dilemmas of action, namely a temptation toward withdrawal, on the one hand, and attempts at mastery through force, on the other. The second response—the attempt at mastery—is the more dangerous, not only because it valorizes violence and force but also because it is the more psychologically unstable. That force or violence lends itself to more predictably reliable results is itself a delusion, a hyper-realist fantasy that sustains state militarism and revolutionary violence alike. The appeal of violence is often tied a hope that the chain of action will come to an end with one last show of force that can secure a final victory. In this hope, advocates of violence imagine the effects of violence to be not only more predictable but more manageable than they have ever proven to be.[57] This is perhaps one of the most important political insights that has emerged from the theory and practice of nonviolence across the last century.

The recourse to violence rests on a belief that unilateral force itself can induce the conversion or at least the compliance of opponents. However, Gandhi tried to show that violence breeds resentment and further resistance. Resistance and recalcitrance were basic to nature of political action; indeed, they might be one of the more expected or foreseeable effects of action. For Gandhi, this was especially acute in the case of violence. As an absolute, irreversible deed, violence initiates definite dynamics of resentment, retrenchment, and retaliation—a dynamic that is often prosaically referred to as the *cycle of violence*. The choice of violent or aggressive action therefore would necessarily escalate conflict and exacerbate tendencies toward polarization and entrenchment.

The problem of unintended consequences is not equivalent to the problem of uncertainty or contingency. Weber and Gandhi were concerned that something about the psychology of action denies acknowledgment of and responsibility for action's consequential effects. Therefore, they tried to make visible the unintended but *foreseeable* consequences of political action. They suggested that acts of provocation and violence often stem from a desire to demonstrate commitment and power and thus can undermine sought after goals. For Gandhi and Weber, excessive attachment to ends and ideals could engender destructive and unstable passions, especially when confronted with the disappointments of political setbacks and failures.

In this vein, consider the parable of the thief Gandhi offered in *Hind Swaraj* to highlight the moral psychology of action. The parable begins with a confrontation with a thief who illegitimately steals your property. In response, you, full of anger, resolve to punish the thief, "not for your own sake, but for the good of your neighbours." You organize an armed band to counterattack; the thief responds defiantly and "collects his brother-robbers" and "pesters your neighbours," who in turn complain that the robber has only resorted to open threats against them "after you declared hostilities against him." You feel badly that you have worsened the situation but feel trapped. Knowing you will be "disgraced if you now leave the robber alone," you instead distribute arms to all your neighbors "and so the battle grows . . . the result of wanting to take revenge upon the robber is that you have disturbed the peace; you are in perpetual fear of being robbed and assaulted; your courage has given place to cowardice."[58]

One of the overt lessons of this story is that improper means chosen to respond to injustice can lead to unintended, deleterious, and unmasterable consequences—more violence, injustice, and instability. The recourse to violence did not diminish but rather excited the resentment and hostility of opponents. Escalation provoked stronger resistance and, in so doing, required more ideological justification, engendering a perverse attachment to principle. In this sense, the parable shows how the investment in, and motivation for, seeking justice and redress is imbricated in the agent's sense of self such that this investment itself becomes a vehicle for escalation. The choice of violence may force you down a certain path, it raises the stakes of justification and hence of retreat or reconsideration. The extreme irreversibility of violence demands hubris in its undertaking and in its continued justification, a precarious subjective orientation that makes acknowledging errors of judgment and policy reversals difficult and rare.[59]

Gandhi's call to "conserve" and "purify" action was a plea to structure nonviolent action in such a way that it can best respond—strategically and tactically—to the hazards of action. Traditional antidotes to the dilemmas of action often fall back upon pleas for individual political responsibility and judgment. Think of Weber's call in the conclusion of "Politics as a Vocation" for an ethics of responsibility that ties the sober calculation of consequences to the cultivation of detached passion and perspective in political judgment.[60] Gandhi's innovation was to seek remedies to action within the terms of action itself, specifically by trying to introduce mechanisms of limitation and control within the very forms that nonviolent action would take.

The key here was to organize and imbue mass action with discipline. Discipline serves to contain and counteract action's irreversibility and unpredictability. In nonviolent protest, actors perform and enact discipline by taking upon themselves the burdens and consequences of action. Acts of protest, resistance, and reform visibly sacrifice benefits (such as money or prestige) and risk severe consequences (such as arrest). In so doing, nonviolent action limits as much as possible the externalizing effects and dangers of action so as to diminish antagonism and negative affect. Moreover, if the act is mistaken, "only the person using it suffers." The disciplined *satyagrahi* does not "make others suffer for his mistakes."[61] By absorbing the consequences of failure, nonviolent actors can more readily retrace their steps. Discipline therefore lent nonviolence an inherent revisability and avenues of self-correction, for in effect its action was never as final or determinate, or dangerous and provocative, as violence.[62] These are some of the ways that disciplined action anticipates and responds to the foreseeable, negative consequences of disruptive action.

The Persuasive Power of Disciplined Action

Disciplined action also aims to positively alter the dynamics of contestation. The function of discipline, here, is to temper the moral-psychological elements of action—the egoistic passions and attachments that drive political conflict—and, thereby, overcome opposition and effect transformative change. This is the broad dynamic at work in the idea of *nonviolent persuasion*. The possibility of persuasion or conversion has been much derided and criticized as either implausible or unnecessary for the successful practice of nonviolent politics. Conversion seemingly implies a change of heart or cooperative resolution as the endgame of nonviolent politics. Critics contend that in fact it is the mobilization of nonviolent power that compels, rather than persuades, the state or opponents to accept and accommodate new claims of justice. I want to suggest that the persuasion sought in disciplined action is not so naïvely dependent on the reality of mutual goodwill, sympathy, or a harmony of interests between the oppressor and the oppressed. Rather, the animating thought is that nonviolent forms of protest are most effective at mitigating psychological resistance when *orientated toward persuasion.* This ties the question of persuasion to the skeptical theory of politics as driven by endemic tendencies toward escalation and coercion.

Disciplined action is built upon the persuasive powers of *direct action.* The emphasis on action recognizes that political persuasion is a difficult task, and that, in particular, moral criticism and rational argumentation on their own cannot effect radical change. Both Gandhi and King thought political arguments were ripe with rationalizations, psychological modes of resistance that disruptive protest tends to intensify. King suggested that "reason by itself is little more than an instrument to justify man's defensive ways of thinking."[63] When "words fail, we will try to persuade with our acts." Nonviolent direct action becomes "the ultimate form of persuasion,"[64] whereby "we present our very bodies as a means for laying our case before the conscience of the local and national community."[65]

Gandhi rarely used the term persuasion and instead spoke of *conversion,* a choice that pointedly foregrounded the limits of rational debate in politics. For Gandhi, deeply held beliefs and principles were almost always less rational than they may appear, and the intellect worked hardest to justify existing interests and prejudices. People are attached to their beliefs as aspects of identity and ego and often cling to them tenaciously when these beliefs are attacked or criticized. In the context of political contestation, rational critique would be ineffectual or, worse still, counterproductive.[66] King likewise argued that "when the underprivileged demand freedom, the privileged first react with bitterness and resistance." Driven by pride, anger, fear, and resentment, "prejudiced and irrational feelings" distort the recognition and progress of justice.[67]

Therefore, those seeking radical transformation, in Gandhi's words, had to appeal "not to the intellect" but rather must "pierce the heart." The central mechanism for appealing to the heart was the work of suffering. Unlike brute force or direct confrontation that can stiffen resistance, suffering works by

> converting the opponent and opening his ears, which are otherwise shut, to the voice of reason. Nobody has probably drawn up more petitions or espoused more forlorn causes than I, and I have come to this fundamental conclusion that if you want something really important to be done, you must not merely satisfy the reason, you must move the heart also. The appeal of reason is more to the head, but the penetration of the heart comes from suffering. It opens up the inner understanding in man.[68]

For King, suffering was "a powerful and creative social force." In its willingness to accept violence without retaliation, self-suffering can "serve to transform the social situation."[69] In this way nonviolent action can "create such a crisis and establish such creative tension that a community that has constantly refused to negotiate is forced to confront the issue." Such creative tension allows for the rethinking of commitments; it weakens entrenched habits and enables people "to rise from the dark depths of prejudice and racism."[70] The idea that direct action provokes creative crisis echoes Shridharani. For King, however, crisis is triggered not simply by mass mobilization but by the way issues of justice are dramatized via suffering.

What Gandhi and King defined and invoked as conscious suffering returns us to the centrality of discipline. Though the idea of suffering is associated with feats of self-sacrifice and the ability to endure violence, for Gandhi and King, its transformative impact depended on the staging of dignity and discipline. For Gandhi, the equivalency between suffering and discipline was definitional. "Self-suffering" was a translation of the Sanskrit term *tapas* or *tapasya* which connotes practices of ascetic self-discipline. King also associated suffering with the performance of dignity and discipline. Militant nonviolent struggle, King insisted, must always be conducted "on the high plane of dignity and discipline."[71] Indeed, King often referred to nonviolent action simply as "dignified social action."[72] Crucially, what was staged in nonviolent protest was not abject displays of suffering so as to evoke pity, but a respect secured via dignity in defiance. What was displayed and dramatized was the protesters' "sublime courage," "willingness to suffer," and "amazing discipline in the midst of the most inhuman provocation."[73]

How precisely can the display and dramatization of discipline in nonviolent protest persuade recalcitrant opponents? Here I turn to another early interpreter of Gandhi, Reinhold Niebuhr, who offered insight into the political dynamics of nonviolent discipline and suffering. Like Shridharani, Niebuhr was an important conduit of thinking about nonviolence in the Civil Rights Movement, especially through his influence on Martin Luther King. King's understanding of nonviolence was shaped in part by Niebuhr's appraisal of Gandhi in his seminal early work, *Moral Man and Immoral Society*. What made Niebuhr such a canny analyst of nonviolence was how he saw its positive potential within a political world riven by irrational sentiments and egoistic drives.

Niebuhr was a political realist, arguably the most influential realist of the twentieth century. As a realist, Niebuhr argued that political conflict was rooted in struggles over power. Major issues of social and political injustice, for Niebuhr, could never be "resolved by moral or rational suasion alone." Rather, entrenched power and privilege had to be challenged by concerted power.[74] But a complete reliance on power was also inherently unstable; "a too consistent political realism would seem to consign society to perpetual warfare."[75] This was because all political contestation generates and is exacerbated by resentments and egoistic sentiments. Any peace established by power could be destroyed by the "social animosities" that a power-induced order "creates and accentuates."[76]

For Niebuhr, nonviolent action diminishes the passions and prejudices that define political antagonism between groups in conflict and thereby interrupts cycles of violence. In this way, nonviolence intimates a form of power that was least dangerous in its effects. Whereas Shridharani extolled the collective power generated by *satyagraha*, Niebuhr, like Gandhi, was much more wary of group egoism. Contestation can generate communal solidarity and sacrifice, but it is a solidarity that arouses egoistic passions and prejudices. Movements that seek social justice will be met with the indignation and resentment of those whose privilege is directly challenged. This is especially the case when criticism takes the form of "personal insults" which will always be felt as "unjust accusations."[77] In a parallel vein, King argued that campaigns fueled by hate, like the use of violence, would further alienate and "confuse the large uncommitted middle group."[78]

For Niebuhr, protests by their very nature aim to disrupt, inconvenience, and coerce. Boycotts are clear-cut cases of pressure, but marches and demonstrations also will be resented by those against whom they are aimed. Even neutral bystanders may respond with hostility and misunderstanding to the inconveniences and disorder of public protest. Niebuhr suggested that the middle classes naturally side with the status quo, and view protesters as enemies of public order. Through its "temper and method,"[79] nonviolence was unusually successful in counteracting and dampening these negative reactions and affective dynamics. Perhaps the most compelling way that disciplined action undercuts resentment is by "enduring more suffering than it causes."[80] By taking upon themselves the burdens and consequences of action, protesters give the impression of a detachment from egoism, of working for a moral purpose beyond reaction, envy, and selfish ambition. Gandhi, Niebuhr, and King recognized that resentment against injustice was morally justified and important. It was decidedly more admirable than complacency or passivity. But, from a tactical standpoint, the more "the egoistic element can be purged from resentment, the purer a vehicle of justice it becomes."[81] In staging goodwill rather than ill will, nonviolence depersonalizes conflict and "protects the agents against the resentments which violent conflict always creates in both parties to a conflict."[82]

In Niebuhr's view of politics, parties to social conflict tend to be extremely partial and self-interested in their analysis of social justice. But the tempering of egoism effected by disciplined action can enable more objective assessment of justice. Here, the key audience or patients of direct action are the potential allies of the movement, what King called the "uncommitted middle," and the public at large. To this audience, adopting self-discipline allows protesters to negate portrayals of them as outside agitators, criminals, and inciters of violence. Indeed, in many circumstances, the hostility of the opposition reveals the latter as the true "instigators and practitioners of violence."[83] The moral conceit of entrenched interests is punctured as propaganda, and the public can see beyond the inflamed situation to more clearly adjudicate claims of justice.

To have such a dynamic impact, the traits expressed via disciplined action—such as enduring suffering, showing good will, suppressing hate, and depersonalizing conflict—need to be incorporated in the style and structure of nonviolent protest. For King and

Gandhi, these traits and impressions did not simply accrue from the moral intentions of protesters or the rhetorical framing or ideology of the movement; they had to be expressed and embodied in the very organization and enactment of mass protest. This is why advocates and practitioners of disciplined action placed such emphasis on following strict rules and codes of conduct during mass demonstrations and acts of disobedience.

Such attunement to the affective dynamics of political contestation and persuasion entailed a more nuanced but also stricter definition of nonviolent action. In collective power, as you will recall, almost everything short of taking up weapons or the threat of direct physical harm could count as nonviolence. And an extensive variety of disruptive boycotts, strikes, and demonstrations are endorsed—no matter how unruly in form or coercive in implication. Advocates of collective power tend to emphasize the size and scale of resistance rather than the *form* it ought to take. By contrast, discipline was the defining, structural feature of the early or classic phase of nonviolence—in the Gandhian era, in the Civil Rights Movement, and the anti-nuclear protests in the UK—where disciplined conduct and comportment were staged in specific actions such as the sit-in, the march, and the freedom ride. This might be usefully contrasted to (sometimes unruly) mass crowds gathering in public spaces, which is more readily associated with collective nonviolence today.

Gandhi and King were well-known for formulating a plethora of rules of comportment and engagement that were meant to instill and express discipline in mass action. In both the Salt *Satyagraha* and the Birmingham campaign, two of the most celebrated in the history of nonviolent politics, protesters had to explicitly assent to these rules in the form of a vow or pledge in order to participate.[84] For protesters, the rules were meant to help muster and exhibit discipline in the face of threats, intimidation, and outright violence. For onlookers, allegiance to these rules showed that activists were willing to bear the costs and burdens of protest themselves, from the costs of self-organization to willingly accepting punishment for breaking the law.

Gandhi's meditations on the rules of disciplined nonviolent action were at the center of his weekly journals, *Navajivan*, *Young India*, and *Harijan*. In these voluminous writings, Gandhi took great pains to establish the precise conditions in which nonviolent tactics could be deployed without inducing escalation or enacting coercion. Gandhi's responses ranged very broadly, from guidelines for large-scale campaigns of non-cooperation and civil disobedience, to delineating rules for specific actions, such as strikes, pickets, marches, work stoppages (*hartal*), and—most controversially—the political fast. Crucially, these rules and distinctions were not only or simply moral criteria about what makes an act more just or legitimate but pragmatic maxims about how to persuasively communicate the meaning and purpose of protest.

Take the case of the *hartal*, or a day-long work stoppage. Gandhi insisted that a *hartal* be announced weeks in advance and that activists refrain from pursuing compliance on the day itself. He contended that a total *hartal*, i.e., with 100 percent compliance, implied coercion, and so the best demonstration of "the voluntary character of the *hartal*" and "a matter of pride . . . from the *satyagraha* standpoint" would be if "some shops stayed open."[85] Indeed, the true *satyagrahi* would go further and protect the shops that chose not to comply from harassment. In dramatizing the voluntary nature of the protest as well as restraint in not intimidating dissenters, the movement demonstrated strength and confidence in the justness of their cause. Tactically, by showing civility toward dissenters, it leaves open the door to their potential conversion and more generally draws more public sympathy than coerced compliance.

In the case of nonviolent pickets, strikes, and boycotts, Gandhi argued against aggressively blocking people from crossing lines or entering shops, factories, and schools. For Gandhi, the adverse consequences of economic boycott, for example, on the livelihood of workers involved in the boycotted industry, while not amounting to an "act of love" was also not an act of violence or coercion if the underlying reasons animating the boycott were just.[86] But this was quite different from the direct physical coercion of blockades and intimidation of social ostracism, which he opposed. Direct coercion not only displayed weakness of will but personalized animosity, which would alienate potential converts to the cause. Gandhi was especially wary of extreme tactics like the political fast, which could very easily become coercive, and thus elaborated especially demanding rules for them. It is worth remembering that Gandhi at no time fasted against the British government or British rule as such, and never in the name of an open-ended demand for independence. For Gandhi, fasting against a political antagonist or enemy functioned only to escalate bitterness and conflict, because one's enemy would necessarily experience the fast as exhortative. One could not "fast against a tyrant" but only against those whose consciences could be stirred by the willingness to sacrifice one's life.[87]

For King, following Niebuhr, the purpose of nonviolent direct action was to cut through or lessen the emotional temperature of mass protest, and make visible and stark who stands on the side of justice. The larger the crowd, the more confrontational the tactic, the more crucial the need to mitigate any sense of intimidation, coercion, and potential unrest that can obscure or distract from the political message of the protest. Discipline could also be displayed and effected via the performance of collective prayers, songs, and silence during large-scale demonstration and marches. Songs or silent prayer communicated inner calm and resiliency that is very different from what we now associate with the paradigm of disruptive protest. For Gandhi and King, this unique combination of mass disruption tempered by discipline made possible more radical acts of dissent, defiance, and disobedience.

Advocates of collective power have also recognized the tactical necessity of self-discipline and restraint in nonviolent action. Gene Sharp argued along very similar lines that nonviolent behavior was not just a moralist preoccupation but a strategic imperative. Self-discipline and refraining from "hatred and hostility" were especially important for winning sympathy and "attracting maximum participation." He likewise suggested that the use of provocative and polarizing tactics like sabotage, as in the case of violence, would shift attention away from the message of the movement, alienate support, and become alibis for state repression.[88] At the same time, in these accounts, nonviolent discipline lacks any distinct theoretical grounding. It becomes simply a contingent, pragmatic choice with little conceptual guidance on why and when nonviolent discipline matters. This is part and parcel of the general lacuna in theories of collective power with regard to the moral-psychological dimensions of political conflict.

CONCLUSION

Nonviolence is one of the most important and surprising political phenomena to emerge over the course of the last century. Along with national liberation, people's war, and socialist revolution, it was one of the most prominent forms of mass politics that had a decidedly global reach. Nonviolence has also seemingly outlasted its many rivals. Moreover, it was a form of politics that self-consciously announced its novelty. *Satyagraha* and nonviolence were new terms in politics. Hannah Arendt once suggested that the appearance of new concepts was rare in politics. The twentieth century arguably witnessed the emergence of two, albeit contrary in implication: totalitarianism and nonviolence. Arendt, along with many other eminent philosophers, made the former—totalitarianism—central to political theoretical reflection and argument. By contrast, nonviolence has been conspicuously absent in mainstream debates in political theory. No major political theorist has written a treatise on nonviolence nor made it a prominent feature of their understanding of modern politics.

Part of my interest in exploring diverse theories of nonviolence, and the history of its interpretation and conceptualization, is to offset this shortcoming. The paradigm of strategic nonviolence, and the array of empirical and theoretical work it has generated, has significantly contributed toward making nonviolent politics an object of sustained political and theoretical engagement. Substantively, these studies of nonviolence have demonstrated and confirmed the extraordinary potency of nonviolent politics. As a prominent example, consider the findings of the much-celebrated work, Chenoweth and Stephan's *Why Civil Resistance Works.* Chenoweth and Stephan tracked more than three hundred campaigns across the twentieth century and conclude that nonviolent political movements have been twice as effective as their armed counterparts in anti-regime resistance, and increasingly so over time. This success, they contend, is due to nonviolence's "participation advantage"—that barriers to nonviolent action are much more minimal than armed struggle.[89] These findings substantiate nonviolence's utility as a tactic of mass mobilization, as a way to organize and display collective power.

Such findings have dispelled long-standing presumptions about the potential scope and range of nonviolent politics. In the wake of the Indian independence struggle and the US Civil Rights Movement, it was commonly asserted that nonviolence might only be viable in and against broadly liberal regimes. But empirical studies have shown that nonviolent insurrections have been increasingly effective in overthrowing non-democratic regimes, no matter how authoritarian such regimes may be.[90] Perhaps even more significant is the cumulative impact of these studies in casting doubt on the capacity of violence to reliably secure popular consent. In this vein, the ongoing theoretical elaboration of the nature of consent and power underlying nonviolence has not only attested to the transformative power of organized mass power but also undercut deeply held conventional assumptions about the political efficacy of violence. To my mind, chipping away at the tenacious hold these assumptions have on our political imagination is one of the most important theoretical and political implications of nonviolent politics. And it is one that the paradigm of strategic nonviolence has done much to draw attention to.

At the same time, strategic studies of nonviolent conflict have overwhelmingly focused on the power dimension of nonviolence. Such focus has had the unintended consequence of constricting our understanding of the theoretical underpinning of nonviolent politics. In elucidating a competing strategic account of nonviolence, nonviolence as disciplined action, I have tried to make visible overlooked premises and implications of an alternative theory of nonviolent politics. The concept of disciplined action foregrounds the affective dynamics of political conflict which, as I hope I have shown, were extraordinarily significant to early practitioners of nonviolence and their theoretical interlocutors and interpreters. In limiting, even denying, a place for discipline, suffering, and persuasion—usually sidelined as dispensable moral commitments associated with principled forms of nonviolence—theories of collective power have misunderstood the political purpose and potential of nonviolence.

In diversifying the ways in which the strategic logic of nonviolent politics is conceptualized, we can think more precisely about what defines and distinguishes nonviolent action not only from armed rebellion but also from other modes of collective action. Acknowledging the different ways in which nonviolence can be and has been practiced also challenges us to think more conceptually about how the political dynamics of nonviolence vary across different political contexts. Among the most recent studies of nonviolent resistance, the paradigmatic example of successful nonviolent politics has been anti-authoritarian, anti-regime resistance. Moreover, a significant determinant of the ability of nonviolent, mass-based movements to topple governments seems to be to their majoritarian character. Despite its proven efficacy in such cases, it is unclear how such modes of collective resistance can be translated to different political situations and forms of conflict, from the struggles of oppressed minorities, economic inequality, and class conflict, to political contestation within democracies. Models of collective power that emphasize mass disruption and cascading revolution might be especially discordant in situations where the primary political antagonist is not a foreign power or a repressive state but is comprised of fellow citizens.

Gandhi and King were particularly attuned to the constraints and possibilities of nonviolent action in conditions of deep social polarization. In such contexts, disciplined action and its orientation toward persuasion were meant to mitigate the negative passions and resentments that are unearthed and intensified by political conflict. Gandhi's campaigns of non-cooperation and mass civil disobedience against British rule are taken to be exemplary instances of nonviolent, anti-regime resistance. But Gandhi also attempted to deploy nonviolent action to resolve various forms of social conflict and domination, such as conflict between Hindus and Muslims and caste oppression. While the results of the campaigns against untouchability and for Hindu-Muslim unity were often mixed and precarious, they involved imaginative experimentation with nonviolent techniques to undo conditions of mistrust and forge alliances and solidarity across entrenched social division.

There is a resonance here with the ways in which King defended disciplined nonviolence as a method with unique advantages in the struggle for racial justice. King recognized that, despite their overlapping moral and political commitments, the political coordinates of the Civil Rights Movement were qualitatively different from anti-colonial struggles. The aim and orientation of anti-colonial movements of self-determination was the overthrow of existing regimes and autonomy from former oppressors. King was arguably the first major theorist of nonviolence to fully recognize the limited applicability of models of anti-regime resistance to minority movements. Securing social equality and integration, in King's eyes, was more complicated and demanding than independence. When oppressed minorities demanded freedom, they did so against a majority that resisted and resented their empowerment. Dramatizing suffering, dignity, and discipline were means by which nonviolent action could be made persuasive within the context of such recalcitrance. Moreover, conflicts between minorities and majorities, between the oppressed and oppressor, were also struggles between citizens who would have to create ways of coexisting in peace, equality, and dignity. Given these challenges, it was, for King, a strategic and tactical imperative that nonviolent direct action orient itself toward reconciliation and not simply the defeat, overthrow, or humiliation of the oppressor.

For analogous reasons, disciplined action is an important concept to revivify in relation to the demands of democracy. The arc of the Civil Rights Movement attests to distinct challenges nonviolent protest faces within the context of democratic politics. The resistance to the movement showed how democracies and democratic publics can be surprisingly hostile to nonviolent protest, especially when waged on behalf of minority interests. As King noted, challenging entrenched interests inflamed and embittered resistance. The democratic demands of living together through crises and conflict require confronting head-on the moral-psychological dynamics of political contestation.

The structures of democratic competition and the continual contest for power fuel resentments, antagonism, and polarization. Democracy also institutionalizes competition and provides mechanisms to express political dissent and effect political change. Insurgent movements, when they take up extra-legal forms of protest, challenge the legitimacy of these institutions and often elicit polarizing and passionate responses. They bear the burden of justifying the necessity of acts of dissent, agitation, and disruption. Scrutiny of political means is a central feature of the politics of protest, but this is especially so in the context of democratic politics. Nonviolent protest, like all protest, becomes subject to public political debate about when and whether direct action is warranted. For Gandhi and King, the use of excessively coercive or aggressive means can distract the public from seeing and engaging with the moral and political message of the movement. This was why the form of protest was so crucial for both King and Gandhi. The dramatization of discipline tries to cut through rancorous debate about the means, lessen affective resistance, and draw people's attention to the underlying issues at stake. At its most imaginative and powerful, disciplined nonviolent protest would involve a perfect convergence of means and ends, with the message itself being mirrored in the form of protest.

ACKNOWLEDGMENTS

I thank José Medina and Tabatha Abu El-Haj for their generous engagement and incisive criticism. I have also benefited enormously from presenting earlier versions of this chapter at the "Ethical Subjects" research seminar at the Rutgers Center for Historical Analysis, the Gandhi workshop at Reed College, and the Political Theory Workshops at the University of Pennsylvania and Yale University. I would like to especially thank Seth Koven and Judith Surkis at Rutgers, and Dennis Dalton, James Tully, Akeel Bilgrami, Darius Rejali, and Jeanne Morefield for their invaluable input at the Reed workshop.

NOTES

1 What is especially key is that Gandhi advocated and practiced *satyagraha* as a novel form of *mass politics*. Here I follow Gene Sharp's claim that what distinguished Gandhi from intellectual precursors like Tolstoy was that he was the first to experiment with nonviolence as practical politics and consciously developed nonviolent organization, tactics, and strategy. Sean Chabot describes the forging of *satyagraha* as a "transformative invention" and qualitatively distinct from forms of contentious politics practiced by mass social movements of the nineteenth century. See Gene Sharp, "Gandhi's Political Significance," in *Gandhi as a Political Strategist* (Boston: P. Sargent Publishers, 1979); and Sean Chabot, "The Gandhian Repertoire as Transformative Invention," *International Journal of Hindu Studies* 18, no. 3 (December 2014): 327–367.

2 On the translation and adoption of Gandhian *satyagraha* by civil rights activists and anti-nuclear protesters in the United States and Britain, see Sean Scalmer, *Gandhi in the West: The Mahatma and the Rise of Radical Protest* (Cambridge: Cambridge University Press, 2011). Sean Chabot's *Transnational Roots of the Civil Rights Movement: African American Explorations of the Gandhian Repertoire* (Lanham, MD: Lexington Books, 2012) analyzes how African Americans came to interpret, adopt, and creatively implement nonviolent techniques. For more overarching accounts of the globalization of nonviolence, see Jonathan Schell, *The Unconquerable World: Power, Nonviolence, and the Will of the People* (New York: Henry Holt, 2003); Peter Ackerman and Jack DuVall, *A Force More Powerful: A Century of Nonviolent Conflict* (New York: St. Martin's Press, 2000); and Gene Sharp, *Waging Nonviolent Struggle: 20th Century Practice and 21st Century Potential* (Boston: Extending Horizon Books, 2005).

3 Gene Sharp's work is the most important in this genre—about which I will say more below. Other key works include: Peter Ackerman and Christopher Kruegler, *Strategic Nonviolent Conflict: The Dynamics of People Power in the Twentieth Century* (Westport, CT: Praeger, 1994); Kurt Schock, *Unarmed Insurrections: People Power Movements in Nondemocracies* (Minneapolis: University of Minnesota Press, 2005) and *Civil Resistance Today* (Cambridge: Polity Press, 2015); Dustin Howes, *Toward a Credible Pacifism: Violence and the Possibilities of Politics* (Albany: SUNY Press, 2009) and "The Failure of Pacifism and the Success of Nonviolence," *Perspectives on Politics* 11, no. 2 (2013): 427–446; Sharon Nepstad, *Nonviolent Revolutions: Civil Resistance in the Late 20th Century* (Oxford: Oxford University Press, 2011) and *Nonviolent Struggle: Theories, Strategies, and Dynamics* (Oxford: Oxford University Press, 2015); and Erica Chenoweth and Maria Stephan, *Why Civil Resistance Works: The Strategic Logic of Nonviolent Conflict* (New York: Columbia University Press, 2014). Popular books promoting nonviolent activism such as Mark and Paul Engler's *This Is an Uprising: How Nonviolent Revolt Is Shaping the Twenty-First Century* (New York: Nation Books, 2016) further attest to the strength and salience of the paradigm of strategic nonviolence.

4 Written as a handbook for activists, Sharp's most popular work is *From Dictatorship to Democracy: A Conceptual Framework for Liberation* (Boston: Albert Einstein Institution, 2003). But the three-volume treatise, *The Politics of Nonviolent Action* (Boston: P. Sargent Publishers, 1973), is the foundational work that covers the theory, method, and dynamics of nonviolent action. The essays collected in *Gandhi as a Political Strategist* (1979) predate this major work but usefully track Sharp's turn to strategic nonviolence. On the development of Sharp's thinking, see Thomas Weber,

"Nonviolence Is Who? Gene Sharp or Gandhi," *Peace & Change* 28, no. 2 (2003): 250–270.

5 Consider, for instance, his popular reputation around the time of the Arab Spring: "Gene Sharp: Machiavelli of Non-Violence," *New Statesman*, www.newstatesman.com. See also the prominent obituaries that appeared in 2018: "Gene Sharp, Global Guru of Nonviolent Resistance, Dies at 90," *New York Times*, February 2, 2018, www.nytimes.com.

6 Alongside Sharp, another influential work that originated the idea of two differing forms of nonviolence is Judith Stiehm, "Nonviolence Is Two," *Sociological Inquiry* 38, no. 1 (1968): 23–30. Stiehm distinguishes between "conscientious" and "pragmatic" nonviolence. For useful overviews of the distinction, see Weber, "Nonviolence Is Who?"; Iain Atack, *Nonviolence in Political Theory* (Edinburgh: Edinburgh University Press, 2012), 9–30; Nepstad, *Nonviolent Struggle*, 4–12, 45–65; and Schock, *Civil Resistance Today*, 25.

7 For more nuanced accounts of principled nonviolence see Stiehm, "Nonviolence Is Two"; Sharp, "Types of Principled Nonviolence" in *Gandhi as a Political Strategist*; Weber, "Nonviolence Is Who?"; and Robert Burrowes, *The Strategy of Nonviolent Defense: A Gandhian Approach* (Albany: SUNY Press, 1996).

8 The term "moderate Machiavellianism" is a reference to Jacques Maritain's "The End of Machiavellianism" and taken up by L. K. Bhardawaj in the short comment, "Principled versus Pragmatic Nonviolence," *Peace Review* 10, no. 1 (1998): 79–81. Clements contrasts this to a principled nonviolence that is based on a "radical ontology" that challenges the "militarized, dominatory, and sovereign nature of contemporary politics" (12). In abandoning this more expansive critical orientation, Clements argues that pragmatic nonviolent movements become "snared" to the coercive logic of the Weberian state (14). In a similar vein, Chabot and Sharifi suggest that in pursuing a purely instrumentalist practice of strategic violence, Egyptian and Iranian resistance movements have limited their political horizon, making them susceptible to, and compatible with, the hegemony of free market liberalism. See Kevin P. Clements, "Principled Nonviolence: An Imperative, Not an Optional Extra," *Asian Journal of Peacebuilding* 3, no. 1 (2015): 1–17; Sean Chabot and Majid Sharifi, "The Violence of Nonviolence: Problematizing Nonviolent Resistance in Iran and Egypt," *Sociologists without Borders* 8, no. 2 (2013). Clements and Chabot and Sharifi point to Gandhi as the purveyor of an ethically transformative model of nonviolent politics. In this they are in line with many scholars who likewise position Gandhi as offering a more radical critique of modern politics. On this point, see especially Uday Mehta, "Gandhi and the Common Logic of War and Peace," *Raritan* 30, no. 1 (Sum-

mer 2010): 134–156 and "Gandhi on Democracy, Politics, and the Ethics of Everyday Life," *Modern Intellectual History* 7, no. 2 (2010): 355–371; and Ramin Jahanbegloo, *The Gandhian Moment* (Cambridge, MA: Harvard University Press, 2013).

9 Chaiwat Satha-Anand, "Overcoming Illusory Division: Between Nonviolence as a Pragmatic Strategy and a Principled Way of Life," in *Civil Resistance: Comparative Perspectives on Nonviolent Struggle*, edited by Kurt Schock (Minneapolis: University of Minnesota Press, 2015).

10 Satha-Anand, "Overcoming Illusory Division," 292. Though Nepstad relies heavily on the principled/pragmatic classification, she acknowledges that the dividing line between the two is not clear. She also notes that what falls under the rubric of principled nonviolence also has a strategic dimension and tries to outline what alternative techniques issue from this perspective. See *Nonviolent Struggle*, 10–12, 50–57.

11 Clements, "Principled Nonviolence"; Chabot and Sharifi, "The Violence of Nonviolence." Howes is particularly innovative here in building on the strength of strategic nonviolence to reformulate pacifism "as a principled commitment to non-violence grounded in a realistic understanding of the historical record and the inherent political liabilities of violence." Howes, "The Failure of Pacifism and the Success of Nonviolence," 428.

12 Satha-Anand, "Overcoming Illusory Division"; Weber, "Nonviolence Is Who?"; Victor Lidz, "A Note on 'Nonviolence Is Two,'" *Sociological Inquiry* 38, no. 1 (Winter 1968): 31–36.

13 Sharp, *The Politics of Nonviolent Action, Part One: Power and Struggle*, 63–64.

14 M. K. Gandhi, "*Satyagraha*—Not Passive Resistance (2-9-1917)," *The Collected Works of Mahatma Gandhi*, Vol. 16, 10. References are to *The Collected Works of Mahatma Gandhi* (Electronic Book), 98 vols. (New Delhi, 1999) and cited hereafter as *CWMG*, followed by volume and page number. King likewise repeatedly contested the implications of passivity, arguing that nonviolence was "not a method for cowards: it *does* resist." And, when socially organized and pursued with unyielding persistence, it becomes a powerful "mass-method" that "disintegrates the old order." See Martin Luther King Jr., "Nonviolence and Racial Justice" and "The Social Organization of Nonviolence" in *A Testament of Hope: The Essential Writings and Speeches of Martin Luther King, Jr.*, edited by James M. Washington (New York: HarperOne, 1986), 7, 33.

15 The term *prefigurative politics* originated in analyses of New Left movements to distinguish forms of organizing and action that enacted radical democratic values from a more strategically oriented politics. See Wini Brienes, *Community and Organization in the New Left, 1962–1968: The*

Great Refusal (New York: Praeger, 1982). For its use as a description of nonviolent action, see B. L. Epstein, *Political Protest and Cultural Revolution: Nonviolent Direct Action in the 1970s and 1980s* (Berkeley: University of California Press, 1991). On the genealogy of the concept and its revival in contemporary left activism, see Uri Gordon, "Prefigurative Politics between Ethical Practice and Absent Promise," *Political Studies* 66, no. 2 (2018): 521–537. For provocative and subtle analyses of Gandhian *satyagraha* as exemplary action, see especially Akeel Bilgrami, "Gandhi, the Philosopher," *Economic and Political Weekly* 38, no. 39 (September 23, 2003): 4159–4165; and Uday Mehta, "Gandhi on Democracy, Politics and the Ethics of Everyday Life." As an aside, it is very unclear if in fact the quote "be the change"—can be directly attributed to Gandhi, as is often supposed. See Brian Morton, "Falser Words Were Never Spoken," *New York Times* (August 29, 2011).

16 Sharp, *The Politics of Nonviolent Action, Part One*, 7–16. It is also referred to as the "consent" theory of power or the "pluralistic" view of power. Sharp himself often turns to the sixteenth-century essay, "Discourse on Voluntary Servitude," by Étienne de la Boétie, to fill out the theoretical roots of this account of obedience.

17 "As force is always on the side of the governed, the governors have nothing to support them but opinion. It is therefore, on opinion only that government is founded; and this maxim extends to the most despotic and most military governments, as well as to the most free and most popular." David Hume, "Of the First Principle of Government," *Essays: Moral, Political and Literary* (Indianapolis: Liberty Fund, 1987), 32.

18 M. K. Gandhi, "Evidence before Disorders Inquiry Committee (9-1-1920)," *CWMG*, 19, 217.

19 M. K. Gandhi, *Hind Swaraj*, *CWMG*, 10, 262.

20 Sharp, "Gandhi on the Theory of Voluntary Servitude," and "Origins of Gandhi's Use of Nonviolent Struggle: A Review-Essay on Erik Erikson's *Gandhi's Truth*," in *Gandhi as a Political Strategist*.

21 Sharp, *The Politics of Nonviolent Action*, Part One, 10–12.

22 Nepstad refers to it as "citizen-based power" to emphasize its non-elite character. Howes calls it a "people-centered" understanding of power. This also resonates with the widespread adoption of "people power" as a moniker for nonviolent resistance, a slogan first made famous by pro-democracy activists in the Philippines in the 1980s. Iain Atack highlights the horizontal character of nonviolent power, and in its positive form, defines it as "integrative" or "cooperative" power. See Nepstad, *Nonviolent Struggle*, 45–49; Howes, "The Failure of Pacifism and the Success of Nonviolence," 435–437; and Atack, *Nonviolence in Political Theory*, 100–121.

23 In *The Politics of Nonviolent Action,* Sharp outlines the theory of power and consent in Part One, and then inventories in great detail an enormous variety of nonviolent methods of protest, noncooperation, and intervention in Part Two: *The Methods of Nonviolent Action.* The concluding volume, *The Dynamics of Nonviolent Action,* presents an analysis of how these methods can lead to the accommodation of protesters' demands, a redistribution of power, and, ultimately, regime change. On Sharp's theory, see Nepstad, *Nonviolent Struggle,* 57–64; and Atack, *Nonviolence in Political Theory,* 114–125.

24 Key works include Ackerman and Kruegler, *Strategic Nonviolent Conflict*; Ackerman and DuVall, *A Force More Powerful*; Schock, *Unarmed Insurrections*; Sharp, *Waging Nonviolent Struggle*; Adam Roberts and Timothy Garten Ash, *Civil Resistance and Power Politics: The Experience of Non-violent Action from Gandhi to the Present* (Oxford: Oxford University Press, 2009); Nepstad, *Nonviolent Revolutions*; and Chenoweth and Stephan, *Why Civil Resistance Works.*

25 Jonathan Schell and Dustin Howes, in particular, developed the Arendtian distinction between power and violence to explore the inherent democratic potential of nonviolent power understood as a form of "action-in-concert." Schell himself was skeptical of Sharp's emphasis on nonviolence as pure technique. By contrast, Howes explicitly tried to build upon the findings of strategic nonviolence to construct a new, "reinvigorated and pragmatic brand of pacifism." Schell, *The Unconquerable World*; Howes, *Toward a Credible Pacifism,* "The Failure of Pacifism and the Success of Nonviolence," and *Freedom Without Violence: Resisting the Western Political Tradition* (Oxford: Oxford University Press, 2016); and Atack, *Nonviolence in Political Theory.*

26 Atack, *Nonviolence in Political Theory,* 8.

27 Krishnalal Shridharani, *War without Violence: A Study of Gandhi's Method and Its Accomplishments* (New York: Harcourt, Brace, and Co., 1939).

28 Richard Gregg, *The Power of Nonviolence* (Philadelphia: J.B. Lippincott and Co., 1934). Both Gregg and Shridharani were directly involved in the Gandhian movement and also closely connected to the Fellowship of Reconciliation's efforts at disseminating and experimenting with nonviolence methods in the 1940s and 1950s. Shridharani had participated in the Salt March, for which he spent time in jail. Soon after, Shridharani attended Columbia University to pursue his PhD—the dissertation eventually became *War without Violence*— while also lecturing on Gandhian politics to student groups, religious groups, and peace activists. On Shridharani and his influence, see Sudarshan Kapur, *Raising Up a Prophet: The African-American Encounter with Gandhi* (Boston: Beacon Press, 1992), 120–121; Scalmer, *Gandhi in the West,* 122–130; Chabot, *Transnational Roots of*

the Civil Rights Movement, 86–99. The revised 1959 edition of Gregg's *The Power of Nonviolence* has recently been republished with a new introduction by James Tully in the Cambridge Texts in the History of Political of Thought series (Cambridge: Cambridge University Press, 2018).

29 Martin Luther King Jr., "Letter from Birmingham Jail," *Why We Can't Wait* (New York: Signet Classics, 2000 [1963]), 85–112. Of particular resonance is King's outlining of the stages of nonviolent direct action and the need for creating crisis via direct action to enable negotiation.

30 Shridharani, *War without Violence*, xxix.

31 Shridharani, *War without Violence*, xxviii.

32 See especially 270–275 and chapter X, 276–294. It is notable that the pamphlet version of *War without Violence* included chapter X which directly compared *satyagraha* and war, alongside chapter I and the concluding remarks.

33 Shridharani, *War without Violence*, 4.

34 Shridharani, *War without Violence*, 285.

35 Shridharani, *War without Violence*, xxxi.

36 Shridharani, *War without Violence*, ch. 1, 3–47. This was the centerpiece of the pamphlet and proved to be especially key for CORE activists. See Scalmer, *Gandhi in the West*, 125–130, 144–147; and Chabot, *Transnational Roots of the Civil Rights Movement*, 86–99.

37 Shridharani, *War without Violence*, 14–47.

38 Shridharani, *War without Violence*, 278–279. Compare with King's account of nonviolent direct action as a form of dramatization that triggers creative crisis. On King's understanding of dramatization, see Karuna Mantena, "Showdown for Nonviolence: The Theory and Practice of Nonviolence," in *To Shape a New World: The Political Philosophy of Martin Luther King, Jr.*, edited by Brandon Terry and Tommie Shelby (Cambridge, MA: Harvard University Press, 2018).

39 Shridharani, *War without Violence*, 116.

40 Shridharani, *War without Violence*, 291–294.

41 Shridharani's project as a whole is framed as a response to James's 1910 essay, "The Moral Equivalent of War." See especially 285–287. See also H.J.N. Horsburgh, *Non-Violence and Aggression: A Study of Gandhi's Moral Equivalent of War* (London: Oxford University Press, 1968).

42 Shridharani, *War without Violence*, 36–41. Both Gregg and Shridharani recounted scenes from the Salt *Satyagraha* made famous by journalists Webb Miller and Negley Farson. Gregg famously described this process as "moral jiu-jitsu." See Gregg, *The Power of Non-Violence*, 41–54.

43 Shridharani, *War without Violence*, 283–285.

44 Shridharani, *War without Violence*, 292.

45 Shridharani was aware that he was deviating from Gandhi on this point. See *War without Violence*, 22, 33.

46 Clarence Marsh Case, *Non-violent Coercion: A Study in Methods of Social Pressure* (London: G. Allen & Unwin, 1923); Reinhold Niebuhr, *Moral Man and Immoral Society: A Study in Ethics and Politics* (Louisville, KY: Westminster John Knox Press, 2001 [1932]); Joan Bondurant, *Conquest of Violence: The Gandhian Philosophy of Conflict* (Princeton, NJ: Princeton University Press, 1958).

47 For a more extensive discussion of this point, see Karuna Mantena, "Mass *Satyagraha* and the Problem of Collective Power," in *Political Imaginaries: Rethinking India's Twentieth Century*, edited by Manu Goswami and Mrinalini Sinha (forthcoming).

48 Karuna Mantena, "Another Realism: Gandhi and the Politics of Nonviolence," *American Political Science Review* 106, no. 2 (2012): 455–470.

49 M. K. Gandhi, "Letter to Jawaharlal Nehru (1933)," *CWMG*, 61, 393.

50 A number of interpreters have read Gandhi's attention to the purity of nonviolent action—and more generally his emphasis on means—as a response to the so-called dirty-hands dilemma and indicative of an overarching concern with protecting the moral purity of political actor. On this point, see Raghavan Iyer, *The Moral and Political Thought of Mahatma Gandhi* (New Delhi: Oxford University Press, 1972); and, more recently, Dipesh Chakrabarty and Rochana Majumdar, "Gandhi's Gita and Politics as Such," *Modern Intellectual History* 7, no. 2 (2010): 335–353. I am not persuaded that Gandhi was so preoccupied with moral corruption of this kind. Rather, the logic ran the other way. The *integrity* of nonviolent action mattered because it was, for Gandhi, closely tied to its political *efficacy*. See Mantena, "Another Realism."

51 Max Weber, "The Profession and Vocation of Politics," in *Weber: Political Writings*, edited by Peter Lassman and Ronald Speirs (Cambridge: Cambridge University Press, 1994), 354–355.

52 Weber, "The Profession and Vocation of Politics," 361.

53 Hannah Arendt, *The Human Condition* (Chicago: University of Chicago Press, 1958), 184.

54 Arendt, *The Human Condition*, 233.

55 See Nagappa Gowda, *The Bhagavadgita in the Nationalist Discourse* (New Delhi: Oxford University Press, 2011); Shruti Kapila and Faisal Devji (eds.), *Political Thought in Action: The Bhagavad Gita and Modern India* (Cambridge: Cambridge University Press, 2013); and Sanjay Palshikar, *Evil and the Philosophy of Retribution: Modern Commentaries on the Gita* (New Delhi: Routledge, 2014).

56 M. K. Gandhi, "Jain *Ahimsa*? (25–101928)," *CWMG*, 43, 131.

57 This point is made in different ways by Niebuhr, *Moral Man and Immoral Society*, ch. 9; Howes, *Toward a Credible Pacifism*; and Schell, *The Unconquerable World*.

58 M. K. Gandhi, *Hind Swaraj*, *CWMG*, 10, 288–289.

59 Bhikhu Parekh, *Gandhi's Political Philosophy: A Critical Examination* (London: Macmillan, 1989), 147.

60 Weber, "The Profession and Vocation of Politics," 365–368.

61 Gandhi, *Hind Swaraj*, 10, 293.

62 On nonviolent action's "principle of reversibility," see Johan Galtung, *Peace by Peaceful Means: Peace and Conflict, Development and Civilization* (London: Sage, 1996), 271–273.

63 Martin Luther King Jr., "Pilgrimage to Nonviolence," *A Testament of Hope*, 36.

64 Martin Luther King Jr., *Stride Toward Freedom: The Montgomery Story* (Boston: Beacon Press, 2010 [1958]), 211–212.

65 King, "Letter from Birmingham Jail," 88.

66 In this vein, Akeel Bilgrami has contrasted the Gandhian practice of moral exemplarity with enlightenment criticism in the Kantian mold. He argues that the latter entails the calling into question of one's opponent's worldview and thereby becomes a moralizing criticism, easily susceptible to corruption (egoistic investments) with "the potential to generate other psychological attitudes (resentment, hostility) which underlie interpersonal violence." See Bilgrami, "Gandhi, the Philosopher," 4163.

67 King, *Stride Toward Freedom*, 214.

68 M. K. Gandhi, "Speech at Birmingham Meeting," *CWMG*, 54, 48. Part of this quote also appears in King in "An Experiment in Love," *A Testament of Hope*, 18.

69 Martin Luther King Jr., "Love, Law, and Civil Disobedience," *A Testament of Hope*, 47.

70 King, "Letter from Birmingham Jail," 90.

71 Martin Luther King Jr., "I Have a Dream," *A Testament of Hope*, 218.

72 King, *Stride Toward Freedom*, 206.

73 King, "Letter from Birmingham Jail," 110.

74 Niebuhr, *Moral Man and Immoral Society*, xxxi.

75 Niebuhr, *Moral Man and Immoral Society*, 231.

76 Niebuhr, *Moral Man and Immoral Society*, 232.

77 Niebuhr, *Moral Man and Immoral Society*, 248.

78 King, "The Social Organization of Nonviolence," 33.

79 Niebuhr, *Moral Man and Immoral Society*, 250.

80 Niebuhr, *Moral Man and Immoral Society*, 247.

81 Niebuhr, *Moral Man and Immoral Society*, 250.

82 Niebuhr, *Moral Man and Immoral Society*, 247.

83 King, *Stride Toward Freedom*, 210.

84 King, *Why We Can't Wait*, 68–69.

85 M. K. Gandhi, "*Satyagraha* Leaflet No. 21," *CWMG*, 18, 41.

86 M. K. Gandhi, "What It Is Not," *CWMG*, 27, 210–212.

87 M. K. Gandhi, "Was It Coercive?" *CWMG*, 61, 377.

88 Sharp, *The Politics of Nonviolent Action, Part Three: The Dynamics of Nonviolent Action*, 594–635. Even the Englers, who especially emphasize the disruptive dimensions of nonviolent protest, acknowledge the tactical necessity of discipline for radical movements. See Engler and Engler, *This Is an Uprising*, 225–250.

89 Chenoweth and Stephan, *Why Civil Resistance Works*, 3–61.

90 Chenoweth and Stephan, *Why Civil Resistance Works*, especially ch. 3.

5

NO JUSTICE, NO PEACE

UNCIVIL PROTEST AND THE POLITICS OF CONFRONTATION

JOSÉ MEDINA

> I've been locked up (for disturbing the peace in Detroit) and I know you got to disturb the peace when you can't get no peace.
>
> —Aretha Franklin[1]

There are forms of protest that are deemed unacceptable because they disturb peaceful coexistence, create or exacerbate conflicts, or are dangerous; they are deemed, in short, *uncivil.* In this chapter I will argue for a view of protest as political confrontation that can and should take many forms, both *civil* and *uncivil.* In my defense of an unconstrained and uncompromising politics of political confrontation, I will argue that concerns about *justice* trump concerns about *peace* (i.e., social peace, or law and order). I will also argue that, given that a lack of justice involves a lack of social peace, the acceptability of any social unrest that a protest may cause has to be evaluated in the context of the social unrest that already exists and that the protest is denouncing and asking us to repair. My approach is contextual and dialectical, assessing the appropriateness of a protest in the context in which it arises and in terms of its dialectical entanglements both with the normative problems that prompt it (i.e., problems of justice) and with the normative consequences to which it is directed (i.e., attempts at restoring justice). Although I will defend a positive view aimed at vindicating the contextual legitimacy of uncivil protest, I will take an indirect route to that positive view by developing negative arguments against views that dismiss the adequacy of uncivil protests and heavily restrict what can count as a legitimate protest.

There are different ways in which so-called uncivil protest come under attack. First, what I call the *conservative* view of protest contends that political protest should be confined to particular spaces and practices designated for political engagement and regulated by strict constraints of law and order. On the conservative view, the charge of politicization of an allegedly nonpolitical space such as sports or the arts is already sufficient to call into question the legitimacy of a protest. Additionally, according to the conservative view, expressions of political dissent and political confrontations should be carefully managed and controlled in order to make sure that the social peace and order are not disturbed, always prioritizing law and order over freedom of expression or freedom of assembly. In the second place, what I call the *liberal* view of protest does not shy away from expressions of political dissent anywhere, but it constrains the acceptability of protest to *civil* protest, alleging that defying the norms of civility is counterproductive if not altogether illegitimate. On the liberal view, it is claimed that political protest must remain *civil* either *on principled grounds*, claiming that protesters must preserve "the purity of action"[2] and discipline their resistance so that their means do not vitiate their ends; or *on strategic grounds*, alleging that undisciplined confrontational tactics will backfire, produce a backlash, and contribute to the escalation of conflict and violence. These two different ways of justifying disciplining political resistance and limiting protest to civil protest result in two versions of the liberal view: the *principled* liberal view and the *strategic* liberal view. In this chapter, I will challenge both versions of the liberal view as well as the conservative view.

The *confrontational* view of protest I will defend does not restrict protest a priori in any particular way and does not rule out in principle any form of confrontation that protest may take. According to my unrestricted confrontational view, we should think of *civil and uncivil* protests as being in a continuum, as situated in a wide and heterogeneous spectrum of cases deploying different kinds of confrontation that may challenge legality and norms of civility to a lesser or fuller extent. As I will argue below, the distinction between civil and uncivil protest is not absolute and categorical, but *gradual and contextual*.[3] There is a complex continuum of cases between the paradigm case of fully civil protest (e.g., a demonstration with a permit that uses only respectful language and a moderate tone) and the paradigm case of fully uncivil protest (e.g., an unruly uprising or riot that includes physical violence and destruction of property). Between those paradigmatic extremes, there is a wide variety of cases in which political confrontation is managed in different ways, and those different forms of confronting injustices can be interpreted as containing different combinations of civil and uncivil elements. Whether an action counts as uncivil in a particular context depends on the norms of civility that apply to that context and how those norms are interpreted. For example, members of the Russian feminist activist organization Pussy Riot protesting topless at Moscow's Christ the Savior Cathedral was considered uncivil in that context, but clearly, topless protesters are not considered uncivil in every context. On the other hand, civility and uncivility are not an all or nothing matter, but qualities that come in degrees. While Rosa Parks's refusal to give up her seat on the bus is an example of maximally *civil* disobedience, other similar acts in the Montgomery bus boycott in 1955–56 exhibited features that were considered *uncivil* (e.g., the appearance or demeanor of the protester which was perceived as undignified, the use of profanity, the tone with which a protester such as Claudette Colvin talked back to the bus driver and the police officers, etc.).[4]

On my gradualist and contextualist view, whether *uncivil* forms of protest are justified cannot be decided a priori and independently of context, not only because civility and uncivility can only be properly interpreted and assessed in context, but also because there are contexts of oppression that only leave room for uncivil protests, and social mobilization by uncivil means may be required for the mitigation of injustice. On my view, the decision that activists, community organizers, and participants in protest must make about what form their political confrontation should take on the civil/uncivil protest spectrum is essentially *strategic*. What needs to be assessed is: What are the most effective means of resisting injustice available to us? Of course, not any form of confrontation will do if we want to minimize conflict and stop the escalation of violence, but the commitment to social peace and nonviolence has to be made compatible with the commitment to confront injustices and the different patterns of violence those injustices may contain. If existing injustices and patterns of violence are left unchallenged for the sake of preserving "the purity of action" and avoiding uncivil confrontation, protest movements may be sacrificing their primary goal of fighting for liberation from oppression and against injustice. The civil/uncivil protest spectrum also contains a nonviolent/violent protest spectrum. The use of physical violence should always be a last resort and only justifiable for the sake of stopping, de-intensifying, or de-escalating already existing violence; but there are milder forms of violence (such as psychological, emotional, or symbolic violence) that are not only difficult, but in fact impossible to avoid in activist practices in an absolute way. In the fight against injustice, we cannot tie our hands and rule out as a matter of principle certain courses of action because they may compromise elusive ideals of "the purity of action" or absolute nonviolence.

Not all injustices involve the perpetration of violence, but, as Iris Marion Young has argued, violence is one of the crucial "faces" of oppression.[5] Structural forms of oppression, such as racism, are grounded in and reproduced through different kinds of violence: indeed, racial oppression has been kept in place through the physical violence that empowered individuals, groups, and institutions (such as the police) have inflicted on oppressed racial groups. But such oppression has also been kept in place through the economic violence that material practices and structures have created, and by the psychological, emotional, and discursive violence that a racist culture and its racially biased systems of representation and forms of communication perpetrate. There is also another form of violence that often accompanies and facilitates oppression: *epistemic violence*,[6] that is, the violence one suffers when one is harmed as a subject of knowledge and understanding, as it happens when people are silenced, systematically misrepresented, or rendered invisible or inaudible. There is a particular kind of activism that is directed against epistemic violence: This is what I have termed *epistemic activism*,[7] which is aimed at breaking silences, giving voice to the victims of injustice, disrupting patterns of social invisibility, and awakening people from their *political slumbers*, that is, from their social blindness, apathy, and insensitivity. Epistemic activism cannot awaken people from their political slumbers without making use of discomfort and (at least mild forms of) epistemic violence. Epistemic activists cannot fight against apathy, insensitivity, and social invisibility without stepping on people's toes and using provocations and confrontations. Think here, for example, of the confrontational politics of ACT UP during the AIDS epidemics and their interventions in public and institutional spaces to disrupt social invisibility and to uproot apathy and insensitivity,[8] to which I will return as one of my central examples of uncivil protest later in the chapter.

To preview, my analysis and argumentation will suggest that the views that affirm a categorical distinction between violent and nonviolent action and insist on "the purity of action" draw on an underlying notion of violence that is overly narrow and not attentive to different kinds of violence and their interrelations. My contextualist perspective calls into question whether we can make sense of a principled distinction between civil and uncivil protest and between violent and nonviolent politics independently of particular contexts of action. Contextually, the question for nonviolent protest movements is how to maximize the likelihood that their interventions will result in decreasing violence in the long run and all things considered. And note that inaction or non-intervention, as well as tamed or disciplined protests that shy away from stepping on people's toes, can be complicit with the normalization of violence in public life and with the toleration of insidious forms of structural violence, whereas uncivil confrontational politics—as exhibited, for example, in epistemic activist interventions of ACT UP or in the counter-protests of Black Lives Matter—can disrupt the complicity of multiple publics (not only those directly addressed, but also those standing on the sidelines).

It is one thing to be committed to the mitigation of violence and another to be committed to "the purity of action" or to nonviolence in an absolute sense. Confrontational politics can remain contextually committed to the mitigation of violence while at the same time not ruling out uncivil protests and disruptive tactics that may include carefully deployed and well-managed uses of (mild forms of) violence for the sake of resisting injustice and mitigating violence. Not only is it conceptually impossible to guarantee that protest will remain fully civil and free from violence in an absolute sense, but there are good arguments for making a politics of confrontation broad enough so as to allow for the strategic use of *uncivil* protest and of disruptive tactics for fighting injustice and stopping violence. In fact, I will argue that well-entrenched injustices and patterns of violence that become pervasive in the social fabric cannot be resisted without using uncivil protests and activism that does not shy away from (mild forms of) violent confrontation (such as the epistemic activism of ACT UP), for social upheavals and difficult cultural shifts are required to trigger the process of eradicating such pervasive injustices and patterns of violence.

In what follows I will argue that only a politics of confrontation that makes room for *uncivil* protest can disrupt complicity with widespread injustices and wake people up from their political slumbers. I will focus on three cases in which uncivil protests involve well-justified confrontations that disrupt established social dynamics and defy what passes for norms of civility and respectability: political protests in sports, the so-called confrontational direct actions of ACT UP, and the staging of counter-protests. First, I will focus on protests in sports and will develop my critical engagement with the conservative view of protest. I will then provide a transition from the conservative to the liberal view through a critical discussion of Martin Luther King Jr.'s view of political resistance, highlighting both the resources and limitations of that view for a politics of confrontation. In this section, I will introduce the notion of *confrontational* direct action (through an elucidation of the AIDS activism of ACT UP) and will formulate a general argument for *uncivil* protest, which will be further elaborated in the third section, "Toward a Politics of Confrontation." I will focus on counter-protests and, arguing against the liberal view of protest, I will defend an unconstrained confrontational view that includes both civil and uncivil protest. All three sections of this chapter aim to articulate reasons for the legitimacy and urgent need of a politics of confrontation that makes room for uncivil protest. Today's political climate and widespread forms of apathy and complicity with race-based and class-based injustices that seem to be deepening make an unconstrained and uncompromising politics of confrontation particularly timely and urgent.

Social Spaces without Political Resistance? Stifling Dissent and the Difficulties of Political Protests in Sports

Sometimes protests are deemed uncivil and characterized as disturbing the peace and the social order because they take place in spaces and within practices that have been depoliticized, spaces and practices where political engagements are either banned or carefully managed and controlled. Because social and political conflicts have already been hidden from view, those deceivingly peaceful and politically manicured spaces and practices—such as sports in the United States—do not tolerate expression of dissent and protest. Protest under those circumstances is depicted by conservative forces (and often perceived by mainstream media) as disturbing provocations and the unnecessary manufacturing of conflict by troublemakers. Protesters in those spaces and practices are asked to take their troubles elsewhere, to find other venues for their political expressions. Sometimes these protests are perceived as intrinsically violent, as endangering the peace; and the demands that they be stopped come with particular threats and intimidations for the sake of protecting "the peace" and "the law and order" that civil society needs. In this section, I will argue that these demands and political (sometimes also legal) pressures to stop protests in depoliticized spaces and practices such as sports are ways of stifling voices and dissent and, therefore, ways of contributing to political repression and depoliticization (that is, the policing of depoliticized domains of social interaction). Compliance with such demands would involve complicity with injustice by silence and inaction, which is precisely what protesters in these cases courageously disrupt.

Why should athletes be protesting racial injustice in football stadiums and other sports venues? Is that the time and place for expressing one's political stance against racial injustices in American culture—against, for example, police homicides of people of color? Are those who criticize these protests and try to stifle the athletes' political voices justified in doing so and in keeping sports "free from politics"?

Sports are full of political symbols and political statements, and yet they are supposed to be "free from politics" or "above politics."

While expressions of political unity are not only expected but demanded in sports (around the national anthem, for example), expressions of political dissent or protest are censured and derided as unpatriotic and as fracturing political unity. But why are protests perceived as destructive of national identity and unity? Why should they not be perceived as alternative ways of relating to one's national identity and culture, and as attempts at rebuilding political communities, as conducive to new forms of solidarity and political unity?

Black athletes have been chastised for using their social visibility and cultural capital for political causes that are perceived as "divisive" or corruptive of the unity and ethos of a political community (instead of seeing those causes as opportunities for rebuilding or regenerating such unity and ethos). When black athletes protest, they are criticized for being unruly and disciplined in official and unofficial, formal and informal, ways. They are pressured to shut up. But what is the social and political cost of keeping their power and agency "pure," apolitical? Isn't the silence of those who have social power and a platform to speak a form of complicity with the perpetuation of injustice? What does it mean to insist on the expectation (sometimes the demand) that athletes should remain silent about injustices happening all around them in a society that they are supposed to represent? Shouldn't athletes (as well as other figures with social power and cultural capital) speak up? Shouldn't they be critically vigilant of the well-being of the social fabric that they are supposed to be instrumental in building and sustaining? Precisely because they are role models and play a key role in building and sustaining the bonds of a community, athletes should be critical of the flaws of their society: they have a prima facie obligation to alert the public that the social bonds of a community become perverted if those who are most vulnerable are not acknowledged and if solidarity with their suffering is not expressed. In this section, I will argue that to insist on the depoliticization of athletes' performance is, implicitly, to claim that athletes should only have a *subordinated* agency, that their power should be blindly at the service of dominant institutions and cultures, no matter how immoral or unjust these institutions and cultures happen to be—in short, to force athletes to become ideological figures of complacency that stifle critique, pawns in the deployment of the repressive ideology of *panem et circenses* (bread and circuses).

The taking-a-knee protest of Colin Kaepernick and other football players to denounce racial injustice has been criticized by many as unpatriotic and uncivil and has brought about a renewed focus on political demonstrations during the performance of the national anthem at sports events. But national anthem protests by black athletes have a long history and, as Zach Johnk puts it, "an equally lengthy tradition of angering mostly white fans, sports officials and politicians."[9] At the Mexico City Olympic Games in 1968, during a medal ceremony, Tommie Smith and John Carlos—African American track athletes who had won gold and bronze—raised their black-gloved fists to the sky in a black power salute. The International Olympic Committee censured them, and the US Olympic Committee suspended them and sent them home. On October 19, 1968, the *New York Times* reported that some members of the American delegation "hailed [the black power salute of Smith and Carlos] as a gesture of independence and a move in support of a worthy cause," but "many others said they were offended and embarrassed. A few were vehemently indignant." The punishment of Smith and Carlos served as a warning to others, and it tempered the behavior of other African American athletes in medal ceremonies in the 1968 Olympics: In accepting their gold, silver, and bronze medals for their 400-meter run, Lee Evans, Larry James, and Ron Freeman wore black berets, but refrained from gestures (such as the black power salute) that would result in official sanctions. At the 1972 Olympics in Munich, Wayne Collett and Vince Matthews—also African American athletes who won medals in track—did not face the flag during the medal ceremony and stood casually, with their hands on their hips and their jackets unzipped. They were quickly censured and suspended, officials fearing a repeat of the Mexico City gesture and controversy. Besides these (and other) well-known political protests by American athletes of color at international sports events, national anthem protests have also happened domestically for quite some time. At a college track meet at Nassau Coliseum on Long Island in January 1973, some black athletes did not stand during the national anthem and, as the *New York Times* reported, "most of the 8,551 spectators joined in booing" them, some chanting "Throw them out!," others shouting racial epithets at the athletes. Twenty-three years later, in March 1996, the National Basketball Association suspended Mahmoud Abdul-Rauf of the Denver Nuggets for his refusal to stand during the national anthem. Abdul-Rauf alleged that he did not believe in standing for any nationalistic ideology and that he viewed the flag as "a symbol of oppression." This reopened a controversy about the role of politics in sports and, in particular, a controversy about whether forcing participation in a patriotic exercise strengthens or undermines democratic values. Many asserted, once again, that athletes should keep their politics to themselves and to their private lives, and that we should keep sports "pure," leaving our politics at the door.

"Sports stadiums are just to have fun, not a place for politics," some people say. Sports stadiums are supposed to be free of politics, and yet they are constantly being used for public mourning, for celebrating political events, for expressing solidarity with wars and political causes. I will not harp on the hypocrisy that can be found in a mind-set that refuses to accept protests as appropriate political expressions during sports events while endorsing celebratory political expressions as an essential (even mandatory) part of such events. I will focus instead on two kinds of considerations that are often invoked to ban political protests at sports events, deeming them uncivil and illegitimate: First, there are explicitly political considerations aimed at policing the political expressions that are appropriate or inappropriate at sports events; and, second, there are also considerations that are purportedly *nonpolitical* and that try to demarcate the limits of the political, leaving sports outside those limits. My objection to both kinds of considerations is that, far from ensuring that sports remain "appropriately political" or "nonpolitical," they make sports highly ideological by silencing dissent, requiring conformity with a particular way of thinking, and stigmatizing alternative ways of inhabiting our political communities.

In the first place, there are those who claim that the only political expressions that should be allowed at sports events are those that are celebratory and community-affirming because sports should contribute to developing a positive sense of identity and community, making us feel good about who we are as a community. According to this mind-set, political expressions that are critical or contestatory should not be allowed at sports events because critique and contestation are intrinsically divisive and undermine a positive sense of identity and community. This may sound like a good idea when a community only has things to celebrate and nothing to criticize and contest. But when problems and injustices are swept under the rug and those with a public voice are gagged and only allowed to speak in a celebratory mode, the "celebration" seems highly ideological, erasing or hiding the suffering of some at the cost of the joy of others, disregarding injustices for the sake of creating or sustaining a false sense of comfort, a sense of "feeling good about ourselves" that is based on a false image of ourselves, a sanitized image from which everything bad and problematic has been carefully erased. If our political expressions (at sports events or anywhere) are forced to be celebratory no matter what, no matter how many injustices our community may be suffering or perpetrating, then those political expressions are *ideological* and they create (or *can* create) a false, positive sense of identity and community, a self-image that is not based on facts or on an accurate sense of who we are and what we do. If we are forced to feel proud of ourselves no matter what we do or who we have become, that pride is highly ideological and based on denial. A sense of identity built on a mind-set that rules in pride and rules out shame out of principle,[10] independent of any factual and normative assessment of social realities, is out of touch and operates ideologically. If sports are supposed to be public forms of expression of a community, they need to be equally open to positive and negative political emotions (such as pride and shame) and to political expressions that are both celebratory and critical, for only a political expressivity that is sufficiently pluralistic can accommodate a sense of identity and community that is appropriately diverse, heterogeneous, nuanced, and in touch with reality.

In the second place, there are those who claim that sports should be kept "pure" and "apolitical" for the sake of unity above politics, that is, for the sake of creating and sustaining a *supra-political* identity and community in which all are welcome, accepted, and respected independent of politics. The rationale behind this view is that leisure activities should not be politicized, that the power of leisure is precisely to bring people together independent of their politics and of other differences (such as differences of religion, language, culture, etc.). This mind-set should have a problem with the inclusion of *any* political expression or symbolism in sports, whether celebratory or contestatory, because that would betray the sought-after "purity" or apolitical character of sports. It is worth noting that such purity is not in evidence, and in all sports events some political symbols and expressions (flags, salutes, pledges) are allowed while others are not. This one-sided and selective use of the purity-of-sports rationale to ban some forms of political expression and not others renders the rationale arbitrary and ideological. The defender of the purity view of sports can allege that the view is aspirational and that, although the apolitical character of sports may not be fully achieved, we must nonetheless strive toward it and engage in the active depoliticization of sports activities, not allowing new forms of political expression within sports and trying to eliminate or minimize those political symbols that have become part of the sports scene. But is this "purification," this way of removing or minimizing political expressions in sports, really a way of making sports any less political, a way of severing *all* ties between sports and *all* political ideologies?

Depoliticizing a social space or practice can be ideological—in fact, depoliticizing can be as ideological as selectively and arbitrarily politicizing. The depoliticization of a social space or a practice can be a powerful way of protecting a political ideology from critical interrogation; and, indeed, conformity with dominant ideology is not enforced only by requiring explicit endorsement, but by arranging social spaces and practices in such a way that the dominant ideology is simply taken for granted by social actors, becoming interwoven in the social fabric in which we move, interspersed in the very air that we breathe, so to speak. We position ourselves politically not only through speech and action; silence and inaction are also political, and we take political positions by refusing to speak and act. For this reason, imposing silence on political issues can itself be a strong political move, a political imposition. If we live in a society in which flagrant injustices are not sufficiently visible and appropriately discussed, any social space or practice that contributes to the social invisibility of these injustices and the silence around them is blameworthy. Athletes (or any public figure for that matter) who use their cultural capital to break the silence around an injustice or to undo its invisibility should not be derided and silenced but praised as courageous epistemic activists. Demanding that athletes remain silent about issues of justice for the sake of the purity of sports is ideological because it is a way of enforcing complicity with a particular ideology, the dominant ideology that encourages people to look the other way in the face of injustice. The silence of the sports world with respect to injustices such as racism and xenophobia, far from being a sign of "purity," is a sign of political complicity.

So, there are good arguments that successfully neutralize and counter the considerations that are typically offered for stifling athletes' political voices and keeping protests out of sports events. But, more importantly, independent of these counter-arguments, there are also powerful *positive* arguments for the adequacy and legitimacy of protesting injustices in sports and in other cultural venues—arguments that trump concerns about the (suprapolitical) unifying power or purity of sports. I will ground these arguments in the view of political protest offered in the writings of Martin Luther King Jr., especially his concept of *direct action*, which I will expand to include *confrontational direct action* in both civil and uncivil protest.

Arguments for Protesting Injustice: "Injustice *anywhere* is a threat to justice *everywhere*"

Urged to refrain from participating in protests for the sake of social peace and the preservation of law and order, in his *Letter from a Birmingham Jail*, Martin Luther King Jr. offered an impassionate justification of the legitimacy of his participation in protest. Some of the considerations he presented in his celebrated discourses and letters can be developed into arguments that have validity today and apply to protests in sports and other forms of public demonstrations against injustice that have come under attack. I will focus on two positive arguments, one about the nature of injustice (and its scope in the social world) and the other about the nature of protest (and its relation to our ethical and political responsibilities).

In the first place, there are good reasons to think that injustices have a holistic character: Given the interrelatedness of social spaces, practices, and communities, when an injustice is committed, it should be expected that it will reverberate throughout the social fabric; and it is appropriate to feel concern for such injustice (and to express it) in every corner of the social fabric, since social spaces, practices, and communities cannot be sealed off from each other. This holistic view about injustice was powerfully invoked by King when he claimed that "injustice anywhere is a threat to justice everywhere," citing "the interrelatedness of all communities and states." Here is the complete reflection in which he develops this idea while rejecting the charge of being an illegitimate "outside agitator" leveled against him:

> I am cognizant of the interrelatedness of all communities and states. I cannot sit idly by in Atlanta and not be concerned about what happens in Birmingham. Injustice anywhere is a threat to justice everywhere. We are caught in an inescapable network of mutuality, tied in a single garment of destiny. Whatever affects one directly, affects all indirectly. Never again can we afford to live with the narrow, provincial "outside agitator" idea. Anyone who lives inside the United States can never be considered an outsider anywhere within its bounds.[11]

As King suggests, a protester of injustice cannot be considered an illegitimate "outside agitator" who is bringing in alien concerns, problems, and conflicts that don't belong there, for, if these are concerns, problems, and conflicts of *justice*, then they belong *everywhere*, given the unbounded character of issues of justice and the interrelatedness of political communities. There is no public space or activity that is completely sealed off from political life and immune from protest. Whether people are enjoying a football game in a stadium or dining out with friends in a restaurant, they are sharing a space in which protest can enter and cannot be simply dismissed out of hand as illegitimate "outside agitation."

In King's reflections, we can also find a second argument for the legitimacy of participating in protests against injustices, even in spaces and practices that don't invite political discussions and demonstrations. This second argument is about the nature of protest as a way of responding to social harms and of discharging our ethical and political responsibilities. The kinds of peaceful interventions that King termed "non-violent direct action"—such as marches, sit-ins, boycotts—were forms of protest through which social actors can shed light on unattended social harms and can disrupt their own complicity with the continuation of these harms while inviting others to do the same. These protests proceed by *confronting publics and institutions* about a problem of justice that has been left unattended and for which negotiations and regular political engagements have failed,[12] that is, by refusing to sweep social tensions, conflicts, and harms under the rug, by creating scenarios and dramatizations in which the existing (even if ignored) tensions, conflicts, and harms are felt and have to be responded to. This is how King explains it: "Nonviolent direct action seeks to create such a crisis and foster such a tension that a community which has constantly refused to negotiate is forced to confront the issue. It seeks so to dramatize the issue that it can no longer be ignored."[13] He also stated:

> We who engage in nonviolent direct action are not the creators of tension. We merely bring to the surface the hidden tension that is already alive. We bring it out in the open, where it can be seen and dealt with. Like a boil that can never be cured so long as it is covered up but must be opened with all its ugliness to the natural medicines of air and light, injustice must be exposed, with all the tension its exposure creates, to the light of human conscience and the air of national opinion before it can be cured.[14]

It is in the nature of a protest to confront issues in order to take (and begin to discharge) *responsibility* with respect to the problems of our communities. Martin Luther King Jr. seems ambivalent as to whether protesters "create" tensions or simply "bring out in the open" the hidden tensions that already exist. But in either case (whether simply providing an outlet for hidden tensions or perhaps also creating further social tensions as the existing ones surface), the engagement of protesters with tensions is for the sake of waking people up from their political slumbers, from their numbness and disinterest, and for the sake of initiating a process of taking and discharging responsibility with respect to social harms. King is providing important insights into the connection between *protesting* and *taking responsibility*.

He is calling attention to the power of protest for sensitizing people and making them morally and politically attuned to the social realities in which they live, making them responsive to social harms and engaged in processes of moral repair and restorative justice. A protest is a form of political *communication* that makes social problems known and felt, and it is a form of political *action* that calls for a response to social harms. In these two senses (epistemic and actional), protest is a way of taking and redeeming moral and political responsibilities. King is also emphasizing that, in assessing protests, we must always direct our moral and political sensibilities, not so much toward the tensions and conflicts in the protests themselves, but first and foremost toward the underlying tensions and conflicts that the protests are responding to. Protests can of course be misplaced. Protesters may be mistaken; they may be overreacting or reacting to illusory social evils. But in assessing protests as acts of communication and as acts of initiating responses to social problems and harms, we need to focus first and foremost on the alleged problems and harms in question. Concern for the tensions that protests themselves create should always be secondary to the concern for the preexisting tensions and social harms that cause the protests. As King forcefully put it:

> You deplore the demonstrations taking place in Birmingham. But your statement, I am sorry to say, fails to express a similar concern for the conditions that brought about the demonstrations. I am sure that none of you would want to rest content with the superficial kind of social analysis that deals merely with effects and does not grapple with underlying causes. It is unfortunate that demonstrations are taking place in Birmingham, but it is even more unfortunate that the city's white power structure left the Negro community with no alternative.[15]

Those who want to suppress or constrain protests out of concern for "social peace" and for "law and order" need to balance that concern against the social harms that protesters are responding to, against the felt injustices that move protesters to speak up and act. They need to take seriously the possibility that there is already a lack of social peace and a failure in the governing law and order that protesters are responding to, even if the critics of the protest don't feel it. Their concern for social peace and law and order should start earlier—not with the protest itself, but with "the underlying causes," as King stated, with the social malcontent that led to the protest and the lack of social peace behind it, for any injustice is a disturbance of the social peace and a failure of the governing law and order that has left people unprotected. This is well articulated in the slogan "No Justice, No Peace," to which I will return in the next section.

As we have seen in this section, *direct action*, as conceptualized by Martin Luther King Jr., was understood within the Civil Rights Movement as a communicative action that involved both an epistemic intervention (aimed at creating a new kind of critical awareness and sensibility that could disrupt complicity) and a practical-political intervention (preparing people for transformative action and changes in social policies and social directions). Direct action, thus conceived, is neutral to the means used for epistemic-political intervention and it can include both civil and uncivil protest. King and other leaders of the Civil Rights Movement insisted on *disciplining* political resistance and *constraining* direct action to those interventions that respected the norms of civility and law and order whenever possible. So, the way conflict was brought into the open and dramatized in the civil protests favored by King and his followers was typically by making social conflict as visible as possible but without confronting publics in an antagonistic way, such as blaming or shaming them for social harms, or without creating or deepening social divisions so that the political body would be fractured (us-versus-them) in the fight against injustice. The dramatization of civil protest of this sort was typically silent or soft-spoken and minimized confrontation. This contrasts sharply with the confrontational tactics of other kinds of activism within civil rights movements, such as the tactics of ACT UP during the AIDS epidemic in the 1980s. ACT UP protests typically were extremely loud and disruptive, expressing rage, angrily confronting people, shaming them, and forcing them to choose a side, with the victims or against them, choosing to speak up and act or choosing to watch people die unattended. "Shame! Shame! Shame!" was one of the chants that ACT UP activists would use in their *confrontational* direct actions. Interestingly, the technique of disrupting public spaces and shaming individuals or publics who are trying to enjoy their work or leisure undisturbed has returned to the contemporary political scene. Think of the heckling of Kirstjen Nielsen, the

Secretary of Homeland Security, at a Mexican restaurant in Washington on June 19, 2018, when she was eating dinner and trying to relax. With tensions continuing to escalate over the Trump administration's immigration policy that separates children from their families after illegal crossings at the border, a group of protesters confronted her, chanting "Shame! Shame! Shame!," with individual protesters articulating the ethical and political claims of the confrontation in various ways, such as one who stated, "If kids don't eat in peace, you don't eat in peace" (as reported by the *New York Times*, June 20, 2018).

As Deborah Gould shows in *Moving Politics* (2009), during the 1980s AIDS epidemic, a new kind of activist intervention was developed by ACT UP: *confrontational* direct action. As Gould puts it, "arguing that confrontational direct action was needed to fight the exploding AIDS crisis, oppositional AIDS activist groups began to emerge in 1986–87 out of lesbian and gay communities around the United States."[16] Defiance and oppositional tactics defined the confrontational politics of ACT UP, which "shook up straight *and* gay establishments with defiant, sex-radical politics" [that] "opened up ways of being gay and of being political that had been foreclosed by the more mainstream-oriented lesbian and gay establishment."[17] ACT UP activists felt that the injustice they were fighting against rose to the level of a political crisis and an emergency situation, in which hundreds if not thousands were dying daily, in which silence was really tantamount to complicity with manslaughter or to contributing to death by inaction, as their slogan "Silence = Death" and the pink triangle vividly and tragically expressed. I will bracket the issue of whether "crisis" or "emergency" politics always calls for different kinds of protest and activism than "regular" or "ordinary" politics. It suffices to point out for our purposes—that is, for making conceptual and normative space for uncivil protest—that, in an important sense, fighting injustice is always fighting a social crisis and an emergency, for, as expressed in what became a slogan in the Civil Rights Movement, *justice delayed is justice denied.*[18] In this sense, the justification of the confrontational direct actions in ACT UP activism can be generalized as a justification of uncivil protest and confrontational politics in any fight against injustice insofar as the injustice in question may be left unattended and complicity with it may be left undisturbed if it is not resisted in every way possible, that is, through both civil and uncivil protest.

ACT UP activists and the affected public on whose behalf they were protesting were utterly unconcerned by the negative reactions against their protests voiced by politicians, the media, and citizens who wanted to be able to go on undisturbed in their daily business and leisure activities as they walked through public squares, went to theaters and restaurants, or attended church. They thought that the lack of civility of their protests was fully justified because civility itself had become a cover or an excuse for looking the other way and conducting business as usual as if nothing was happening, or as if the suffering of AIDS victims was not worthy of disturbing the regular flow of social life. In the eyes of ACT UP activists, the demand to remain *civil* was itself a way of hiding the crisis that was ongoing, growing, and kept in the dark, unattended by the silence of institutions and publics. Maintaining the appearance of normalcy in the face of the AIDS crisis was itself a breach of civility, a way of withholding respect for one's fellow citizens, and, therefore, demanding observance of an *unjust* civility—one that was complicit with injustice—was unwarranted. Similarly, today's activists fighting against the "zero tolerance" immigration policy of the Trump administration justify their disruptive techniques (such as the heckling of Secretary Nielsen) by alleging that maintaining the appearance of normalcy in the face of a political crisis in which violations of human rights become immigration policy involves a complete disrespect for the dignity of human beings, and that, therefore, in the face of this utter lack of civility, demanding civility and that people be left undisturbed as they conduct their business (professional and personal) in public life (e.g., watching a game or enjoying a dinner out) is unwarranted. In this sense, the justification for breaching norms of civility in uncivil protest is analogous to the standard justification for breaking laws in civil disobedience: Norms of civility, like laws, can be a sham; they can be unjust and not worthy of observance under certain conditions because they have no force and, in fact, they are "norms of civility" or "laws" in name only. This is the general argument and rationale for the justification of *uncivil* protest. In the next section I will provide further arguments in favor of *uncivil* protest and confrontational politics by challenging different versions of the liberal view that restricts political resistance to civil protest.

Toward a Politics of Confrontation: Uncivil Direct Actions and Counter-Protests

Direct action is the kind of activist intervention that does two things: (1) It disrupts the flow of social life, creating an interruption within a particular space or activity which can then be used for interrogating and reconfiguring social life in particular respects; and (2) It puts emotional, political, and/or economic pressure on individuals, groups, and institutions to change unjust laws, policies, and practices, or to discontinue their complicity with them. This definition is neutral regarding whether the direct action is *civil* or *uncivil.* Disrupting social life and putting pressure on social agents can be done in civil or uncivil ways; that is, it can be done in ways that abide by the norms of civility and minimize defiance and antagonizing confrontation, or it can be done in ways that don't shy away from, and in fact *exploit,* defiance and antagonizing confrontation. The former can be illustrated by what has become the most iconic direct action in the Civil Rights Movement: the Montgomery Bus Boycott in 1955–56. The latter can be illustrated by the *confrontational* direct actions of ACT UP during the 1980s AIDS epidemic.

Most activist interventions can be described both as civil and as uncivil protest depending on whether we highlight or minimize the most disruptive and confrontational elements in them. And, in fact, some protests have been re-described such that they have moved from one category to another, being perceived at some point as uncivil and at another point as civil protest by mainstream American publics. Think, for example, of Tommie Smith's and John Carlos's black power salute at the 1968 Olympic Games. This protest contains elements of *civil* engagement: It is performed by the athletes in a silent, orderly, and composed way; it makes a political statement by carefully displaying symbols without fully disrupting the ceremony in question or the larger event. Indeed, the Black Power Salute protest is often celebrated today as a fine example of civil protest that, while antagonizing the establishment of the world of sports, inspired many athletes and sports fans to cultivate more critical attitudes both within and outside sports. But the Black Power Salute protest also contained elements that were perceived at the time (and could still be perceived today) as *uncivil*: it was a markedly defiant and confrontational gesture through which the athletes were trying to shame a nation and to distance themselves from those who pledge allegiance to a political community that had crossed moral boundaries and violated principles of justice. There is no question that the Black Power Salute protest was considered a divisive, uncivil protest by many (if not most) in 1968, and analogous protests in sports are similarly judged by some (if not many) today.

Which direct actions are considered civil and uncivil seems to be a contested issue depending on the criteria that we use. But whatever criteria we may settle on, the distinction between civil and uncivil protest does not seem to be a categorical distinction but rather a *gradual* one in the sense that there is a wide spectrum of possible ways to protest, with some, more clearly *civil* protests at one end of the spectrum and other, more clearly *uncivil* protests at the other end of the spectrum. I propose a confrontational view of protest that leaves it to the activists themselves whether to resort to civil or uncivil direct actions, that is, whether to dramatize the social conflict and stage the confrontation in polite, cooperative, and unthreatening ways or in defiant, antagonizing, and provocative ways. The unqualified view of protest that a politics of confrontation needs is opposed not only to conservative views that impose strong restrictions on protest, but also to liberal views that open all spaces and practices to contestation but restrict that contestation to *civil* protest. In this section I will question the grounds on which liberal views constrain legitimate protests by the norms of civility.

We identify an intriguing case of direct action that contains both civil and uncivil elements in the die-ins that ACT UP activists staged in the 1980s when they blocked streets, squares, and entrances to public buildings or businesses with their own bodies by laying on the ground like corpses, with signs and provocations that made people think about the social silence and inaction that contributed to the rising death toll of the AIDS epidemic. With their own inert bodies on the ground, activists blocked (or at least made difficult) the path of city dwellers so that they were unable to continue their business or personal activities as usual. The activists forced citizens to suspend their regular activities by having to wait for the dramatization to end; diverted their paths to other venues or other activities; or created a sea of "dead bodies" that they would have to jump over. And how long can someone impatiently wait, or take a different path, or jump over symbolic dead bodies before realizing the deep insensitivity of pursuing business as usual? By dramatizing the public health crisis in this way, ACT UP activists tried to highlight the cost of silence and social inattention, and they were also sending a message to apathetic and complicit institutions and publics that they would no longer tolerate silence and inaction, and that their continued silence and inaction would have consequences and would not leave their lives undisturbed. ACT UP activists were engaging in what I described in the introduction as *epistemic activism*: They staged epistemic interventions that could awaken people from their political slumbers, creating epistemic friction with apathy and insensitivity and ensuring that people felt uncomfortable and realized the social cost of inaction. The active use of emotional warfare and the aggressive deployment of discomfort employed by ACT UP were often paired with the use of (mild forms of) epistemic violence, e.g., heckling, disrupting communicative dynamics (by chanting or shouting over speakers), discrediting politicians and institutions, etc. There are both civil and uncivil aspects that can be recognized in this epistemic activism. For example, the die-ins of ACT UP exhibited some *civil* elements: They were often performed in silence and with decorum, and activists often endured violent reactions against them without retaliation. But they also exhibited some *uncivil* elements: They could include shaming and antagonizing proclamations, graphic provocations, and even (in some cases) threatening gestures. Where to put die-ins in the spectrum of civil and uncivil protests is a difficult question; and no less difficult is the question of whether (and how) the *uncivil* aspects of this confrontational direct action can be justified. These questions remain timely today.

More than two decades after the die-ins organized by ACT UP during the AIDS epidemics, some activist organizations have recently staged die-ins to protest what they describe as an *epidemic* of racial violence and police homicides against people of color.

Perhaps the most successful and publicized of these confrontational direct actions was the massive die-in organized by Black Lives Matter at the Mall of America in December 2014 at the peak of the holiday shopping season. Many protesters participating in the die-in were detained and the protest, while considered highly successful by many (including its organizers) in providing visibility to a worthy cause, was also heavily criticized by others for its disruptive and confrontational nature. There are other activist tactics used by protesters that disrupt economic activity and the flow of social life, such as stopping traffic by occupying intersections or marching on roads. These tactics have come under heavy criticism by some publics and legislators (with new regulations being issued designed to avert them or to punish participants forcefully).[19] They have been deemed *uncivil* by many, in contrast with the civil disobedience espoused by Martin Luther King Jr. and the Civil Rights Movement. Contemporary antiracist movements and organizations such as Black Lives Matter are certainly in continuity with the Civil Rights Movement. But are they going too far in their tactics? Are the uncivil protests of ACT UP activists, or of current antiracist activists, radical and illegitimate responses to injustice? And, whether legitimate or not, could they be counterproductive in creating a backlash instead of procuring the support of publics and institutions for a worthy cause? Can they inadvertently contribute to the often feared "escalation of conflict and violence"?

As discussed in the previous section, Martin Luther King Jr. has taught us many lessons about fighting injustice and about taking that fight to the streets and to every corner of the social world. But King and many of his followers also talked about *disciplining* resistance, participating in protests and demonstrations in a *disciplined* way that minimizes disruption and keeps our actions "pure" and free of violence. Limiting resistance to civil protest is what I call *the liberal view*, which can be defended on principled grounds or on strategic grounds. In the first place, as a matter of principle, uncivil protest is argued by many to be ruled out by the principle of nonviolence. According to the principled liberal view, defiant and disruptive tactics are at odds with self-disciplining and the cultivation of "the purity of action," promulgated by the Gandhian philosophy of nonviolence followed by King and other Civil Rights leaders. Second, at the strategic level, the *disciplining* of resistance recommended and exercised by many of King's followers involved carefully choosing and practicing one's presentation and demeanor in order to maximize the positive reception of the actions of activists by the general public: for example, wearing respectable clothing, being trained in how to move and look composed, practicing how to speak and how to remain silent, and so on. The strategic argument for this disciplining relates to appealing to mainstream sensibilities and maximizing the chances of garnering social support for one's cause, avoiding any kind of backlash. The confrontational direct actions of ACT UP, for example, were often criticized on these strategic grounds. The strategic liberal view of protest raises general concerns about playing into the hands of dominant sensibilities, about forcing activists to show the most palatable—and often most conservative—side of their social movement. These are general concerns that have been widely discussed—especially by black feminist scholars—under the heading "the politics of respectability."[20] But I want to focus here on what is at the core of the liberal view of protest, both in its principled and in its strategic variety: Should disobedience and resistance be bound and tamed by *civility*? Could there be contexts that also call for *uncivil* disobedience and *uncivil* resistance?

Arguing for a politics of confrontation that makes room for uncivil protest, in what follows I will offer two sets of considerations against the liberal view of political resistance. As a claim against the principled liberal view, I will argue that those who affirm a categorical distinction between violent and nonviolent action and insist on "the purity of action" draw on an underlying notion of violence that is overly narrow and not attentive to different kinds of violence and their interrelations. I will argue that whether activist interventions or direct actions run the risk of contributing to the dreaded "escalation of conflict and violence" is not an issue that can be settled on principled grounds, that it is a *contextual* issue, and that principles of nonviolence (at least the general commitment to the mitigation of violence) do not by themselves rule out uncivil protests as illegitimate forms of resistance. In the second place, against the strategic liberal view, I will argue that it is far from clear that uncivil protests (such as the confrontational direct actions of ACT UP or of Black Lives Matter) are always counterproductive and self-undermining because they result in a backlash or the escalation of conflict and violence, turning people against their cause instead of garnering social support.

Is there such a thing as a *nonviolent* protest in an *absolute* sense? Is there a process of *self-purification* that can extricate activists and their actions from all possible violence? When we pay attention to how structural forms of violence work, it is far from clear that we can draw a sharp boundary between the violent and the nonviolent, and that it is possible to identify forms of action or inaction that are "pure" and in every possible way devoid of violent aspects or consequences. My contextualist perspective calls into question whether we can make sense of a principled distinction between *violent* and *nonviolent* interventions independent of particular *contexts of action*, suggesting that, instead, we should focus on what counts as *more or less violent* (or more or less likely to increase or decrease violence) in particular contexts, given the positionality of actors and the surrounding practices. Contextually, the question is not so much how we can guarantee "the purity of action," extricating our actions from violence altogether; rather, the contextual question for nonviolent social movements is how to maximize the likelihood that activist interventions will result in decreasing violence in the long run and all things considered. Note that inaction or nonintervention, as well as civil protests that shy away from upsetting people and deploying epistemic violence, can be complicit with the normalization of violence in public life and with the toleration of insidious forms of structural violence, whereas confrontational politics, as exhibited, for example, in counter-protests, can disrupt the complicity of multiple publics, challenging not only those they directly confront but also other publics standing by.

Counter-protests are criticized both on principled and on strategic grounds. On principled grounds, counter-protests are criticized for being too disruptive and antagonizing, and for violating "the purity of action" by inciting conflict, provoking opponents, and being unable to stop the escalation of a confrontation. Critics of Black Lives Matter claim that there should not have been a counter-protest in Charlottesville (or anywhere else, for that matter) because counter-protests are responsible for exacerbating conflict and for the escalation of violence. But, of course, the entire aim of such counter-protests is precisely to stop the normalization and escalation of violence (and the deepening of vulnerabilities to violence) that have been occurring while complicit publics look the other way. Were they to refrain from staging counter-protests and speaking up against racism, they too (counter-protesters say, and they are right) would have been complicit with the normalization and escalation of violence. Confrontation or complicity—that is the question; that is the dilemma confronting us, all of us who are committed to the mitigation of injustice and violence (and not only the members of Black Lives Matter and other antiracist violence movements). Rather than the illusory attempt to keep our actions "pure" in a categorical way, the desideratum of nonviolent social movements should be to learn how to mitigate the violent aspects and consequences of our political actions, that is, to learn how social actors can coordinate and calibrate their *chained actions* to eradicate injustices and patterns of violence.[21]

Should one counter-protest against those who have been authorized to protest, those who have been vetted and granted a permit? An authorization to march or demonstrate on a street or a square does not give a group license to monopolize the public discourse in the designated space, to express itself politically without contestation. Such monopolization would involve silencing those who are not part of the authorized protest and it would curtail the freedom of speech of passers-by who would be forced to stand by silently, taking in without contestation whatever the authorized demonstrators want to say. Of course, that is not what authorizing a march or demonstration means. So, what is the problem with participating in counter-protest? Shouldn't it be expected in a democratic society to find publics countering the message of those who demonstrate? Counter-protests are often criticized as if they somehow endanger the freedom of speech of those who protest. However, if counter-protesters are not preventing protesters from speaking (if they are not literally destroying their signs or making them shut up), if they are only responding to their political statements while letting their discourse continue, then such counter-protesters are simply exercising a democratic freedom and a civic duty to participate in public discourse. Moreover, when protests contribute to a harm, as for example when protesters in white supremacist marches intimidate or silence a group—turning them into a target of hate, or inciting publics to participate in the perpetuation of violence or unjust treatment—there is actually a prima facie civic *obligation* to respond, to neutralize and counter their message, not to let the march go uncontested.

Of course, not just any form of confrontation will do if we want to minimize conflict and stop the escalation of violence; rather, the commitment to nonviolence has to be made compatible with the commitment to confront injustices and the different patterns of violence those injustices may contain. If patterns of violence are left unchallenged for the sake of preserving "the purity of action" and avoiding confrontation, protest movements may be sacrificing their primary goal of fighting for liberation and the mitigation of injustices. Confrontational politics can remain contextually committed to the mitigation of violence while at the same time not ruling out disruptive tactics in our politico-communicative practices—such as storming into public hearings or staging counter-protests—and in our socioeconomic practices—such as blocking traffic or interrupting economic activity (as in, for example, the die-ins). It is always a contextual matter how patterns of violence can be mitigated more appropriately, and disruptive tactics are legitimate when nothing short of them is guaranteed to contribute to a status quo that normalizes and institutionalizes existing patterns of violence—whether physical, structural, socioeconomic, emotional, psychological, symbolic, or epistemic violence.

Can *all* violence be avoided in nonviolent resistance movements? As Karuna Mantena has pointed out in her elucidation of Gandhian philosophy, nonviolent resistance as noncooperation and the withdrawal of consent at a collective level involves the process of breaking the material and ideological infrastructure of legitimacy.[22] This process could include the economic violence of boycotting and blocking the streets, as well as communication warfare that makes use of psychological, emotional, symbolic, and epistemic violence—think here, again, of the confrontational politics of ACT UP during the AIDS epidemic and their epistemic-political interventions in public and institutional spaces to disrupt social invisibility and to uproot apathy and insensitivity, which included shaming people and institutions, satirizing them, stopping their speech and actions. Disrupting complicity with oppressive communicative dynamics could also include tactics in epistemic activism such as shouting to make people shut up, shaming people, refusing to speak and participate in epistemic cooperation, disrupting hearings, and blocking deliberative processes that marginalize and stigmatize oppressed groups. In other words, the non-cooperation and withdrawal of consent in communicative practices that epistemic activism often involves seems to make unavoidable use of different kinds of violence, most distinctively epistemic violence, but also symbolic, psychological, and emotional violence, and even in some cases economic and physical violence, at least if physical violence is thought to include the damage or destruction of property such as tearing up papers, taking down public signs, or writing graffiti on public or private property. Is it possible to avoid the use of violence in resistance if we understand violence in all these different forms? And if we refuse this broad understanding of violence, how is a narrow notion of violence (reducible, for example, to bodily injury) going to do justice to the different layers of the phenomenon of violence and explain how vulnerabilities to violence are generated and reproduced? The mitigation of violence is a contextual issue, and, therefore, the commitment to the mitigation of violence can be upheld in many ways and not simply through self-discipline, self-purification, and refraining from participating in uncivil protests (such as confrontational direct actions).

A nonviolent movement of resistance does not need to uphold the normative principle of the purity of action, but only the commitment to the mitigation of violence. How this commitment needs to be implemented is a contextual matter. And the advisability of uncivil protests then becomes a *strategic* issue. Even after principled objections against uncivil protest are rejected or neutralized, there are those who defend the liberal view of resistance and reject uncivil protest as inadequate on strategic grounds. A strategic liberal view that restricts resistance to civil protest seems to be endorsed by Mantena's interpretation of *satyagraha* and nonviolence. Mantena argues that the nonviolent politics of *satyagraha* avoids confrontational and disruptive tactics that, as she puts it, could "exacerbate tendencies toward polarization and entrenchment" that would threaten the coherence and success of the movement or campaign.[23] It is important to note that there are no good reasons to think that the kind of polarization often precipitated by confrontational tactics will "threaten the coherence and success of the movement or campaign." As the famous activist chant "What side are you on, my friend?" makes explicit, disrupting complicity often requires the kind of head-on confrontation that polarizes publics and forces people to put their cards on the table, as it were, and choose a side—this is also what political satire often does. This involves a *tactical polarization*, but one that can have fruitful consequences for denouncing and disrupting complicity. The chant "What side are you on, my friend?" may invite polarization, but it can also block evasive moves such as, for example, Donald Trump's infamous claim that there are "good people on both sides, on both sides" in the aftermath of Charlottesville in August 2017. Confrontational and coercive tactics, even if polarizing, can be crucial—and in some cases, perhaps even necessary—for triggering a process that disrupts apathy and complicity and can facilitate social change. The Freedom Riders and the activists organizing sit-ins and other forms of civil disobedience within the Civil Rights Movement did not compromise the coherence or effectiveness of their movement when they antagonized people by using coercive pressure on complicit publics, no matter how polarizing the public opposition they encountered was. Martin Luther King Jr. himself powerfully articulated how dangerous it is to tame resistance for the sake of avoiding conflict in his "Letter from Birmingham Jail." In response to the criticism that "our actions, even though peaceful, must be condemned because they precipitate violence,"[24] King reminded us that the violence was already there and they were simply bringing it "out in the open."[25] In this way, he foreshadowed the response of activists today when they are accused of disturbing the peace and they reply that there is no peace to be disturbed to begin with: *No Justice, No Peace.* The fear of disturbing the peace has been used as a rationale for "disciplining" resistance, but when there is no peace to be disturbed in the first place, this rationale has no purchase.

Recent antiracist violence movements and organizations, most notably Black Lives Matter, have been criticized for disturbing the peace and challenging law and order by protesting without a permit and staging counter-protests. And think here not only of Charlottesville, but also of all the Trump rallies during the presidential campaign and afterward where there were counter-protests, with violence very often erupting sometimes verbally, sometimes physically. Some argue that the very presence of counter-protesters on the streets where others are voicing their racist views exacerbates tensions and contributes to the escalation of violence. The counter-protesters rightly reply that they are confronting what is already violent (i.e., discourses and attitudes that instigate violence) and that not confronting and countering them in any way would be to remain complicit with such violence. US civil society needs to confront public affirmations of racism and public expressions of attitudes that normalize and legitimize violence, because refusing to stand up to threats and to stand with those being threatened is to leave them unprotected and to indirectly contribute (by silence and inaction) to their vulnerability to patterns of violence. But what kind of confrontation is most appropriate?

Movements of resistance should of course be concerned with whether or not their interventions exacerbate conflict and violence, but when conflict and violence are all around us, it is not at all clear how "the purity of action" can be maintained and how we can fully extricate activist interventions from potentially violent reactions. A transformative politics must *confront* the different forms of social conflict and violence that already exist without limiting itself for the sake of minimizing disruption. Confrontation *might* lead to escalation of tensions and conflicts, but it might not if the confrontation is well managed. This is a contextual and strategic issue. And perhaps a carefully managed confrontation is part of the tactical "disciplining" of resistance that Karuna Mantena and others have argued for; so perhaps a politics of confrontation is after all compatible with the Gandhian model of *satyagraha* in an interpretation such as Mantena's. But the demand of being "disciplined" and exercising "restraint" is problematic not only as an ethical demand, but also as a strategic demand. At the very least, this demand needs to be contextualized and properly qualified in a way that avoids domesticating resistance movements at the will of "the normal" or "the mainstream." The contextualization and qualification of the demand for restraint and discipline are especially important under conditions of oppression. It is very problematic to demand that those who exercise restraint be those who are oppressed and marginalized and those who have the courage to come out, denounce the existing tensions, and confront oppression, while the beneficiaries of oppression and those invested in perpetuating violence are left unchallenged and unencumbered to take the streets. Those trying to normalize violent attitudes and subordinating speech, such as white supremacist groups, view any kind of confrontation as the illegitimate instigation of conflict and violence. But racial conflict and violence are not created by those who confront white supremacists; the racial conflict and violence are already out there. The marches of white supremacists are intrinsically violent and those who call them out and confront them are simply, as Dr. King put it, bringing "to the surface the hidden tension that is already alive"; they "are not the creators of tension."[26]

There are no good strategic reasons that force us to purge a resistance movement of uncivil protests that exploit defiance and disruption and stage epistemic-political interventions that wake people up and disrupt their apathy and complicity. Strategic arguments claiming that uncivil protests are counterproductive are of two kinds. First, there are those who argue that uncivil engagement is the worst way to address your opponents because you are never going to appeal to their conscience or convince them of anything by shouting louder than them, shaming them, or being rude to them; in fact, they argue, such uncivil engagement with one's opponents typically emboldens them and can lead to the escalation of conflict and violence. Second, there are those who argue that, independent of its effect on those who are being directly addressed, confrontational uncivil actions have a negative impact on the wider public, leading to backlash, loss of social support, and failure to achieve changes in policies and attitudes. Both arguments are misguided.

The first strategic argument fails to see that protests are complex communitive actions with multiple audiences and multiple publics being addressed in different ways and through different kinds of speech acts; and that the lack of civility in uncivil protests is not deployed as a form of persuasion, especially not as a way of changing the minds of the perpetrators of injustice themselves. For example, in the confrontational direct actions of ACT UP during the AIDS epidemic, activists didn't naively think that by shouting, shaming, or disrupting activities, they were going to convince politicians and regular citizens of their views and that a change in health policy would ensue automatically. Instead, their political actions had different and more complex short- and long-term communicative goals: As an immediate communicative goal, these activists were addressing those affected directly and indirectly by the AIDS epidemic, telling them that they were not alone and that others were also outraged by the apathy and inaction of politicians and of a general public that simply watched while going about their business as if what was happening had nothing to do with them; in the short run, the communicative goal of ACT UP activists was to give visibility to a health crisis and to break a social silence that was complicit; in the long run, their communicative goal was to continue putting pressure on institutions and publics until attention, resources, emergency measures, research, educational programs, and policy changes were mobilized to fight the AIDS epidemic. ACT UP activists made a lot of people mad, but they were willing to take the risk of upsetting people while achieving success in their communicative goals of consoling victims and affected populations, putting a health crisis on the social agenda, and making it difficult (if not impossible) to avoid having a discussion about the AIDS epidemic in public discourse. Similarly, those who heckled Secretary Nielsen at a Mexican restaurant didn't naïvely think that they were going to change her mind or heart by chanting "Shame! Shame! Shame!" or yelling "If kids don't eat in peace, you don't eat in peace"; nor did they think that they would change the minds and hearts of Trump supporters when they witnessed the heckling on the news. Neither Secretary Nielsen nor Trump supporters were the primary audience these hecklers were trying to reach. Rather, with the heckling of Secretary Nielsen (which is reminiscent of the confrontational direct actions of ACT UP), activists were addressing those affected directly and indirectly by a cruel immigration policy that separates children from their parents, telling them that they are not alone and that others are also outraged by such violations of human rights being committed by politicians who go out to dinner as if nothing was happening and by a public that goes about their business as if nothing out of the ordinary was happening. Activists such as these hecklers are also trying to appeal to the conscience of a general public, which either by active support or by silence and inaction, is complicit with an ongoing injustice. Similarly also, counter-protesters who confront white-supremacy marches are not addressing only or even primarily the white supremacists to whom they direct their voices and signs (they do not naïvely think that white supremacists will be converted on the spot to their antiracist cause). Their primary audience is not the white supremacists they confront, but rather, those who are being threatened or intimidated by the message of white supremacists, telling them that they are not alone and that they will be protected and supported when targeted by racism. Their primary audience also includes the wider public, telling members of the general public that they would not allow hate and prejudice to go unchallenged and uncontested, and neither should they.

The second strategic argument against uncivil protests does acknowledge that these protests have multiple audiences and are typically trying to reach a wider public that goes beyond those who are directly and explicitly addressed in confrontational actions and interventions. But this second argument claims that uncivil protests are counterproductive because they fail to secure social support for their cause and, far from paving a path toward social change, they typically bring about a backlash and embolden the opposition. Public reactions to protest must first be put in a temporal context, and an initial backlash does not necessarily mean the failure of the resistance movement, but simply an obstacle that may be overcome if the protest is sustained long enough. And sometimes it can be the beginning of progress to trigger *any* reaction at all from publics who were previously indifferent and apathetic. It is true that a negative reaction can be worse than no reaction, but reactions have a dynamic life and they can be transformed, with an initial negative reaction leading to other reactions later on and to the possibility of productive conversations that can solidify a public concern that did not exist before. In the third place, although there is no guarantee that confrontational and disruptive tactics will meliorate things, it is not clear that it is not worth trying even the most confrontational and disruptive tactics, especially when other tactics are not working. Even without winning over public opinion, continued emotional, political, and/or economic pressure can lead to victories, institutional reforms, and policy changes. As ACT UP activists knew well, unpopular and divisive politics can lead to political victories; confrontational and disruptive interventions, if sustained long enough, can achieve (at least some of) its goals. In fact, ACT UP activism, although often vilified, has a success story to tell, even if it is one of partial and tragic success. While the backlash that ACT UP produced is often overemphasized, its achievements are often underplayed. As Gould points out, the relentless confrontational activism of ACT UP secured a "long list of victories":

> ACT UP forced the Food and Drug Administration to speed up the drug-approval process and to adopt policies that allowed people with life-threatening illnesses access to experimental drugs *prior* to approval. The movement's efforts reconfigured scientific procedures, and thus scientific research itself, by securing the inclusion of people with HIV/AIDS in government and corporate AIDS decision-making bodies, allowing affected populations to have input into drug trial design and other aspects of drug research. ACT UP pushed the Centers for Disease Control to expand the definition of AIDS to include infections and diseases commonly occurring in HIV-infected women and poor people. [. . .] ACT UP forced pharmaceutical companies to lower the prices of AIDS drugs; prodded insurance companies to reimburse for non-FDA approved, experimental drugs; pushed government bodies to create needle-exchange programs; and prevented the passage of extremely repressive AIDS legislation.[27]

What we can say about ACT UP's disruptive technique of confrontational direct action with more historical distance and more evidence seems analogous to what we can say about the die-ins and counter-protests of Black Lives Matter. Black Lives Matter activists may have upset many and they may have emboldened white supremacists and other conservative groups, but they have also had important successes. They have managed to put racial violence and police homicides on the political agenda; they have mobilized publics; they have created more critical awareness and vigilance with respect to racial violence; and, although their sustained protests and interventions—including the confrontational and perhaps uncivil ones such as die-ins and counter-protests—have not yet led to widespread structural changes and institutional reform, such as nationwide police reform, they have had at least some local and partial successes—for example, by triggering investigations into particular police departments[28] and into the criminal justice system, and garnering support for institutional reforms such as mandatory police body cameras. It is still too early to have a full assessment of whether the most disruptive and uncivil tactics of Black Lives Matter have paid off, but there is certainly no knock-down strategic argument against uncivil protest supported by the empirical evidence now available in the realm of antiracist activism. So, in short, there is no compelling case for limiting political resistance to civil protest, as the liberal view tries to do, either on principled or on strategic grounds.

Conclusion

Should organizations such as Black Lives Matter shy away from counter-protests because some of the chained actions linked to their interventions (whether by their own members or by others joining in) result in violent interactions? Can networks of actors maintain "the purity" of their chained actions? And what is the point of maintaining the ideal of such "purity" in a social world full of conflict and violence? What can this *aspirational* "purity"[29] mean? An uncompromising politics of confrontation can still abide by the commitment to minimize violence and conflict whenever possible, but without tying its hands or retreating when dealing with "impurity" and having to confront intrinsically violent social realities, with the aim of not exacerbating the violence, but to do *whatever* it takes to eradicate it.

In this chapter, I have argued against the conservative view that severely constrains protests for the sake of "law and order" and maintaining social peace, and I have also argued against the liberal view that limits political resistance to civil protest for principled or strategic reasons. In a positive vein, I have argued for a confrontational politics that is not bound by the norms of civility and includes both civil and uncivil protests that can produce epistemic-political interventions of various kinds. I have argued elsewhere[30] for a politics of confrontation that calls people out and disrupts complicity, a politics that brings confrontation to everyday life by asking people to counter micro-aggressions with micro-resistance, a politics that brings confrontation to institutional life by asking citizens and organizations to put pressure on institutions to stop oppressive policies and practices and to discontinue or restrict their cooperation with the institutions until they do so. It is true that a politics of confrontation runs the risk of exacerbating conflict and even violence, and that such risk should be carefully managed (in fact, a lot of the discussions of activist tactics are about mitigating risks). But the risk is worth taking because the alternative of not taking such a risk is to prolong one's complicity for the sake of an illusory social peace that only the privileged can enjoy. Confrontational activism refuses to let people enjoy their complicity and the comfort of their insensitivity to injustice, availing itself of disruptive tactics. Social justice activism cannot always have the luxury of being constrained by the norms of *civility* or "the purity of action." Social justice activism should be conceptualized as the centerpiece of a full-blown *confrontational politics* that can help us disrupt our complicity with ongoing injustices and discharge our responsibilities as active citizens and moral agents. Justice trumps everything; and, therefore, the fight for social justice should proceed unconstrained by concerns about civility, law and order, or social peace: *No Justice, No Peace.*

Notes

1 Independent Staff, "Aretha Franklin: How the Queen of Soul Offered to Post Bail for Angela Davis, Saying 'Black People Will Be Free,'" *The Independent*, available at www.independent.co.uk.

2 I am invoking the notion of "purity of action" that has been so influential in the Civil Rights Movement and nonviolent movements of resistance following the Gandhian principle of *Satyagraha*. This will be addressed later in this chapter when I discuss the notion of *disciplined* resistance that Martin Luther King Jr. advocated.

3 Although I am very sympathetic to Candice Delmas's conceptual analysis of the notion of uncivil disobedience in her chapter "Uncivil Disobedience" (this volume), she seems to be invested in drawing a principled conceptual distinction between civil and uncivil disobedience. Although for analytic purposes a conceptual distinction can be drawn—and Delmas draws it well—it is a distinction that, when applied to specific cases, becomes a *contextual* matter, because civility and incivility can be differently interpreted in different contexts. It is also a *gradual* matter, because civility and incivility are achieved in degrees, rather than appearing as absolute qualities of political action.

4 For a comparison and contrast between the different acts of disobedience and their civil and uncivil elements, see section 5.3.2 of my book *The Epistemology of Resistance: Gender and Racial Oppression, Epistemic Injustice, and Resistant Imaginations* (New York: Oxford University Press, 2012).

5 See Iris Marion Young, *Justice and the Politics of Difference* (Princeton, NJ: Princeton University Press, 1990).

6 The concept of *epistemic violence* was coined and elucidated by Gayatri Spivak in "Can the Subaltern Speak?," in *Marxism and the Interpretation of Culture*, edited by Cary Nelson and Lawrence Grossberg (Urbana: University of Illinois Press, 1998), pp. 66–111. This concept has been further elaborated and discussed in the recent literature on epistemic injustice—see especially Kristie Dotson's "Tracking Epistemic Violence, Tracking Practices of Silencing," *Hypatia* 26, no. 2 (Spring 2011): 236–257. Epistemic violence is any kind of violence inflicted on us as subjects of knowledge and understanding, which includes silencing, discrediting, systematic misrepresentation or distortion of one's meanings and beliefs, etc.

7 My notion of *epistemic activism* refers to the critical activities of denouncing, contesting, and resisting the cognitive-affective attitudes and sensibilities (or insensitivities) that facilitate oppression. See José Medina's "Epistemic Injustice and Epistemologies of Ignorance," in *The Routledge Companion to the Philosophy of Race*, edited by Paul Taylor, Linda Alcoff, and Luvell Anderson (New York: Routledge, 2017), pp. 247–260. See also José Medina and Matt Whitt's "Epistemic Activism and the Politics of Credibility: Testimonial Injustice Inside/Outside a North Carolina Jail," in *Making the Case*, edited by Nancy McHugh and Heidi Grasswick (Albany: SUNY Press, forthcoming).

8 See Deborah Gould, *Moving Politics: Emotion and ACT UP's Fight against AIDS* (Chicago: University of Chicago Press, 2009).

9 See the *New York Times* article by Zach Johnk titled "National Anthem Protests by Black Athletes Have a Long History," September 25, 2017.

10 Note here that an enforced negative self-image that rules in shame and rules out pride would also be equally ideological for the same reasons.

11 Martin Luther King Jr., *I Have a Dream and Letter from Birmingham Jail* (Logan, IA: Perfection Learning, 1963/1990), p. 5.

12 For Martin Luther King Jr., direct action is the fourth step to which members of a nonviolent resistance movement resort after the existence of an injustice has been factually established, after negotiations have failed, and after they "purify" themselves in preparation for action. As he puts it: "In any nonviolent campaign there are four basic steps: collection of the facts to determine whether injustices exist; negotiation; self-purification; and direct action." (ibid., p. 1).

13 Ibid., p. 8.

14 Ibid., pp. 18–19.

15 Ibid., p. 5.

16 Gould, *Moving Politics*, p. 4.

17 Ibid., p. 5.

18 As King put it: "We must come to see, with one of our distinguished jurists, that 'justice too long delayed is justice denied.'" (*I Have a Dream and Letter from Birmingham Jail*, p. 11).

19 For an excellent discussion of these issues, see Candice Delmas's "Uncivil Disobedience" (in this volume).

20 See Brittney Cooper's *Beyond Respectability: The Intellectual Thought of Race Women* (Chicago: University of Illinois Press, 2017) and Frances White's *Dark Continent of Our Bodies: Black Feminism and Politics of Respectability* (Philadelphia: Temple University Press, 2001). For a longer history of the critique of "the politics of respectability" within African American communities, see Evelyn Brooks Higginbotham's *Righteous Discontent* (Cambridge, MA: Harvard University Press, 1994). Higginbotham has criticized the self-management strategies of black leaders to appear more "dignified" (and even more "human") in the eyes of white Americans by adopting white American values, religion, dress, and so on. Higginbotham's critique of the politics of respectability also addresses the control and management exercised over black women's bodies by black church leaders.

21 For an elucidation of the kinds of agency involved in social movements and an account of what I call *chained action* (i.e., the kind of hybrid agency characteristic of activists that is both individual and social), see section 5.3 of my *Epistemology of Resistance*.

22 Karuna Mantena, "Competing Theories of Non-Violent Politics" (in this volume).

23 Ibid., p. 207.

24 King, *I Have a Dream and Letter from Birmingham Jail*, p. 19.

25 Ibid., p. 18.

26 Ibid.

27 Gould, *Moving Politics*, p. 4.

28 In this respect, particularly noteworthy is the Department of Justice report released on January 13, 2017, which recognized widespread misconduct and institutional racism in the Chicago police department. The federal investigation into the Chicago police department was motivated by mobilizations of Black Lives Matter and other activist groups in the aftermath of the murder of Laquan McDonald in 2014 and other police homicides after that.

29 If the concepts of nonviolence and "the purity of action" in *satyagraha* are understood as aspirational ideals, rather than as categorical

notions, then Mantena's model can accommodate the contextualist and gradualist approach to nonviolent politics that I propose. But, in order to determine whether or not gradualism and contextualism are compatible with *satyagraha*, more needs to be said about how to deploy the notion of "the purity of action" and the distinction between violence and nonviolence contextually.

30 See Medina, "Epistemic Injustice and Epistemologies of Ignorance," and Medina and Whitt, "Epistemic Activism and the Politics of Credibility."

6

PROTEST FATIGUE

RICHARD THOMPSON FORD

My wife and I both participated in numerous marches, sit-ins, and demonstrations during our college and professional school years. We sat-in to pressure our respective universities to divest from South Africa during the apartheid era, to address sexual assault, and to maintain a commitment to affirmative action and faculty diversity.

More recently, my family joined the Women's March in San Francisco, emerging from the Muni station at Civic Center into an energetic, diverse crowd of people in stylish workwear, tech industry standard hoodie sweatshirts and, of course, pink "pussy" hats. As we joined the crowd marching up Market Street, several spontaneous chants broke out—most of which involved the inappropriateness of sexual assault or the general vulgarity and unfitness of our forty-fifth president. We enthusiastically joined in, and for a while a good time was had by all. Eventually my wife thought something was missing: "What about other women's issues, like the glass ceiling or equal pay? Let's start chanting equal pay for equal work!" I was all for it in principle, but for whatever reason, I had a bad feeling about the idea. Maybe it was just a premonition or perhaps somewhere in my subconscious I sensed that this relatively well-heeled crowd might not see wage equity as a pressing or unambiguous issue. Anyway, we tried it for several minutes, but almost no one joined in. The few who did commiserated with us after the effort fizzled: "Half of these people probably don't have to work," one middle-aged woman with a greying bob haircut grumbled.

As we drifted back to the Muni station to go home, we wondered whether the march was worthwhile. On the one hand, it was great to let the world know that millions of Americans disagreed with Trump and found his character deficient and his behavior appalling. But didn't everyone already know that? Would anyone be shocked to discover that a lot of people in San Francisco were against Trump? It was important to keep women's issues in the public consciousness. But did the march really do that? We couldn't even get support among people *at the demonstration* for pay equity. What did all of those people marching really stand for anyway? Just that the president shouldn't brag about grabbing women's genitals? Trump was going to say or do something appalling on a regular basis—could we shut down Market Street for a demonstration every time he did?

Almost two years later I was downtown in San Francisco with a friend and had an hour to kill, so we decided to go to my favorite hotel bar. But as I walked up, I heard a noisy labor protest outside: People were pounding on drums, banging gongs, and chanting. We gave a couple of the picketers high fives and kept walking. I know that the hotel workers' union in question stages similar protests every time their contract expires, and that they make sure the contracts expire just before the holidays to give themselves maximum leverage. Most of the hotels in downtown San Francisco were being picketed. The strike has required at least one major conference to change its plans at a cost of several hundred thousand dollars. And of course, the workers were forgoing their wages, and several spent Thanksgiving outside on the picket line. This was a noisy, annoying, costly, and disruptive protest. Worse, it was completely predictable—it arrived, like leap year, on a predetermined schedule. My friend and I both reflexively support organized labor but even we wondered, as we found a bar that wasn't attached to a hotel, whether it would be better if there was another way to bring management to the negotiating table.

***

Mass demonstrations, protest marches, organized boycotts, and other forms of political activism have been tools of the left and disempowered classes and factions for centuries. Mass protest was central to the black Civil Rights Movement, as it had been to the women's suffrage movement before it, and as it would be to the antiwar movement, the gay rights movement, and countless other social causes.

At its best, mass protest is a powerful tool of political opposition, a bold and striking reflection of society's most serious frustrations and noblest ambitions. But increasingly, mass protest and civil disobedience has become safe, predictable—and frequent. Organized pressure groups of every political perspective clamor on an almost weekly basis for an overstimulated and inured public's attention. Mass protests are a rite of spring on college campuses, a yearly initiation into the world of higher learning as conventional as the tailgate party or the dorm room one-night stand.

The phenomenon of the counter-demonstration proves that protest has now become a readily available tactic in any ideological disagreement, available to both the "woke" and the reactionary right alike. Today, when one group in ideologized conflict plans a demonstration, it's not uncommon for its ideological enemies to plan a counter-demonstration at roughly the same forum, in order to counteract the first group's message. Not only does the counter-demonstration prove the ease with which a mass protest can be organized, it also suggests diminishing returns: If any protest can be met with an equal and opposite counter-protest, perhaps everyone involved would have been better off staying home.

This chapter will look at the use and misuse of political protests, civil disobedience, and mass demonstrations. I'll use the term "protests" to cover all of these. I aspire to evaluate this set of tactics *without regard to the underlying political goal.* This is important: Historically, protest has been associated with organized labor, oppressed minority groups, and progressive political movements, so it's probably inevitable that some will see any criticism of protest as a criticism of progressives or "the left." But part of the trend that has led to protest fatigue is the growing use of protest by interest groups from across the political spectrum. When considering my arguments, I ask the reader to bear in mind the use of these tactics and methods by those she disagrees with as well as those she agrees with; by those with trivial grievances and claims better pursued in conventional politics as well as serious concerns that have been unfairly ignored. Consider the men's rights movement and the patriarchal Christian organization the "Promise Keepers" as well as the suffragettes and the women's marchers; Nazis marching through a community of Holocaust survivors as well as the March on Washington; the disruptions caused by cyclists in San

Francisco's "Critical Mass" demonstrations as well as Take Back the Night rallies.

Mass demonstrations certainly can still serve their historic function as a powerful wake-up call to a somnambulant establishment, but it's just as certain that they are overused and often misused. This chapter will explore the overuses and misuses that have caused what I'll call "protest fatigue"—a sense of weariness and cynicism about social protests and movements—and try to distinguish legitimate and potentially useful protests from those that are needlessly irritating or downright counterproductive.

Social protest can be a reaction to an inadequate or corrupt political process or market economy—mass demonstrations for women's suffrage are a paradigmatic example of such a protest, since it was a protest movement that aimed to correct the political process itself. But any protest that advances a cause that hasn't gotten a fair shake in the political process qualifies. Protest can also be a reaction to a violation of fundamental rights—here the fairness of the political or market processes that brought about the challenged result are irrelevant because a violation of rights is never justified. Protest can also be an established part of a political system or market—such as labor picketing sanctioned under the National Labor Relations Act.

Protest, then, can be a disruption of the political and economic status quo, or it can be an expected part of the day-to-day operation of the system—politics by other means. A proviso. When I criticize certain protests, I do not intend to imply a legal argument concerning the "rights" of individuals and groups to assemble and express themselves. Although some of my argument has implications for First Amendment doctrine, which I will explore in a brief conclusion, my central argument concerns the wisdom and civic-mindedness of protest—not its legality.

Costs

There are costs to the overuse of protest.

Inconvenience and Disruption

Most obviously, protests and mass demonstrations are time-consuming and inconvenient for nonparticipants: They block streets in congested cities, disrupting normal commuting and commerce. This may seem trivial as compared to the importance of a political cause, but inconvenience is not the only problem. Blocked streets can impede the movement of emergency vehicles, resulting in life-threatening delays. Large, unruly crowds are magnets for criminals, sociopaths, and disruptive elements—as a consequence, violence and destruction are always a risk, and police must be deployed at significant public expense.

Dilution of Sympathy

Moreover, with too many protests, serious injustices must compete with superficial gripes; the profoundly aggrieved share space with narcissistic attention-seekers, and well-considered propositions are drowned out by unreasonable demands and half-baked proposals. Civil disobedience loses its capacity to rouse us from complacency. The faceless corporations and governments, the implacable bureaucrats and self-satisfied bourgeoisie are supposed to sit up and take notice of the rage and indignation, spontaneously bursting forth in the form of a mass demonstration, their comfortable daily routines disrupted and their fragile illusion of stability and control shattered. But when social protest becomes an expected part of life in every post-industrial mass democracy on the planet, it no longer challenges the status quo; it *is* the status quo. Governments are resigned to mass protest: Cities issue permits for political demonstrations, assign extra police (who appreciate the inevitable overtime pay), and prescribe planned gathering sites and march routes to maximize exposure and minimize inconvenience.

The bourgeois-capitalist-white supremacist-patriarchal state may even welcome such domesticated mass demonstrations as a useful safety valve for frustrations that, if pent up, might lead to more serious unrest. Corporate managers, ensconced in the high towers of capital, coolly calculate which losses occasioned by boycotts and strikes are manageable and which must be appeased with some symbolic gesture or acceptable sacrifice; meanwhile they compensate for any losses by taking advantage of the boycotts and strikes their competitors will inevitably face and by marketing the accoutrements of radical chic to an all-too-receptive buying public. Bureaucrats study mass demonstrations as a social phenomenon, taking photographs, gathering data, making calculations, and comparing incidents. And the complacent bourgeoisie, far from quaking in their boots, merely sniff in annoyance when *yet another demonstration* threatens to delay happy hour or picking up the kids from day care, but of course everyone understands—the day care will waive the late pickup fee, the martinis will be just as cold a half hour later, we all know this is just part of living in a big city, and after all I did it when I was a bit younger and more naïve or idealistic—what did Churchill say: *If you're not a socialist at twenty you have no heart*—hell, maybe I'll just pull over and join them . . . what are they protesting this time, anyway?

Undermining Liberal Institutions

The implicit premise of a social protest is that the conventional means of settling disputes, distributing resources, and mediating divergent preferences are inadequate. This message may be desirable to true radicals who wish to undermine existing institutions and hasten their collapse, but it is risky for those who support liberal democratic ideals and institutions but simply wish for more targeted reform. Today's highly polarized political environment highlights the risks as well as the appeal of social protest: Many people are deeply dissatisfied with government and feel for various reasons that elected officials are either derelict in their duties or illegitimate. These are perfect conditions for a protest movement opposing specific policies and also calling into question the legitimacy of the current administration generally. But the same tactics are available to supporters of the current administration should their favored candidate fall from power. The risk is that government—and ultimately the very institutions of liberal democracy—will be under perpetual assault, not simply with respect to discrete issues but with respect to their legitimacy generally.

IDEAL PROTESTS

The paradigmatic mass protests have had three characteristics: legitimacy, efficacy, and self-sacrifice. Mass protests like the March on Washington, the Montgomery bus boycott, or the demonstrations for women's suffrage were politically legitimate because the causes they advanced were undeniably just and because the conventional means of advocacy (the democratic process, the courts, and participation in the market economy) were corrupt or unjustly exclusive. They were efficacious because they were unexpected, daring, and disruptive: They shook the organizations in control of the economy and politics out of their comfortable complacency, inspired public sympathy, and implicitly threatened further and more serious disruption should their demands be ignored. They involved self-sacrifice because the participants ran a very real risk of retaliation: Mass demonstrations were considered unlawful and protesters were routinely arrested, jailed, often physically abused by law enforcement officers, and ostracized by others in their communities. Self-sacrifice contributed to efficacy by demonstrating the commitment of the protesters, thereby potentially enhancing both public sympathy and the implicit threat of additional disruption if demands were not met. And this suggested legitimacy because protest was a costly alternative to the conventional political process or private enterprise.

Problematic Protests

Problematic protests lack one or more of these characteristics. To be sure, a protest can be worthwhile even if it lacks self-sacrifice and the questions of efficacy and legitimacy are often debatable. Still, many of today's protests are less than ideal: Some are clearly unlikely to result in meaningful social change, some pursue agendas better advanced in the normal democratic process or through the market, and many do not involve the kind of self-sacrifice that inspires admiration, suggesting that participants have undertaken a sober and responsible assessment of costs and benefits.

Here I will list four signs that a protest is problematic. Again, I am not arguing that any protest with one of these faults is necessarily ill-considered—I only suggest that they are telltale signs that a protest might have been a bad idea.

"Selma Envy": Protest as False Nostalgia

Conservative Lutheran pastor Hans Fiene coined the term "Selma envy" to describe a contemporary longing for the heroic and morally unambiguous social justice struggles of past eras. Selma envy is inspired by the desire to find today's equivalent of the civil rights struggle: "[m]ore than we wanted to find the perfect prom dates, we wanted to find our own bigotry to eradicate. After years of hearing those saints sing 'We Shall Overcome,' we were overcome with jealousy. We coveted Selma. We envied that march."[1] Fiene claims—I think unfairly—that liberal support for causes like gay rights is motivated by Selma envy. One doesn't have to covet the experience of the Civil Rights Movement to oppose irrational discrimination and thoughtless animus. Moreover, conservatives have been surprisingly adept at exploiting the mystique of the Civil Rights Movement for its causes—Selma envy seems to be a non-ideological condition.

Indeed, the critique of "Selma envy" seems less apt as a description of substantive political commitments than as an account of the attraction of the *experience* of social protest. For instance, during the wave of protests in 2007 surrounding the "Jena Six"—six black students charged with attempted murder for a schoolyard assault—one protester actually said, "This is the first time something like this has happened for our generation . . . You always heard about it from history books and relatives. This is a chance to experience it for ourselves."[2] This is an odd way to describe a true social injustice—it sounds more like what one would say about a solar eclipse or a seat on the last flight of the Concorde.

Similarly, when Baltimore Mayor Kurt Schmoke participated in 1995's Million Man March, he actually tried to distance himself from much of the substantive agenda: "I don't accept hate-filled, anti-white, anti-Semitic language coming from anybody," he said; nevertheless, he joined the march, which was organized by notorious demagogue and anti-Semite Louis Farrakhan, "because I think it is an important event [that] will probably *be seen* as significant in the history of African Americans."[3] Like the student who enthused that the Jena Six protest was his generation's "chance to experience" the Civil Rights Movement, Schmoke marched to be part of the march itself—not for any substantive cause.

The idea that social protest is an *experience* that has "happened for" the participants, rather than a sadly necessary response to injustice, suggests that some mass demonstrations are organized for the benefit of the *participants* rather than the cause. This contributes to protest fatigue: We suffer through more disruptive demonstrations than are warranted by actual social injustices. It's hard to avoid the conclusion that some of today's social protests are motivated by the self-image of those protesting as much as by the urgency of the cause. Like a Che Guevara t-shirt or a Palestinian keffiyeh scarf bought at Urban Outfitters, social activism has become a fashion statement for impressionable young people searching for a personal style and for older folks who really ought to find more age-appropriate attire.

Preaching to the Choir: Protesting as Psychotherapy

It is often said that social protests "speak truth to power"—suggesting that one needs to go where power is located before speaking. But often social demonstrations are organized, not where the objectionable decision, policy, or practice was made, but in the location convenient for people who object to it. This means that many demonstrations speak truth, not to power, but to a powerless but highly sympathetic audience. Racial justice rallies in black communities, marriage equality protests in San Francisco and West Hollywood, religious liberty demonstrations in the bible belt—these demonstrations are superficially modeled on high stakes protests in potentially hostile environments, but they actually serve more as morale-building events. There's nothing wrong with morale-building, but it doesn't necessarily require the closing of public streets or a heavy police presence. Again, protests that preach to the choir are fatiguing because they inconvenience innocent bystanders and do little to advance the cause: Why block traffic to press a point on people who already accept it?

The Opiate of Mass Protest

Karl Marx famously claimed that religion was the opiate of the masses—a soothing belief system and set of rituals that mollified the oppressed, distracting them from meaningful political action. Ironically, mass demonstrations may now serve a similar function. Mass democracies have developed means of containing and domesticating demonstrations, they now rarely threaten the status quo. Instead, they provide their participants with the psychological satisfaction of meaningful action but have little real effect on public policy.

Consider, for instance, 1995's Million Man March. It brought no specific racial injustice to the attention of a complacent public; it pressed no landmark racial justice legislation. It only rehashed the familiar set of social problems that had plagued inner-city black communities for decades: crime, joblessness, broken homes, failing schools. Nor did the Million Man March call for a renewed public commitment to racial justice: There was no demand for more aggressive civil rights laws, no impassioned plea for investment in inner-city neighborhoods, no emotional reminder of the nation's unfulfilled commitment to integration.

Instead, the Million Man March was to be a "day of atonement" and "reaffirmation" for black men. Black men were to confess their sins—drugs, gang violence, promiscuous sex—and reaffirm their commitment to their families and communities. But self-reliance didn't require a march on Washington. The result was an assembly whose substance was in direct opposition to its form: a group rally for individual self-reliance; a mass protest in service of personal responsibility. It was the *form* of the Million Man March that was responsible for much of its appeal: buoyed by nostalgia for the Civil Rights Movement, for the moral certainty of an unambiguously noble cause, the courage and heroism of speaking truth to power, and the solidarity of a community united in resistance to a common oppressor.

The central message of personal atonement and the primacy of the family echoed the prevailing neoconservative ethos of the time—far from a courageous challenge to the status quo, it harmonized with a growing popular exasperation with racial politics, hostility to social welfare policies, and celebration of a narrowly defined conventional family. As Louis Farrakhan, the organizer of the march, put it: "We wanted to call our men to Washington to make a statement that we are ready to accept the responsibility of being the heads of our households, the providers, the maintainers and the protectors of our women and children."[4] The subtext—made unmistakable by the exclusion of women from the march itself—was that black men had allowed overbearing black women to control their families to the ruin of all concerned and that men must reassert their dominance and lay claim to the role of patriarch.

The Million Man March inspired others. The Promise Keepers, a men's fundamentalist Christian organization, planned their own gathering and day of atonement on the mall. Like Elvis to the Million Man March's Junior Wells, the Promise Keepers sang the same tunes to a larger, white audience: *Stand in the Gap: A Sacred Assembly of Men* was the largest gathering ever at the National Mall. Like the Million Man March, Stand in the Gap sought, not a political revolution, but a personal one. Like the Million Man March, the Promise Keepers traced many social ills to the decline of the traditional, male-dominated family and admonished men to seize control of their households from potentially recalcitrant wives. As the National Organization for Women noted in alarm, Promise Keeper Tony Evans insisted: "I am not suggesting that you *ask* for your role back, I am urging you to *take* it back. There can be no compromise here."[5] Meanwhile, at a sister rally, ambiguously named "Chosen Women," a female speaker told the faithful throng: "Our job is to submit to our [husbands as we would to our] teachers and our Professors . . . even when we know they are wrong."[6]

The similarity between the Million Man March and the Promise Keepers was neither coincidental nor the result of simple mimicry. Both movements grafted the style of the Civil Rights Movement onto what was basically an encounter group, staged on a scale undreamed of by the practitioners of EST and Gestalt therapy. The goal—other than that of aggrandizing the movement leaders—was to disguise group therapy in the macho garb of political activism.

Both the Promise Keepers and the Million Man March offered the balm of amateur therapy packaged as the strong medicine of social activism: "Solidarity" was bonding on steroids; "empowerment" a macho synonym for self-actualization; "speaking truth to power" was the talking cure with a Y chromosome; "pride" a tough guy's self-esteem; the call for "atonement," a fist-pumping way of saying: *The first step to recovery is to admit you have a problem.* As in any therapy session, the experience was all: Although there was vague talk of economic investment in black communities and voter registration in the Million Man March, this was an afterthought. Any practical goal, political agenda, or policy objective would only impede the gestalt—as counterproductive as asking an analyst how you'll know when you're no longer neurotic and can quit your weekly therapy sessions.

The biggest irony was that both the Million Man March and the Promise Keepers—for all of their patriarchal muscle flexing and boys' club exclusivity—had lifted their blend of the personal and the political directly from 1970s feminism. Even the targets of social critique—the home, the family, and the individual trapped in an oppressive domestic relationship—were those first identified by feminists. The difference was that *feminists* had good reason to politicize the intimate and the private. The home, family, and intimate relations were (and are) the mechanisms of women's inequality, and women have been conditioned from the earliest years of life to accept that inequality. Thirty years after Betty Friedan wrote *The Feminine Mystique,* men were using the syntax of feminism to bemoan their loss of male authority and prestige and deploying the tools of the women's movement to keep women in their place.

Protesting as Politics by Other Means

As protests become a regular and predictable part of life in mass democracies, they are no longer the tools of only the downtrodden and the marginalized. Increasingly they are used by powerful interest groups as an alternative to the normal political process. When the wealthy and influential fail to influence elections, they now try to get a second bite at the apple by provoking a mass demonstration or protest movement: For instance, the activism of the NRA—essentially a lobbying arm of shadowy weapons manufacturers—uses mass protest to undermine or roll back regulations that would limit the market for guns. Or consider Ammon Bundy, who led an armed protest against the federal Bureau of Land Management in order to graze his livestock on federal land.[7]

Legitimacy

Mass demonstrations are more than simple expression. If the organizers of marches and demonstrations fail to receive permission from local authorities or exceed the terms of their permits, they cross the line into civil disobedience. And even if organizers comply with legal formalities, demonstrations are unusually disruptive—indeed, that's the point. Given the large number of conventional media for expression—newspapers, radio, television, private conversation, and social media—it's fair to ask when such extraordinary means are warranted. Citizens in mass democracies can encourage change in public policy through the political process. People unhappy with the behavior of private actors (say, labor practices or the sale of arguably inhumane products such as fur coats or foie gras) can deny offending businesses their patronage. For the most part, viewpoints that fail to persuade elected representatives or a majority of voters are not entitled to influence policy; similarly, individuals are not entitled to intervene in private contracts between other consenting parties.

Sometimes protests become a way for causes that have simply lost in a fair political fight to try for a second bite at the apple, using the pressure tactics of social activism. Consider for instance the Critical Mass cyclist protests in San Francisco. San Francisco is home to some of the most crowded streets in the United States. With its crowds come the vibrant street life, energetic public culture, an avant-garde arts scene, and gritty subculture that the city is famous for. And with those crowds come a more mundane day-to-day local culture of frayed nerves, raised elbows, and bruised ribs; a daily push and shove that continually threatens to transform the city's lonely crowd into a violent mob.

Gridlock in the Bay Area rivals that of Los Angeles and metropolitan Atlanta for the worst in the nation. San Francisco's pedestrians seize the right of way whether they are entitled to it or not, strolling into rush hour traffic mid-block, purposefully oblivious to oncoming traffic. They are, all too often, proven dead right: The city's hilly streets are now marked with white chalk outlines, symbolizing the bodies of pedestrians struck dead by cars. The outlines are a form of protest-cum-public art painted by an anonymous provocateur whose motives remain unknown: They serve to warn motorist and pedestrian alike to slow down and take care.

And San Francisco cyclists are a growing fellowship bound together by a sense of moral superiority borne of their commitment to transportation without a carbon footprint. And what thanks do they get for reducing global warming, air pollution, and dependence on foreign fossil fuels? They are regularly run off the road, cut off at intersections and bullied into the gutter by callous motorists. Cyclists began to fight back against the hegemony of the horseless carriage, forming the San Francisco Bicycle Coalition, which has successfully lobbied the city to convert street parking and traffic lanes into designated bicycle lanes, with the stated goal of making all of San Francisco's roadways "bike friendly." They also fought back by biking as aggressively as the worst motorists: Professional and weekend warrior alike adopted the bike messenger's daredevil maneuvers, darting in and out of traffic, sailing through stop signs and red lights, jumping curbs, bullying pedestrians off of sidewalks, and heaping abuse—verbal and physical—on drivers who get in their way.

Most notoriously of all, the bicyclists fought back by forming a monthly mob scene known as Critical Mass in which hundreds of cyclists with axes to grind or time to kill ride through the city's major thoroughfares in a parade so dense as to block motorist, pedestrian, and chicken alike from crossing the road. These unauthorized events can stretch for miles and tie up traffic for blocks in every direction. Pedestrians who dare to breach the column find themselves quickly run down—numerous injuries have resulted and police—powerless to stop the events—warn both motorists and pedestrians to steer clear. Motorists have inadvertently steered into it (because Critical Mass is not authorized, its route is neither publicized nor marked) and have been made to regret it: In April 2007, a mother and her two children visiting from a nearby suburb made the mistake of steering their car onto a Japantown street that had been commandeered by Critical Mass. Cyclists surrounded their car and pummeled it with fists, feet, tire pumps, and bicycle frames, breaking windows and causing more than $5,000 in damages.

If Critical Mass was supposed to inspire public sympathy for cyclists, it has achieved precisely the opposite. Public opinion in liberal San Francisco is overwhelmingly negative, even among many cyclists. Here's a sample: "Critical Mass isn't a recreational activity, it is an invitation to thuggery and vandalism. Prior to the first Critical Mass, I actually had a lot of respect for cyclists. Not anymore." "No other organization routinely breaks traffic laws, impedes other road users and, in general, acts like a bunch of three-year-olds on a playground. As a bike rider, I'd love to see Critical Mass shut down." "Critical Mass is a Critical Mistake. I can't believe they have been allowed to terrorize the City this long."[8]

When mass demonstrations are simply pressure tactics deployed when ordinary means have failed, their legitimacy is questionable.

Again, I ask readers to consider causes with which you disagree: If you support demonstrations against the sale of fur coats, consider how you would feel about demonstrations against the sale of homoerotic literature. In each case the demonstrators make a moral claim that they feel transcends normal commerce. But in each case the moral claim is debatable: For the most part, we expect citizens to use civil persuasion to press their moral claims rather than attempt to disrupt lawful transactions.

Of course, many protests—perhaps even all—could be described as sidestepping ordinary politics. How can we tell the difference between a legitimate protest against an unjust use of power, and a rejection of the results of democratic contestation? I'll suggest three instances in which protest is justified as a correction or part of democratic politics. None of these offer a formula for determining when protest is legitimate and when it is not, but they at least provide a way for thinking through the question.

Process Failure

The ideal social protests were legitimate because the normal avenues to social change were unfairly closed. Suffragettes obviously could not press their claims at the ballot box; similarly, black civil rights demonstrators were denied a meaningful political voice due to numerous discriminatory tactics that became the focus of the Voting Rights Act. Formal access to the vote may not be sufficient: The political process might be systematically biased against a particular group or point of view. Legal scholar John Hart Ely's famous conception of process failure is instructive here.[9] Although Ely thought of process failure as a constitutional justification for judicial review of legislation, we could extend it to apply to the legitimacy of social protests. Ely argued that "discrete and insular" minorities are at a systematic disadvantage in popular politics: Elected representatives can safely disregard their concerns and may also be irrationally biased against them. In this respect, it is not surprising that minorities have been among the most important social protesters.

A similar claim can be made with respect to private transactions in the market. Liberal economic theories posit that private rights to contract and property guarantee that market transactions are legitimate: Any voluntary transaction or relationship by definition makes both parties better off, at least in terms of the expected outcome. Of course, there is ample theoretical debate over whether private transactions characterized by unequal bargaining power and asymmetrical information might be illegitimate, but these are at most exceptions to the general rule. Protests targeting private enterprises or relationships are often premised on some failure or corruption of normal market processes: Animal rights protests insist that the if animals themselves are considered parties to transactions that involve animal products, rather than property, the transactions lack legitimacy because the animals do not consent. Human rights activists point out that labor conditions that involve underage or coerced labor fail to meet liberal standards of meaningful consent. Organized labor advocates argue that non-union labor suffers from unequal bargaining power in negotiations with large employers, rendering any consent to wages and labor conditions suspect.

Ely's "process failure" account has been criticized on numerous grounds. For instance, Bruce Ackerman pointed out that "discrete and insular minorities" are not necessarily at a disadvantage in the political process.[10] In fact, they can form a powerful political faction that, because of its discreteness and insularity, will vote as a block and deliver reliable support (or opposition) to representatives. In fact, it may be that anonymous and diffuse minorities—such as gay men and lesbians—are at a greater disadvantage in terms of the political process. Ackerman's criticism seems apt: Indeed, political victories for gay rights came only after large numbers of people openly identified as gay—becoming discrete rather than anonymous—allowing for political organization and efforts to combat pernicious stereotypes. The point is not that discrete and insular minorities—like African Americans in the 1970s—are never at a political disadvantage. But if diffuse and anonymous minorities can also be at a disadvantage, then a general theory that seeks to identify politically disadvantaged groups by their characteristics is in trouble. In a democracy, minority positions are *supposed* to lose: The process is flawed only when a minority position doesn't have a fair chance to garner broader support.

So, appeals to a failed process are tricky: Other than blatant suppression of the vote, it's hard to identify the features that make a facially reasonable democratic political process flawed. Any democratic system must balance deliberative with direct democracy and the registration of breadth versus intensity of support; it must also make controversial judgments about how to define the relevant political subunits, such as cities, states, and electoral districts. All of these necessarily controversial decisions can be described as unfair to some constituency or other, justifying extra-democratic measures, such as judicial review or direct action in the form of mass demonstrations.

"Rights" and Other Concerns That Transcend Normal Political Debate

Ackerman's ultimate conclusion in his critique of Ely's process failure theory was that extra-democratic measures had to be justified substantively. Similarly, we might say that protest is legitimate when it advances a cause that transcends normal politics. A protest movement for paving the roads or raising the speed limit seems wrongheaded because these are mundane concerns of precisely the type we expect normal politics to deal with. It's not an injustice that the advocates of an 80-mph speed limit haven't gotten their way—it's simply the outcome of a well-functioning democracy in which most people value the safety of a lower speed limit more than the efficiencies of speedier travel. By contrast, a demonstration against police brutality involves human rights. Human rights should not be subject to the normal give and take of politics—a government that fails to respect fundamental rights is itself illegitimate and should be met with mass resistance.

But almost any political position can be put in terms of rights. Savvy activists of every ideological stripe have become extremely adept at manipulating rights discourse and making a plausible claim that their preferred policies are required as a matter of fundamental rights. The abuse of First Amendment rights to freedom of expression are a good example of this phenomenon. When the University of California at Berkeley refused to offer conservative speakers Ann Coulter and Milo Yiannopoulos their preferred venues and schedules, they and their supporters insisted that they had been denied their right to free speech. Berkeley was inundated by demonstrations both for and against the two speakers, and extremists threatened armed confrontations.

The idea that Coulter and Yiannopoulos had been denied their right to speak was almost ludicrous as a legal matter: Berkeley did not bar either person from speaking; in fact, it made venues available, just not their preferred venues at their preferred times—preferences that posed insurmountable logistical and security challenges. The First Amendment allows government to place reasonable time, place, and manner restrictions on expression in order to serve legitimate public purposes—public safety being foremost among them.[11] Moreover, government is not required to provide a venue for expression—it need only make existing public fora available, subject to reasonable time, place, and manner restrictions.

Of course, the legalities did not stop Coulter and Yiannopoulos from claiming that their right to free speech had been violated—thus justifying a mass demonstration. And because the premise of the mass demonstration is that conventional politics are flawed, it is no answer to insist that the cause in question does not implicate formal rights recognized by the judiciary. The claim of right is inherently ambiguous: it is both a descriptive and a normative claim; a statement of positive law and a demand for law reform. When animal rights activists insist that foie gras farming practices or the manufacturing of mink coats violate the "rights" of geese or minks, they mean to insist on natural rights that preexist any actual court, legislation, or international treaty. The trouble is that two—indeed an unlimited number—can play that game: If animals have "rights" despite the lack of legal precedent or support, then new rights can be asserted on behalf of fundamentalist Christian business owners who refuse to serve gay couples in defiance of anti-discrimination laws, or survivalists who walk through city streets with firearms strapped to their belts in defiance of local and state criminal laws, or cyclists who ignore stop signs and traffic signals. Most such disagreements and divergent preferences are exactly what democratic institutions and voluntary commercial transactions are designed to mediate. Civil society cannot function when any interest group feels entitled to disrupt peaceful social intercourse unless and until their demands are met.

As was true of "process failure," the idea that some claims transcend conventional politics is at best indeterminate—rather than offering a way to decide ideologically charged controversies, these arguments are simply subsumed within them—rights become politics by other means.

Institutionalized Protest

Labor picketing is a special case that requires a short discussion of its own. Picketing is a familiar form of social protest; it is inconvenient and it is also routine—in a sense it would seem to be politics by other means and hence an example of a problematic form of protest based on my discussion so far. But there is an important distinction: Picketing is an institutionalized and highly regulated part of conventional negotiations between management and labor. It is part of the political compromise established in the nation's labor laws. It is, in this sense, unquestionably legitimate: The labor picket is not politics by other means—instead, it is part of a process established by democratic politics to ensure a reasonable balance of power between management and labor.

With that said, however, one still can ask whether an institutionalized mass protest is the best way of reaching that laudable end. Isn't the decision to routinize protest also a way of neutering it, making it safe and relatively unthreatening? And isn't the right to picket a sort of consolation prize, a substitute for more durable and reliable forms of power? Today, a growing number of progressives in the United States are discovering the German model of labor relations, in which labor is guaranteed a permanent role in corporate governance. Instead of pressuring management for higher wages, greater benefits, or more favorable working conditions, labor is part of the process that sets these terms. An advantage, according to the advocates of the German approach, is that everyone involved comes to see the business—investors, management, labor, and consumers—as an organic whole that either thrives or suffers together, instead of antagonistic factions struggling in a zero-sum contest for advantage. As a result, management is more solicitous of labor and labor, now given greater insight into the constraints facing the business as a whole, is less likely to make unreasonable demands. Admittedly, some aspects of the German approach may not be workable in other national contexts for reasons of political will and constitutional law. And of course, no arrangement is a guarantee of perfect harmony. But picketing—legally authorized or not—would always be available if negotiations failed. And such an arrangement seems a more sensible, efficient, and straightforward way of ensuring that labor is fairly treated than a legally guaranteed and limited entitlement to picket.

Efficacy

Of course, there are instances in which the dysfunction of conventional politics justifies a mass demonstration and civil disobedience. In my view, the almost daily outrages of the Trump administration present such instances on an alarmingly regular basis. Unfortunately, because mass protest is so often deployed as a substitute for conventional politics, it is less effective in response to truly extraordinary political crises.

Assuming a social protest is legitimate, in order to be justified it must also be efficacious. Demonstrations pressing legitimate concerns and voicing valid complaints will nevertheless cost more than they are worth if they are unable to persuade or cajole those in a position to address the concerns.

Speaking Truth to Power

Political protests are often designed to force people in positions of authority to face up to some inconvenient truth. A mass demonstration can put an issue on the agenda: Environmental activism has led many businesses and governments to prioritize sustainability and zero-impact policies; feminist activism has forced universities and law enforcement to address sexual assault and sex trafficking. Demonstrations can also convey the power of an overlooked or marginalized group: For instance, the "Day Without Immigrants" protest was well conceived to illustrate the contributions that immigrants make to the American economy.

Speaking truth to power requires a fairly simple message and a good sense of who is in power. Not all causes have these attributes, and too often, activists oversimplify their message in order to craft a catchy protest slogan. For instance, protests against mass incarceration and police abuses typically target police and local officials and demand the accountability for individual officers involved in questionable conduct or changes to specific and easily identified practices, such as stop-and-frisk. But individual officers are relatively powerless to change policing practices driven by department leaders, lawmakers, and public opinion—to a significant and disturbing degree most police are doing more or less what the majority of their constituents want done when they target low-income men of color for scrutiny.

The proliferation of firearms is largely responsible for fatal encounters with police, as Berkeley Professor Frank Zimring notes in *When Police Kill*: American police are twenty-five times more likely to be killed in the line of duty than their counterparts in the United Kingdom and forty times more than their counterpart in Germany. Fear of a deadly encounter explains why police themselves use deadly force: Roughly 60 percent of police shootings involved a suspect with a gun or something that looked like a gun.[12] Meanwhile, mass incarceration is largely a function of prosecutorial discretion and incentives to secure high conviction rates. Unsurprisingly, mass protests do not focus on these diffuse causes of injustice in law enforcement, which are too removed from the visceral encounters that can be captured on video and become the flashpoint for social activism. There is much to protest in contemporary law enforcement, but activism that focuses exclusively on individual accountability of officers can promote lopsided or even counterproductive reforms and give the misimpression that officer misbehavior is the primary cause of injustices in the criminal justice system.

Similarly, the Occupy Wall Street protests famously fizzled out because the target of protests and the specific demands were vague. The inequality of the modern post-industrial economy has many causes: globalization, job redundancy caused by technological advances, monetary policy, trade policy, and financial deregulation. While "Wall Street" was a convenient symbol for the polarization of wealth, Wall Street financial institutions were only one of many responsible institutions, playing a role largely determined by other forces, both domestic and global. Many of society's most pressing injustices have this character: they are systemic, caused by a web of interrelated forces with no obvious center of command or "head" to be cut off. A mass demonstration may simply be poorly suited to confront such injustices.

Conveying Sense of Unusual Urgency/Threat

The ideal protest conveys the urgency of the social injustice and the intensity of commitment of those fighting it. Implicit in most effective social protests is a threat of escalation: When thousands of people take to the streets in protest, there is an unavoidable—and to some extent intended—sense of menace. The famous tradition of nonviolent protest is in one sense an exception that proves this rule and in another sense an example of the rule in practice. It is an exception that proves the rule because nonviolent protest was a novel and remarkable idea when Mohandas Gandhi and Martin Luther King Jr. practiced it in the mid-twentieth century. Before then, it was assumed that any social protest could easily turn into a violent riot where life and property were threatened—and many did. Nonviolent protest is also an example of the rule because it always carries an implicit threat: *Deal with us now while peace-loving leaders are in charge—if peaceful activism does not work, hotter heads may prevail next time.* This synergistic relationship between nonviolent and militant activism is well known in the context of the American Civil Rights Movement, where Martin Luther King Jr.'s leadership was contrasted with the more radical nationalist message of Malcolm X.

This suggests that the efficacy of protest is related to the willingness of participants to turn to violence—at real personal risk. This raises two issues: one of efficacy and one of legitimacy.

With respect to efficacy, it suggests that the easier, more enjoyable, or more fashionable it is to protest, the less efficacious it is likely to be. The person who joins a protest movement in order to have the "experience" of activism is unlikely to stay the course if real risk or sacrifice is required—and those in power know it. Easy protests may make headlines, but they are unlikely to provoke fear—or inspire change. Zeynep Tufekci, a sociologist and participant in the Gezi Park protests in Turkey, argues that protests organized through social media are "going to be not as effective or powerful in proportion to the energy that can garner . . . these protests that appear very empowering but are actually introducing new weaknesses." She specifically cites mass demonstrations as a source of new weakness:

> A lot of people think that if you can pull off a big march, then that's a huge sign of success. . . . [after] the big anti-war march in February of 2003 right before the Iraq war . . . I thought, "surely that can't ignore this, this is a huge demonstration of strength." And Bush just said, "Why should I pay attention to a focus group?." . . . In the past, if you wanted to hold a . . . large march, say the 1963 March on Washington, it took 10 years of sustained movement-building to get to the point where you could even think about it and then it took six months of organizing. . . . if you're a person in power, you look at that, and you're thinking, "If they can pull this off, they have logistics, they have organizational capacity, they have collective decision-making ability. . . .
>
> [By contrast] if you look at the Women's March . . . if you're a legislator or if you're a person in power, you know it came together very quickly. You know it came from a Facebook post. . . . it's not the same length of time and the same building of capacities as the 1963 march. While it looks the same, it's not signaling to the powerful the same thing . . . digital technologies . . . give us springs on our feet . . . that means when you need to do the next thing, you don't necessarily have the muscle.[13]

With respect to legitimacy, the relative ease with which protests can be formed means that organizers and participants do not face the same set of incentives as people in the past did. As barriers to entry fall, in some sense mass demonstrations are an example of moral hazard: The participants bear a decreasing share of the overall cost of their behavior, while a greater share is borne by the communities in which the demonstrations take place. This can mean that the overall social cost of demonstrations is actually increasing—not because each individual demonstration is costlier, but because the ease of organizing demonstrations leads to more of them.

Once again, let's consider this aspect of protest without reference to the desirability of the underlying goal. It's easy to say that the cost to the community is trivial in comparison to the importance of the goal when you agree with the goal. But consider the implicit threat of violence from an alt-Right group pressing a free speech claim on behalf of professional provocateurs like Coulter or Yiannopoulos, or the white supremacists rallying at the University of Virginia against the removal of a statue of Confederate General Robert E. Lee. For those who value the contributions of higher education, the focus of far-right protest movements at universities should be especially disquieting: Just as leftist activists targeted the symbols of conventional wealth and power—government offices, banks, large businesses—right-wing agitators target the institutions they see as powerful forces of liberal ideology and political correctness.

In both cases, the cost of the demonstration is, in some sense, an independent *goal*: Even if protest does not achieve the stated end, at least it has disrupted the functioning of a hated institution. In a sense, the psychological satisfaction of inconveniencing some representative of the hated "power structure" compensates for the overall lack of efficacy. It's very hard not to see the recent so-called free speech protests at UC Berkeley in any other light: It was already clear that Berkeley would not accede to Coulter's or Yiannopoulos's demands, and the arrival of additional agitators only strengthened the university's position that public safety required a change in venue. But the agitators were able to disrupt the normal functioning of a hated elite university, with its privileged, politically correct snowflakes and pampered liberal professoriate. Tom Wolfe's account of the "confrontation" suggests this, less savory, aspect of most protest movements:

> It wasn't just that you registered your protest and showed the white man that you meant business and weakened his resolve to keep up the walls of oppression. . . . There was something sweet that happened right there on the spot. You made the white man quake. You brought fear into his face . . . A demonstration, like the civil rights march on Washington in 1963, could frighten the white leadership, but it was a general fear, an external fear, like being afraid of a hurricane. But in a confrontation, in mau-mauing, the idea was to frighten white men personally, face to face. . . . "You—yes you right there on the platform—we're not talking about the government, we're not talking about the Office of Economic Opportunity—we're talking about *you*, you up there with your hands shaking in your pile of papers."[14]
>
> [But] later on you think about it and you say, "What really happened that day? Well, another flak catcher lost his manhood, that's what happened." Hmmmmmmm . . . like maybe the bureaucracy

> isn't so dumb after all . . . All they did was sacrifice one flak catcher, and they got hundreds, thousands . . . They've got replaceable parts. They threw this sacrifice to you, and went away pleased with yourself . . . You did your number and he did his number, and they didn't even have to stop the music . . . The band played on.[15]

It's human nature to seek personal retribution along with social justice. It's understandable that people with legitimate grievances might also seek a bit of psychological gratification on the side. But it is worth asking whether such a goal is politically legitimate. Moreover, it's possible that the personal eclipses the political—especially when one is dealing with diffuse and systemic injustices that are hard to describe or put in the crosshairs. The protest, then, rather than being a threat to "the establishment," becomes a sort of safety valve, allowing the discontented to blow off steam in a relatively unthreatening way. *Go ahead and hassle some investment bankers, park service police or college professors, vent your spleen—we'll wait for you to get tired and go home, then get back to business as usual.*

This raises the disquieting possibility that "the system" has found a way to domesticate social protest. Today, mass demonstrations are not shocking or unsettling—they are an expected part of life and a conventional alternative to other forms of political activity, such as voter registration drives or political canvassing. It's not so much that people in positions of power ignore social protests—it's just that they don't understand them as "protests" anymore—instead they are closer to an impromptu opinion poll, a face-to-face petition or, as President Bush put it, a "focus group."

Conclusion: Post-Protest

What can we do to preserve and conserve the power of social protest for the most serious injustices and still confront issues that aren't good targets for a mass demonstration? Ideally, activists would limit disruptive mass protests to issues where they enjoy legitimacy and are likely to be effective. Given the prevalence and effectiveness of organizing through social media, this will require a great deal of introspection and self-discipline. Every activist believes her cause is important and under-appreciated, and it's hard to tell in advance which efforts will be effective. The most I can suggest is a healthy skepticism: Mass protests—even on behalf of causes you personally support—are not always a good idea. The disruption and inconvenience can alienate potential allies—all the more so if a protest disintegrates into violence. The powers-that-be have found a way to accommodate mass demonstrations and even turn them to their own advantage. Protests suggest that normal liberal political institutions are corrupt or inadequate—an appealing message for true radicals and subversives, but a risky one for anyone else, especially at a time when liberalism and Enlightenment values are under attack. And any innovative tactic will surely be copied by disreputable movements and causes. Mass protests are not a panacea—they are more like an antibiotic, which has side effects and can encourage the growth of resistant strains. Use when necessary, but handle with care.

Thankfully, social media, which makes protests easy and potentially less effective, also offers new approaches to political engagement. Social media campaigns can quickly raise large sums for preferred causes—or in opposition to irresponsible or corrupt politicians. Grassroots social media organizing could serve as ballast to the large donations and lobbying efforts of the wealthy.

Consumer activism and boycotts are another fruitful strategy. The recent "Grab Your Wallet" campaign[16] is an apt example: By threatening to politicize day-to-day commerce, Grab Your Wallet can deter big businesses from supporting political campaigns, taking money out of politics. Notice that here the aim is simply neutrality: By punishing businesses that support conservative politicians, Grab Your Wallet doesn't necessarily encourage the support of liberal causes—instead, it raises the threat of a politicized commercial sphere, in which markets are split along ideological lines. Since this threatens to cut the customer base of merchants in half, the businesses have a powerful incentive to stay out of politics altogether. Effectively then, Grab Your Wallet achieves a sort of campaign finance regulation by alternative means.

My personal favorite is humorous counter-protest. When confronted with an offensive or vile protester, such as the alt-Right, white supremacists, and neo-Nazis, the natural inclination is to match their belligerence with your own implacable sense of moral purpose. But Germans facing neo-Nazi demonstrations have devised a more clever and perhaps more effective approach: They have turned the neo-Nazi march into a joke and a fund-raiser for anti-Nazi causes. "Rechts Gegen Rechts" or Right Against the Right is billed as the nation's "most involuntary walkathon" in which local residents donate 10 euros to an anti-Nazi organization for every meter of the Nazis' march. "Someone stenciled . . . 'start,' a halfway mark and a finish line, as if it were a race. Colorful signs festooned the route . . . a sign at the end of the route thanked the marchers for their contribution to the anti-Nazi cause . . . someone showered the marchers with rainbow confetti at the finish line." At a fascist rally in Charlottesville, counter-protesters "dressed as clowns. They held signs reading 'wife power' and threw 'white flour' into the air." *New York Times* contributor Moises Velasquez-Manoff argues that such humor can "highlight the absurdity of absurd positions and . . . deflate the puffery that, to the weak minded . . . might resemble heroic purpose . . . by undercutting the gravitas white supremacists are trying to accrue, humorous counter-protests may blunt the events' usefulness for recruitment. Brawling with bandana-clad antifas may seem romantic to some disaffected young men, but being mocked by clowns? . . . not so much."[17]

These alternatives succeed by capitalizing on the relative ease with which a protest can be organized on social media. If hundreds of thousands of people can be encouraged to march in cities across the nation for awareness of police brutality or women's issues, the same number could be induced to contribute five or ten dollars to a political action committee—a sizable war chest for elections. Organization and outreach to coordinate fund-raising and assure contributors that funds will be well spent might be a better use of time and energy than a march in a city where most people already support the cause or a demonstration that can't zero in on the right targets.

With these observations, I don't mean to suggest that mass demonstrations are never appropriate. To the contrary, much of my ambition is to preserve the full communicative and emotional force of mass protest for those times when it is most needed. So I leave you with the timeless observations of perhaps America's most eloquent advocate of timely and necessary protest.

> Those who profess to favor freedom
> And yet deprecate agitation

Are men who want crops
Without plowing the ground.
They want rain without thunder and lightning.
They want the ocean without the awful roar of its waters.

Power concedes nothing without a demand.
It never did, and it never will.
—Frederick Douglass, August 4, 1857

NOTES

1 Hans Fiene, "Gay Marriage Isn't About Justice, It's About Selma Envy," *The Federalist*, March 15, 2015.

2 Maria Newman, "Jena Update: Crowds, Activism and Outrage," *New York Times*, September 20, 2007. https://thelede.blogs.nytimes.com.

3 "Who's In and Who's Out: Which Black Leaders Supported the March," *Time*, October 13, 1995.

4 "Farrakhan Inspires and Infuriates at Once," *USA Today*, February 16, 1996.

5 James Dobson, *Seven Promises of a Promise Keeper* (Nashville, TN: Thomas Nelson Press, 1994).

6 "Myths and Facts About the Promise Keepers," National Organization for Women.

7 www.nbcnews.com.

8 "SFPD to End Critical Mass?," SF Gate, March 2, 2010, www.sfgate.com.

9 John Hart Ely, *Democracy and Distrust* (Cambridge, MA: Harvard University Press, 1980).

10 Bruce Ackerman, "Beyond Carolene Products," 98 *Harv. L. Rev.* 713 (1985).

11 *Clark v. Community for Creative Non-Violence*, 468 U.S. 288, 293 (1984).

12 Frank Zimring, *When Police Kill* (Cambridge, MA: Harvard University Press, 2017), p. 86.

13 Issac Chotiner, "Has Protesting Become Too Easy?," *Slate*, May 8, 2017. www.slate.com.

14 Tom Wolfe, *Radical Chic and Mau-Mauing the Flak Catchers* (New York: Farrar, Straus and Giroux, 1970).

15 Ibid.

16 www.grabyourwallet.org.

17 Moises Velasquez-Manoff, "How to Make Fun of Nazis," *New York Times*, August 17, 2017.

7

"NO WAYS TIRED"

AN ANTIDOTE FOR PROTEST FATIGUE IN THE TRUMP ERA

SUSAN J. BRISON

We have witnessed a resurgence of mass demonstrations and other public forms of political protest in the Trump era, but are protests becoming less effective and delegitimated—counterproductive, even—precisely because of their frequency and ubiquity? Granted, more and more of us may be, in the immortal words of Fannie Lou Hamer, "sick and tired of being sick and tired" and, at marches against ever more virulent manifestations of sexism and racism, signs like "I Can't Believe I Still Have to Protest This Shit" evince a certain weariness and frustration among the dissenting masses. In this chapter I argue, however, that *more*, not less, protesting—by more people, in more places, on more occasions—is what we need now, since it can have a galvanizing, reinvigorating effect and be no less legitimate than past protests such as demonstrations for women's suffrage and the March on Washington. Mass protests today, far from sapping our energy and yielding diminishing returns, have the potential to tap and replenish the ever-renewable resources of hope and solidarity.

The most indefatigable protester I've ever known was Grace Paley, a friend and neighbor of mine in Thetford, Vermont, who was not only an extraordinary poet, essayist, and short story writer, but also an antiracist, antiwar, antinuclear, and feminist activist.[1] Every summer on August 6, for nearly three decades, Grace, her husband Bob Nichols, and a few friends of theirs, stood on the village green in Thetford in the late afternoon light with handmade signs, silently protesting the US atomic bombing of Hiroshima. Why did they do it? I wondered. At most a few dozen people driving home from work saw them. This annual ritual took place well before protesters posted selfies on social media, and even the local paper, for which nothing seems too parochial or trivial to write about, never covered these silent vigils.

What did this tiny protest accomplish? What did the sum of all of Grace's protests—small and large—accomplish? Grace didn't live to see Obama elected. Thank God she didn't live to see Trump elected. But she lived through the Bush years and protested the invasion of Afghanistan and, then, of Iraq. How did she keep going? Why did she never succumb to protest fatigue? Someone once asked Grace, in her later years, why she continued to protest—and to protest so *many* things—when humanity appeared to be making so little progress and she replied, "It's a good way to live your life."

In his engaging and provocative chapter, "Protest Fatigue," Richard Ford, while lauding past protests such as "the March on Washington, the Montgomery bus boycott [and] the demonstrations for women's suffrage," argues that contemporary protests have largely lost their force by becoming too safe, too predictable, and too frequent.[2] They also, increasingly, on his view, give rise to counter-demonstrations, leading him to speculate that "if any protest can be met with an equal and opposite counter-protest, perhaps everyone involved would have been better off staying home."

Ford begins by noting some of the costs of contemporary protests: inconvenience and disruption, dilution of sympathy, and the undermining of liberal institutions. I'm persuaded that some of the protests he discusses, such as the monthly Critical Mass cyclist protests in San Francisco, do indeed have these costs and may very well be counterproductive. But I'm not persuaded that his analysis of these protests and the others he focuses on—the 1995 Million Man March and the subsequent Promise Keeper's Stand in the Gap: A Sacred Assembly of Men—generalizes to most, or even very many, of today's protests.

Although I agree with Ford's lists of "ideal" versus "problematic" protests, I disagree with the way he attempts to distinguish between the two. On Ford's view, the "ideal" protests of the past had three characteristics: legitimacy, efficacy, and self-sacrifice on the part of the protesters. "Problematic" ones "lack one or more of these characteristics." Although he qualifies this by acknowledging that "a protest can be worthwhile even if it lacks self-sacrifice and the questions of efficacy and legitimacy are often debatable," he asserts that "many of today's protests are less than ideal: Some are clearly unlikely to result in meaningful social change, some pursue agendas better advanced in the normal democratic process or through the market and many do not involve the kind of self-sacrifice that inspires admiration, suggesting that participants have undertaken a sober and responsible assessment of costs and benefits."

I don't take Ford to be using the word "ideal" in its literal sense here, but, rather, to mean something more like *worthwhile all things considered.* Surely it was less than ideal that black women who were leaders in the Civil Rights Movement were not invited to speak at the 1963 March on Washington (with the one exception of Daisy Bates, who delivered a very brief "Tribute to Negro Women Fighters for Freedom").[3]

So let's reframe the question: What are the distinguishing features of a *worthwhile* protest? This gives rise straightaway to the question: *Worthwhile for whom?* What each of us needs to decide before organizing, funding, or participating in a protest is, "Is this worth *my* while?" or, rather, since no one protests as an abstract individual or a bare particular, but as a member of a group that is *for* or *against* something, "Is this worth *our* while?" The answer, of course, will depend on who *we*, the protesters, are and what our aims are.

Ford seems to approach the question of whether a protest is worthwhile from a society-wide consequentialist perspective. In order to determine whether a protest is worthwhile—or pointless, or, worse, counterproductive—we need to consider the costs and benefits to *all* those affected by the protest. And, presumably, we should also take into account the costs and benefits of all the foregone alternatives, asking whether all the person-hours and dollars could and should have been spent on some other more worthwhile activity. Or perhaps he is saying that our cost-benefit analysis needs to take under consideration only what the protest does for (or against) the cause in question.

In either case, the question of whether the protest is worthwhile *for the protesters* is largely neglected. Things look different if we take, as our starting point, the perspective of the protesters and if we look at a wider range of contemporary protests, in particular those focused on oppressed or victimized groups, people fighting for their rights. Yes, protests can spark counter-protests, and victim-talk gives rise to counter-victim-talk, as Martha Minow has pointed out.[4] Likewise, as Ford notes, "almost any political position can be put in terms of rights." But this doesn't mean we have to accept such talk at face value. We need to critically evaluate claims of victimization and rights violations, and fortunately, we are able to do this.

I have doubts that the three characteristics Ford lists—legitimacy, efficacy, and self-sacrifice on the part of the protesters—are *the* earmarks of worthwhile protests. Of the three, "legitimacy" seems least controversial, but I'm not sure what he means by it. It strikes me as perhaps tautologically true that worthwhile protests must be legitimate.

But must they involve self-sacrifice and be efficacious? Granted, most of *us*—highly privileged academics—most of the time risk nothing or very little when we protest (although post-Charlottesville, that may be changing). But why *should* self-sacrifice—or putting oneself at significant risk of harm—be an earmark of a worthwhile protest?

And when asking whether a protest is efficacious, we need to specify *toward what end?* Toward what end did the mothers of the Plaza de Mayo march weekly in Buenos Aires from 1977 until the end of the so-called Dirty War (in 1983) and beyond, until 2006? They had met while trying to find their sons and daughters who had been "disappeared." Was their protest effective? It did not bring back their sons and daughters, but it brought the world's attention to the atrocities committed by the military regime in Argentina. Did it involve self-sacrifice? In the early years, the mothers did put themselves at risk, but not after 1983. Did their protest become less worthwhile after that? Less worthwhile *for whom?*

As Mari Matsuda has observed, of civil rights era protests, "[i]n focusing only on the material changes attained and, particularly obvious today, the material changes *not* attained, we fail to acknowledge the ways in which the civil rights movement dignified its participants by giving them a forum for resistance. In addition to moving the dominant culture toward its more progressive ideals, protest movements claimed human dignity for participants. After years of stoic silence, of backing down, of enduring the daily insult of name-calling, of Jim Crow, and of second-class citizenship, the civil rights movement offered a chance to claim one's personhood."[5]

But Ford seems to disparage any agent-centered ends protesters might have for themselves. Three of the four "tell-tale signs that a protest might have been a bad idea" focus on what he takes to be suspect attitudes on the part of the protesters. In the section on "Selma Envy"—a phrase that, to me, has the false ring of "victim envy" since no one *really* envies those who marched across the Edmund Pettus bridge on "Bloody Sunday" or those who have been genuinely victimized—Ford derides "mass demonstrations [that] are organized for the benefit of the *participants* rather than the cause," as if the only benefit to the participants might be a purely self-regarding special sort of experience, something akin to watching a solar eclipse or getting "a seat on the last flight of the Concorde." In the section on "Preaching to the Choir: Protesting as Psychotherapy," Ford trivializes the morale-building that protests can accomplish as mere self-indulgence, and, in "The Opiate of Mass Protest," he argues that demonstrations "now rarely threaten the status quo," but, rather, "provide their participants with the psychological satisfaction of meaningful action," while having "little real effect on public policy."

But this assessment of the efficacy (or lack thereof) of contemporary protests ignores powerful national and global movements that *are* making a difference. Here are just a few examples: the Puente Human Rights Movement in Phoenix led by currently and formerly undocumented immigrants; anti-rape activism on college campuses; One Billion Rising; Black Lives Matter; the fight for a minimum wage of $15. In *"We Are All Fast Food Workers Now": The Global Uprising Against Poverty Wages,* historian Annelise Orleck describes the galvanizing effect of recent protests for higher wages. "On April 15, 2015," Orleck recounts, "low-wage workers in two hundred US cities, in 40 countries on six continents struck and rallied for a living wage. They marched in New York, Boston, Los Angeles, Chicago and hundreds of other American cities. They marched in London, Brussels, Paris, Stockholm, Manila, Seoul, Tokyo, Rio, Tegucigalpa, Buenos Aires, Brasilia, Capetown, Freetown and Accra."[6]

As Orleck notes, "It wasn't only economic gains that moved them. The marchers sought to reoccupy cities where all but the wealthiest have been marginalized by rising costs, to make visible the people whose labor makes cities run."[7] Orleck marched alongside tens of thousands of low-wage workers that day in Manhattan, noting that "many were legal residents but many others were undocumented" and "made a conscious choice to come out of the shadows, riding subways and commuter trains from apartments in East New York, Flatlands, Brownsville and the Bronx. . . . It took a leap of faith for them to come out into the light . . . to lift their heads, to walk freely down the streets of the center city where they worked but could not afford to live."[8]

Orleck tells the story of Tampa fast food worker-activist Reika Mack who, in February 2015, "was one of 500 *Fight for $15* activists from 10 states who traveled to the Ebenezer Baptist Church in Atlanta, where Martin Luther King Jr. was once pastor. There, the young workers were tutored by some of the sanitation strikers who marched with King in Memphis in 1968. . . . 47 years later, the white-haired activists led young fast food workers as they marched to a nearby McDonalds. On a traffic-clogged Atlanta avenue they sat down and sang 'We Shall Overcome.' . . . 'It was a beautiful thing,' Mack says, 'to know that we were marching for the same cause as they did so many years ago. For our humanity, for our rights.'"[9]

This isn't "Selma envy." And it's the opposite of narcissistic self-indulgence. Such protests *do* provide a much-needed boost to the morale of the protesters, but this comes from the realization that the protest one is engaged in now is much larger than oneself and more long-lived than one's own generation, that one is not only being inspired by those who protested before, but providing inspiration for those who will protest later. Such protests have an electrifying force that spans not only spatial, but also temporal boundaries.

The protests I've participated in have been, most often, about matters of life and death, or that's how they've felt to me—*my* life (reproductive rights marches, Take Back the Night rallies, One Billion Rising dances) or *others'* (antiwar demonstrations, Black Lives

Matter protests, anti-Fascist/anti-Nazi vigils). Putting my white body on the street with black bodies to protest police brutality against blacks is essential, not only to demonstrate cross-racial solidarity, but also to show that I recognize that *I* have a responsibility to do something, that this issue concerns me. Truly worthwhile protests can blur the usually sharp distinctions between self and other, revealing the interconnectedness of all our fates.

Making our bodies visible in protests can help to counter media coverage that presents racism as something that only blacks have reason to protest, as when the *New York Times* reported, on January 15, 2019, after Trump attacked Representative John Lewis of Georgia on Twitter, "Blacks around the country have reacted to Mr. Trump's remarks with fury." The article continues: "The angry reaction is driven not only by Mr. Trump's Twitter posts but by what many blacks say they reveal about the president-elect's lack of understanding of the reverence with which the civil rights movement and its leaders are viewed by African-Americans."[10] Of course, blacks have more at stake in dealing with the racism of a president-elect, but white people need to show that it makes us angry, as well, and one way to do that is to take to the streets.

Here are some features of a protest that indicate to me that it's worthwhile.

- It dignifies the protesters. It helps them to overcome the stigma of oppression and victimization and the self-blame and shame that so often accompany these things. So, yes, it's therapeutic, but not in an individualistic, self-indulgent way.
- It energizes the protesters, especially those who suffer from invisibility fatigue, status quo fatigue, and indifference fatigue.
- It unites the protesters, creating or enhancing solidarity among them.
- It makes visible and audible something that had been shrouded in silence.
- It raises awareness of widespread, long-standing, systemic injustices—things that are so ubiquitous that they can be as invisible as the air we breathe.[11]

Granted, mass demonstrations aren't the *only* way to draw attention to such injustices. Sometimes other efforts can have this effect. Amartya Sen's *NYRB* article, "More Than 100 Million Women Are Missing," made vivid and concrete something that had not been apparent to most of us.[12] But protests are *one* way—and a way with distinct advantages over other methods. (Compare the vicious infighting among liberals and leftists on social media after the presidential election with the extraordinary solidarity of the Women's Marches in DC, across the nation, and around the world on January 21, 2017.)

* * *

"*You* will not replace *us*, *Jews* will not replace *us*," the neo-Nazis and white supremacists chanted on the lawn of the University of Virginia in Charlottesville on August 11, 2017. At this time in the United States, it's crucial to respond to this call, and there are occasions when one can do so only by physically showing up.

As a University of Virginia professor said, of the candlelight vigil at which thousands protested the earlier neo-Nazi march, "The marchers last weekend stained our University and we had to do something to reclaim it. We need to show that we as a community reject their values and to come together and affirm that to each other."[13] And, as Matsuda urges, we academics "need to do more than study. We need to participate. Students in SNCC were fond of asking, when armchair liberals and intellectuals express sympathy for the movement, 'Where is your body?'"[14]

My experience of the 2017 Women's March in DC was very different from Ford's in San Francisco. The solidarity we experienced was exhilarating. I had been skeptical about the pink pussy hats—I thought they didn't display sufficient gravitas—but I was wrong. The differences among us that had been amplified on social media since the election were muted or gleefully ignored (as when the men's and women's rooms at Union Station spontaneously became unisex in order to more easily accommodate so many women). Later, watching the online videos of millions of protesters around the globe was thrilling. Being part of that was *not* entirely unlike the experience of watching a solar eclipse, or watching videos of it as it sweeps across the planet, in that it was awe-inspiring, reminding one of the vastness of the planet, of the cosmos, and of one's participation in something much larger than oneself. But it was quite different, I imagine, from the highly exclusive experience of getting a seat on the last flight of the Concorde. On the contrary, the global march had a humbling, leveling effect, that facilitated an expansive sense of solidarity. In DC, most marchers got nowhere near the stage—and didn't even mind. With 500,000 people present, packed tightly together for hours, I witnessed no pushing or shoving, no frayed nerves or flaring tempers, but, instead, strangers looking after each other, offering water and snacks.

Those of us who were close enough to the stage at the DC rally joined Janelle Monae in a "Say Her Name" call-and-response tribute to black women murdered in acts of police brutality. What effect did shouting their names, again and again, have? It didn't put an end to such murders, but it kept the memories of these women alive, showed their mothers that they were not alone in their pain, and strengthened our resolve to do whatever we could to end the racism and misogyny that fueled their murders and, then, rendered them invisible.[15]

In my opinion, a truly worthwhile protest should include music (and, ideally, dancing). Unlike writing letters, op-eds, and blog posts, unlike calling or emailing elected officials, unlike voting—all things we typically do in isolation, on our own—singing we do together, with one voice. The Women's March in DC was not merely a call to action, but more like a call-and-response, an action in itself. Those of us who had felt, in isolation, defeated and demoralized, found renewed strength in our visible—and audible—solidarity with others. And I can't imagine a more fitting end to the rally than Toshi Reagon leading us in singing "Ella's Song," the words of Ella Baker set to music by Toshi's mother, Bernice Johnson Reagon: "We who believe in freedom cannot rest. We who believe in freedom cannot rest until it comes."

Notes

1 For those not familiar with the life and writings of Grace Paley, I recommend starting with this *New Yorker* profile: George Saunders, "Grace Paley, The Saint of Seeing," *The New Yorker*, March 3, 2017, available at www.newyorker.com, and this review of *A Grace Paley Reader* (2017): Alexandra Schwartz, "The Art and Activism of Grace Paley," *The New Yorker*, May 8, 2017, available at www.newyorker.com.

2 Richard Ford, "Protest Fatigue," this volume.

3 Daisy Bates stood in for Myrlie Evers (listed on the program as "Mrs. Medgar Evers," following the norm at the time) who was invited qua wife of the slain civil rights leader who had been murdered two months prior to the march. ("About," Anna Julia Cooper Center, http://ajccenter.wfu.edu.

4 Martha Minow, "Surviving Victim Talk," *UCLA Law Review* 40 (1993): 1411.

5 Mari Matsuda, *Where Is Your Body? And Other Essays on Race, Gender, and the Law* (Boston: Beacon Press, 1996), 75.

6 Annelise Orleck, "*We Are All Fast-Food Workers Now": The Global Uprising Against Poverty Wages* (Boston: Beacon Press, 2018), 56–57.

7 Orleck, *Fast-Food Workers*, 57.

8 Orleck, *Fast-Food Workers*, 57.

9 Orleck, *Fast-Food Workers*, 75.

10 Yamiche Alcindor, "In Trump's Feud with John Lewis, Blacks Perceive a Callous Rival," *New York Times*, January 15, 2017, available at www.nytimes.com.

11 The Fight for $15, Puente, ACT UP, Mothers of the Plaza de Mayo, Black Lives Matter, and the Women's March all did this.

12 Amartya Sen, "More Than 100 Million Women Are Missing," *New York Review of Books*, December 20, 1990, available at www.nybooks.com.

13 Caroline Newman and Sanjay Suchak, "Taking Back the Lawn," *UVA Today*, August 17, 2017, available at http://news.virginia.edu.

14 Matsuda, *Where Is Your Body*, 78.

15 Or, rather, relatively invisible, in comparison to the murders of black men that have been the focus of #BlackLivesMatter.

PART III

THE DEMOCRATIC SIGNIFICANCE OF PROTEST AND DISSENT

8

DEFINING NONVIOLENCE AS A MATTER OF LAW AND POLITICS

TABATHA ABU EL-HAJ

Those who predicted outdoor assembly would be relegated to the status of a quaint political practice with the rise of the digital age have been sorely mistaken. A range of forces, including rising economic inequality and partisan polarization, have converged to reinvigorate a politics in which disruptive protest is a central tactic. In the United States, recent protests have been notable for their spontaneity—from the sweep of protests in the wake of police shootings in city after city in 2015 to the outpourings in opposition to President Trump's first travel ban in January 2017. Social media appears to have invigorated the form by significantly lowering the costs of mobilizing and organizing. Overall, these protest movements have engaged and energized individuals from various walks of life and political stripes, mainstream and fringe, many of whom had not previously engaged in public politics. One-third of the participants at the Women's March in Washington, DC in January 2017, likely the largest march in US history, had never been to a demonstration at the capitol before.[1]

Not surprisingly, this wave of public protests has renewed scholarly interest in the history, practice, and normative implications of protest and dissent. Karuna Mantena's "Competing Theories of Nonviolent Politics" and Richard Ford's "Protest Fatigue," both in this volume, offer skeptical perspectives, with Mantena attempting to locate "the political purpose and potential of nonviolence,"[2] and Ford highlighting the potentially self-defeating, even undemocratic, consequences of contemporary forms of disruptive protest.

In "Protest Fatigue," Ford seeks to interrogate contemporary political protests and mass demonstrations, setting out "to distinguish legitimate and potentially useful protests from those that are needlessly irritating or downright counterproductive."[3] Provocatively, he argues that there is little value in the vast majority of "noisy, annoying, costly and disruptive protests"[4]—characterizing contemporary social activism as a mere "fashion statement"[5] and wondering whether we would all be "better off staying home" and engaging in normal electoral politics.[6] While Ford assures us that his aim is not "to imply a legal argument concerning the 'rights' of individuals and groups to assemble and express themselves,"[7] his repeated characterizations of contemporary coercive protest strategies as illegitimate and anti-democratic do seem to imply that some forms of assembly are less worthy of constitutional protection.

Mantena, more measuredly, seeks to correct for the fact that while "[n]onviolence is one of the most important and surprising political phenomena to emerge over the course of the last century,"[8] it remains significantly undertheorized. Among the most important undertheorized aspects of the political form, she argues, is the question of coercion, including its necessity and definition. Toward that end, Mantena seeks to explain and motivate Gandhi's "strict insistence that satyagraha ruled out all forms of coercion"[9]—including not only sabotage, hunger strikes, and ostracism but even physical obstructions during demonstrations.[10]

Unlike Ford, Mantena does not go so far as to suggest that more coercive forms of protest are inherently antithetical to democracy. Still, like Ford, she implicitly holds up Gandhi and King's particular form of nonviolence, which adhered to a "stricter definition of nonviolent action,"[11] as a normative model for the practice.

I have grave concerns about any effort to give the protest strategies of Gandhi or Martin Luther King Jr. primacy when defining nonviolence insofar as the emphasis on their "stricter" version of nonviolence will inescapably infiltrate constitutional doctrine. Mantena might be right to emphasize, with Gandhi and King, the externalities associated with "coercive tactics that relied on intimidation or veiled force,"[12] but it is important not to blur their status as nonviolent or to criticize the practice on the grounds that it "suggests that normal liberal political institutions are corrupt or inadequate."[13]

The fact is that disruptive protest has been a central tactic of American democratic politics since the Founding—one that was explicitly protected by the First Amendment, notwithstanding its well-known coercive tendencies. To elide this constitutional history at a moment when the president of the United States is a critic of any act of dissent—even acts that are peaceable by any measure, such as kneeling during the national anthem to protest racism—is, to my mind, unconscionably risky. President Trump recently went so far as to opine, when his unpopular nominee for the US Supreme Court was greeted by protesters before a congressional hearing, that "it's embarrassing for the country to allow protesters."[14] His attacks on the freedom of assembly, sadly, cannot be laughed off.

Around the country, legislatures have been introducing and passing bills that render a wide swath of protest tactics unlawful precisely because they have been effective in drawing attention to claims and issues that typically fall off the legislative radar. More important, these legislative efforts are part of a broader pattern of eroding fundamental democratic norms—from partisan redistricting to rewriting legislative procedures and traditions for judicial nominations—and are importantly related to the routine attacks on the free press and the loyalty of dissenters.[15]

Now more than ever, therefore, whatever our personal normative views on either the tactics of contemporary protesters or the parameters of current constitutional doctrine, it is our duty as a scholarly community to reaffirm that recent acts of protest and dissent operate well within the bounds of our American tradition of outdoor assembly and its constitutional protections. We may personally question the millennial iteration of the people outdoors, but we should take care not to inadvertently reinforce the wild suggestions of President Trump and various legislators that recent acts of protest and dissent are somehow at odds with, or an embarrassment to, American democratic traditions. My comments, in this regard, are limited to the recent politics of protest and dissent in the United States.

Disorderly Assembly and the American Constitutional Tradition

The notion that public dissent—given its implicit threat of violence—poses a threat to legitimate political processes and thus to liberal democracy fundamentally misconstrues both the history and practice of popular sovereignty in the United States. Discordant protest has been a central tactic of our democratic politics since the Founding—one that was explicitly protected by the First Amendment. It is, therefore, simply inaccurate to suggest that disruptive protest, given its coercive tendencies, is in tension with liberal democracy. In the United States, nonviolent protest is *not* "an extra-institutional form of politics"[16]—let alone a threat to the normal channels of democratic politics.[17]

Equally important, the nonviolent political movements of the mid-twentieth century do not have a monopoly on the definition of *nonviolence* in our constitutional tradition. While it may be interesting to interrogate, at a granular level, the tactics of nonviolent movements and how they have changed over time, it is a mistake to suggest, even inadvertently, that contemporary protesters should be bound to Gandhi's narrow conception of nonviolence—or, in the American context, that of his disciple, Martin Luther King Jr.

In every era, American democracy (or republicanism as it was once called) has involved and required a continuum of political practices. As practiced, versus as theorized, American democratic politics involves far more than elections, and responsiveness occurs in many places other than legislatures.[18] In fact, as practiced, deliberation and discourse play (and have long played) a narrower role in our democracy than democratic theory often supposes.

Outdoor assembly and protest, in particular, have held a central place within the repertoire of democratic political practices since the Founding, notwithstanding their associated risks of violence.[19] In the early nineteenth century, as I have documented elsewhere, elections were part of an array of political practices recognized as legitimate ways of making claims on the government, including public meetings, petitions, parades, politicized celebrations of local and national holidays, juries and mobs.[20] Today, we have embraced political parties and replaced the jury with litigation, but both elections and the politics of the people outdoors remain central to the normal repertoire of democratic politics in the United States.

Indeed, the centrality of protest and dissent to the American form of liberal democracy was baked into the First Amendment.[21] The text of the First Amendment articulates two rights: the freedom of speech and "the right of the people to *peaceably* assemble."[22] Like the term "freedom of speech," the term *peaceably* is not self-defining. While riots and unlawful assemblies have always been understood to fall outside constitutional protection, what constitutes a riot or unlawful assembly and, in particular, how much violence must be involved, has been much less clear.[23]

Americans in different eras have held radically different understandings of "how violent or disorderly a crowd may be before it loses First Amendment protection," with our contemporary understanding among the most restrictive.[24] From the Founding through the late nineteenth century, American law was significantly more tolerant of the disruption and inconvenience associated with the people outdoors, placing great value on the right of assembly as a privilege and immunity of American citizenship—greater value, in fact, than on the freedom of speech.[25]

Nineteenth-century Americans had a much higher social and legal threshold for the irritations that come with democracy.[26] Through the nineteenth century, the right of assembly—established to protect not only assemblies of the people for purposes of drafting lists of grievances but also the actions of the Sons of Liberty—was understood to require tolerance for the unruly, uncivil, and incoherent elements of protest.[27] The crimes of "unlawful assembly" and "riot" required an actual and imminent threat of violence.[28] It was, therefore, not uncommon for Americans, both enfranchised and disenfranchised, to gather in public places and parade through the streets at will. These gatherings, planned and unplanned, were considered lawful—even when they occurred without advanced permission, at night, and involved the burning of public figures in effigy.[29] Government officials could not regulate such assemblies without showing a breach of the peace, defined in terms of levels of actual violence.[30] Merely blocking a highway, in the absence of an imminent threat of violence to persons or property, for example, would have been considered peaceable conduct during much of the nineteenth century.

This nineteenth-century constitutional history is critical at this moment when the very legitimacy of any dissent is under attack. It demonstrates that the distaste of Ford and others for the inconvenience, disruption, and potential violence associated with outdoor assembly like the modern Supreme Court's willingness to permit authorities to dampen its disruptive tendencies through elaborate permitting regimes and broad definitions of riot and unlawful assembly are only *one* moment in our constitutional history, as discussed further below. A moment that significantly undervalues protest, including its ability to facilitate the forging of a collective political identity and active political engagement.[31] Indeed, whatever the limits of the millennial conception of nonviolence, it is hard to deny that it has inspired and energized Americans from across the country, regardless of political persuasion or socioeconomic status, to engage in our democracy at a time when many are disenchanted with electoral politics. Moreover, a significant body of research suggests that these initial forays into protest politics are likely to develop into engagement with electoral politics. Indeed, the notion that the proper measure of outdoor assembly is its success in achieving its political and social goals misses the full array of ways outdoor assembly contributes to our democracy.

The Contemporary Repertoire of Nonviolence and the American Tradition

To be sure, millennial nonviolent politics has developed its own distinctive characteristics and tactics. The ritualized and orderly form of protest associated with the politics of the late twentieth century has been replaced with a more vibrant practice—one that is more tolerant of disorder. And still, the tactics that we have seen in recent years—notwithstanding their divergence from the practice of *satyagraha*—largely operate within the bounds of our constitutional tradition. Only rarely have they posed significant threats of violence to persons or property. Thus, any move to render assemblies like the ones discussed below illegitimate—let alone beyond constitutional protection—for their passion, inconvenience, or disruptiveness constitutes a significant step backward, especially given how central they have become to the repertoire of contemporary American politics.

From the late 1970s through the 1990s, major protests focused on the National Mall in Washington, DC. Many marches during the period—for example, those in opposition to the Persian Gulf War in 1991 and the Million Man March—were organized by established nonprofits. Their organizers frequently acquiesced to high levels of advanced regulation and prided themselves on their cordial relationships with relevant authorities.[32] Orchestrated to remind the public of the large marches on Washington, DC that took place at the height of the civil rights and antiwar movements of the 1960s and early 1970s, these demonstrations were frequently read as feeble replicas of marches past. Those organizations that broke the orderly mold—ACT UP and certain radical environmentalists, in particular—were both discredited for their lack of civility and dismissed as fringe. The environmentalists, who spiked or sat in trees, were even labeled eco-terrorists.

The tenor of contemporary protests has been far more disruptive. Few protests in recent years have manifested the degree of discipline, let alone the top-down discipline, that marked either the independence movement led by Gandhi in India or the civil rights marches led by Martin Luther King Jr.

Social media has facilitated the fluidity of the new form both by making it much easier to organize quickly in response to current events and by enabling mobilization through personal ties rather than established organizations—although the latter certainly help.

The actions of the Occupy and Black Lives Matter movements illustrate how millennial nonviolent protest differs from that of the mid-twentieth century. Occupy constitutes the first prominent example of millennial protest and dissent. Organized to call attention to income inequality and the pervasive influence of special interests in democratic politics, the movement began with the occupation of Zuccotti Park, located near Wall Street in New York City, on September 17, 2011.[33] Although Occupy, like protest and dissent movements of prior eras, was conceived and initially orchestrated by established organizations, the Occupy assemblies evidenced an energy and spontaneity that was unusual at the time.

Two tactics emerged as its signature: first, its persistence, and second, its nightly assembly. In defiance of the norm that public assemblies must be time limited to mitigate public inconvenience, Occupy aimed for permanent occupation of public space in cities and towns across the country. Many occupations proceeded without even obtaining required permits from local authorities—thereby establishing the movement's rejection of the conciliatory tactics of the previous era of social movement politics. Second, each encampment held a nightly assembly in which participants debated and addressed pressing political, strategic, and administrative concerns, using a human loudspeaker.

These two strategies were complemented by disruptive daily processions. For Occupy, the routine disruption its street processions caused and the daily eyesore its encampment presented were ways to direct the attention of many mainstream Americans to its cause. One early procession blocked traffic on the Brooklyn Bridge for hours—garnering important attention to the movement's cause early on.

Still, its assemblies and marches were largely notable for their peacefulness, until municipal efforts at removal took hold. Only then did we hear stories of alleged rioting and violence. In the end, the movement was relatively short-lived. Between October and December, city officials across the country, relying on a host of established legal precedents, had cleared the major encampments.

The Occupy movement was shortly succeeded by the rise of Black Lives Matter ("BLM"). Far more than Occupy, BLM embraced the power of disruption and harnessed the distinct potential of social media to permit immediate responses to current events. By broadcasting incidents of police shootings in real time as well as incidents of over-policing the subsequent protests, BLM has produced some of the most genuinely spontaneous marches of the recent era. In doing so, it has drawn and maintained the mainstream media's attention to an issue that is not new in America. More distinctively, through the use of social media, BLM appears to have mobilized individuals who may not be especially well-connected to existing civic and political organizations through their personal ties.

As with Occupy, mitigating the inconvenience of vigils and marches has been low on the priority list of the BLM movement. In a symbolic rejection of the tactics used in prior eras,[34] BLM demonstrations routinely proceed without obtaining requisite permits, even when practical—sometimes opting to demonstrate precisely where authorities are least likely to grant permits.[35] Many of the movement's signature four-and-a-half minute "die-ins"—representing the four-and-a-half hours that Michael Brown's body lay on the street in Ferguson—have occurred in locations meant to heighten inconvenience and, as such, attention. The most prominent was a 1,000-plus-person die-in at the Mall of America on Black Friday, but there were others. In Philadelphia, where I live, a die-in was staged at the central Amtrak station and was followed by a march to City Hall, during rush hour. Altogether the event, prompted by a grand jury's decision not to indict the police officer responsible for Michael Brown's death, lasted four hours and, as it happened, coincided with the city's annual lighting of the Christmas tree at City Hall.[36] Similarly, activists in the Twin Cities orchestrated a 150-person effort to shut down a local freeway for about an hour following the grand jury's decision not to indict the officer responsible for Eric Garner's death.[37] The incident was orchestrated as "a stop" on the march to City Hall.

Only a handful of major BLM protests have spiraled out of control. Rioting typically involved violence to property, including setting fire to police cars and other acts of vandalism, and was a reaction to the intimidating crowd control tactics used to police BLM protests. In Ferguson, Missouri, crowd control tactics included the presence of military vehicles and the use of LRAD (long-range acoustic device) sound cannons.[38] In this regard, the experiences of BLM are typical: It is well documented that assemblies most frequently descend into mayhem in response to efforts to police them.[39]

Taken together, Occupy and BLM demonstrate the ways in which millennial forms of nonviolence reject the sort of discipline that Gandhi sought to instill within the independence movement through the practice of satyagraha. While Gandhi eschewed even those forms of nonviolence that merely bordered on the coercive, contemporary political activists embrace a much broader definition of what constitutes nonviolent action. Occupy recreated the classic democratic town hall but did so in central squares and parks, dramatizing the power of the people as sovereign without much attention to the inconveniences it produced. BLM was most successful when it was able to quickly orchestrate through social media outpourings in streets across the country to protest police shootings. Both movements appeared to outsiders as fluid and leaderless. In neither were participants encouraged to signify their respectability by appearing well dressed, respectful, silent, or prayerful. Equally important, neither movement prioritized formulating a concrete political demand or offering authorities advanced notice.

Of greater interest, over the past decade, such protest tactics have migrated from the fringe of radical politics to the center of national politics. The efforts of the Standing Rock Sioux Tribe to halt the construction of the Dakota Access Pipeline nicely illustrate this migration.

The Standing Rock Sioux Tribe operates within the mainstream of American interest group politics on the left. Unlike either Occupy or BLM, the Tribe, therefore, began with a single defined demand: to reroute the construction of the 1,170-mile-long, $3.8 million project of the Dakota Access Pipeline so that it would not run under Lake Oahe, a sacred body of water for the Tribe. Its encampment was from the start part of a larger political strategy that involved, among other things, litigation. The Tribe, moreover, had cultivated organizational allies before embarking on its action.

In the spring of 2016, when it first established the encampment outside Cannon Ball, a small town not far from the Standing Rock Sioux Reservation, it was joined by both environmental activists and other Native American allies.[40] Dozens of teepees and hundreds of tents were set up, and those congregating regularly engaged in prayer, traditional ceremonies, and peaceful resistance.[41]

In most ways, the tactics of the Standing Rock Sioux hewed closely to the classic script for nonviolent protest.[42] The Tribe, however, made one critical choice to break with that tradition: It decided to indefinitely camp on federal land without a permit—rendering the protest technically unlawful.

Ultimately, it was the persistence of the unpermitted encampment (an act that can *only* conceivably be considered violent in a symbolic sense) that led to both violent confrontations with police and public awareness of their claim. The longer the unpermitted encampment dragged on, the more strained the relations between activists and law enforcement officials became.[43] The tension reached a breaking point in late October 2016, when law enforcement sought to forcibly relocate the protesters. As is often the case when the police arrive to clear a protest, the scene quickly turned violent:

> Scores of officers dressed in riot gear walked in a wide line, sweeping protesters out of the area as face-to-face yelling matches broke

> out. Several vehicles, including at least one truck, were set ablaze. A standoff unfolded beside a bridge known as the Backwater Bridge, where protesters set fire to wooden boards and signs and held off the line of officers over many hours.[44]

Like in the Indian nationalist and the US Civil Rights movements, state violence drew sympathy to the cause and resulted in a (temporary) victory for the Standing Rock Sioux. It was a second confrontation a month later that really drew national media attention.[45] Two thousand veterans vowed to serve as human shields to protect the demonstrators from what they perceived as unjustified militarized policing. North Dakota's governor responded by vowing to evacuate the camps immediately because of an impending heavy snowfall. Within days of the ordered evacuation, President Barack Obama intervened to halt construction of the Dakota Access Pipeline. The victory, however, proved short-lived. President Trump revived the Dakota Access Pipeline project shortly after taking office.[46]

While the Dakota Access Pipeline protests illustrate the migration, the election of Donald Trump crystallizes just how thoroughly Occupy and BLM have reshaped the tenor of contemporary politics. Few could have predicted how many hundreds of thousands of Americans, including many who had never protested before, would take to Washington, DC and to their own local public squares to resist (and to a lesser degree defend) President Trump's messages of xenophobia, sexism, racism, scientific skepticism, and official corruption. And no one could have envisaged the degree to which established interest groups would embrace outdoor assembly as an integral element of the repertoire of contemporary American democratic politics.

The results: One in five Americans report participating in a street protest or political rally in the two years since Trump's election, according to a Washington Post Kaiser Family Foundation poll.[47] The poll, which was the most extensive study of public protest in more than a decade—itself a data point—was conducted before the most recent, and third-largest, nationwide day of protest. On March 24, 2018, the one-month anniversary of the Parkland school shooting in Florida, nearly a million students walked out of class to join March for Our Lives in protest of the absence of sensible gun regulation.[48] They marched in Washington, DC but also at 763 other locations. Altogether, more than 1.3 million Americans marched that day.[49]

The Women's March was the catalyst. Like the marches on DC that took place in the 1980s and 1990s, it was organized by activists, who drew together a coalition of nearly four hundred existing organizations. Lawyers were hired, permits obtained, buses chartered, and microphones rented. Now, however, there was Facebook, which helped spread the word. The result caught the nation's attention. The first Women's March was recorded as "the largest single-day demonstration in recorded US history."[50] These numbers accrued from the fact that the march in Washington, DC was accompanied by 653 marches around the nation. The sheer number of these satellite marches, in both urban and rural settings, was unprecedented, as was the size of the crowds in many cities. An estimated 450,000 turned out in Los Angeles and also in New York City.[51] Altogether, it is estimated that 4.2 million marched.[52]

The staggering and unexpected numbers at the Women's March caught many, including President Trump, off guard and marked the beginning of a movement to resist the new administration.[53] Not long after, President Trump signed an Executive Order banning entry into the United States of citizens from certain Muslim countries. The Order, which appeared to fulfill his campaign promise of a Muslim ban, was immediately greeted with spontaneous airport protests—thousands of activists, many of them lawyers, swarmed major US airports.

The airport protests were the first indication of the degree to which political crowds have come to operate in conversation with ordinary electoral politics. In Philadelphia, Mayor Jim Kenny joined protesters at Philadelphia International Airport on the first night of the protests. Along with Pennsylvania Governor Tom Wolf and the two highest ranking Democratic members of the state's delegation to Congress, Senator Bob Casey and Representative Robert Brady (some still in formal attire), they helped the protesters negotiate with customs officials.[54] The visibility of the initial wave of airport protests reinforced the salience of litigation but also built organizational capacity for other political strategies to oppose Trump's immigration policies.[55]

The extent to which those who have participated in recent marches come from backgrounds of socioeconomic privilege provides one further measure of the degree to which outdoor protest has reasserted itself as an integral part of mainstream contemporary American politics. In the spring of 2017, researchers reported that "[m]ore than three-quarters of participants at [the Women's March, the March for Science and the People's Climate March] had at least a bachelor's degree." Moreover, among participants surveyed at the Women's March in DC, "53 percent . . . had a graduate or professional degree." These figures are astounding given that, nationally, only about one in three Americans holds a bachelor's degree.[56] The more extensive study of the Washington Post Kaiser Family Foundation poll confirms these initial results, reporting that those who have engaged in protest in the last two years are older and more affluent than in bygone eras.[57] Despite the relative privilege of those who have participated in anti-Trump marches, many are new to outdoor protest.[58]

Dissent during the Trump administration—with a few exceptions—has been notable for its orderliness despite the adoption of certain signature tactics from the more radical movements.[59] Still, while anti-Trump actions have been overwhelmingly nonviolent, this does not mean that they have not been fractious—or coercive in Gandhian terms. Protesters have not emphasized civility, decorum, respectable attire, measured movements, or silent prayer. Indeed, the signs at the Women's March were affirmatively provocative, and town halls with Republican officials in the spring of 2017 to oppose, among other things, efforts to repeal the Affordable Care Act frequently degenerated into shouting matches.[60] In one recorded example, Utah Congressman Jason E. Chaffetz, then chairman of the House Oversight Committee, struggles to get a word in edgewise, when confronted by an auditorium full of voters concerned about President Donald Trump's conflicts of interest, who are chanting "Do your job!"[61] Many Republicans officials responded by cancelling town halls.

Taken together, these diverse examples of protest illustrate the ways that contemporary social and political movements operate with a much broader conception of nonviolence than Gandhi's. Individuals are mobilized through their social ties (frequently online) rather than through institutional or organizational affiliations, generating the appearance of spontaneity. Protesters are more willing to take to the streets and to remain in public spaces *without* official permission, as evidenced by Occupy, BLM, protests of the North Dakota Access Pipeline, and the outpouring at airports across the country when President Trump issued his first Executive Order. Some groups even question legal requirements that give authorities advanced warning. The existence of social media has also permitted the rise in actions that are coordinated across cities—significantly amplifying participation rates for both fringe and mainstream interests as well as the capacity to draw out individuals who have not previously participated in protests.

Mitigating the levels of inconvenience associated with protest actions has become a low priority. Millennial protesters have instead embraced the disruptiveness of the form. They have embraced opportunities to derail the mundane routines of American life, from traffic to holiday shopping. They have interrupted speeches and performances and detained senators in the elevator. In some cases, actions have clearly been orchestrated to approach the line of unlawful assembly. This is especially true of those that have opted to gather in places that are technically private—most famously, Zuccotti Park in New York City.

Still, the signature tactics of millennial protest are fundamentally disruptive rather than violent, in the traditional sense of damage to persons or property. While the decision to eschew the practice of negotiating informally with relevant authorities about order maintenance plans has meant that these protests are frequently "time-consuming and inconvenient for nonparticipants,"[62] the tactics of millennial protesters have operated well within legal and constitutional boundaries despite their disruptiveness. Outbreaks of actual violence toward persons and property remain atypical, and groups that espouse the judicious use of violence (such as Antifa) remain marginalized.[63]

Nevertheless, individuals have frequently been arrested on charges of disorderly conduct, trespass, unlawful assembly, and riot—even when they were simply exercising their First Amendment rights.[64] In one instance, officials arrested twenty people for participating in a BLM sit-in at a St. Louis gas station, and then more than one hour later arrested a National Lawyers Guild

("NLG") Legal Observer who was on site; all were arrested for unlawful assembly. In another, participants in a die-in at the Mall of America—a classic instance of nonviolent, symbolic, and performative action—were initially charged with unlawful assembly and disorderly conduct, even though the die-in was significantly less aggressive than the eighteenth-century long tradition of burning figures in effigy during political parades.

These charges rarely stick.[65] But the arrests successfully remove the individuals from public places. More critically, legislators in thirty-one states have introduced numerous bills—to date around sixty-four—seeking to render unlawful a wide range of the disruptive tactics previously described.[66] To be sure, many of these efforts have stalled, and many are likely unconstitutional. Still, it would be a mistake to ignore their discursive significance as efforts to delegitimize the disruptive tactics of recent resistance movements. To suggest, as Ford does, that a cost of public protest is the "[u]ndermining [of] liberal institutions"[67] is, therefore, to play into the hands of those who do indeed seek to undermine the legality of public assembly.

The ways in which these state legislative efforts have been tailored to the emergent tactics of nonviolent protest is particularly striking. Recent state legislation has sought to enhance criminal penalties for obstructing traffic while participating in a public assembly. Since January 2017, no less than eleven legislatures have considered bills that would increase fines and jail sentences for individuals charged with obstructing traffic during a public assembly. Some of these bills specifically target efforts to block highways—a signature tactic of BLM. A bill introduced in Mississippi in 2017 would have made it a felony to "sit[], stand[] or [lie] in a public road or highway," so as to impede or hinder the passage of emergency vehicles. It died in the judiciary committee.[68] A bill introduced in the Florida legislature sought to criminalize the act of obstructing traffic during an *unpermitted* demonstration.[69] In Minnesota, the governor recently vetoed three bills that would have heightened penalties for protesters who obstruct traffic, including access to airports.[70] Elsewhere, seven legislatures have considered bills that would relieve motorists of liability should they hit individuals deliberately blocking traffic during protests. To date, none of those bills have passed.

Some efforts, however, have been successful. In 2017, South Dakota passed a law that makes obstructing a highway a misdemeanor punishable by up to a one-year jail sentence or a $2,000 fine.[71] Meanwhile, in Massachusetts, legislation that, among other things, would impose up to $5,000 in fines for intentionally obstructing "normal and reasonable movement of vehicular or pedestrian traffic" is pending before the legislature.[72]

The last two years have also seen the introduction of bills seeking to expand the definition of unlawful assembly to cover nonviolent acts. Traditionally, as previously discussed, the offense was limited to situations of threatened violence to persons or property.

A bill introduced in the Missouri House in February 2017 is particularly revealing for the ways it muddies the definition of unlawful assembly. The proposed bill lays out a new offense, "unlawful traffic interference," and renders it a class D felony if the offense occurs "as part of an unlawful assembly."[73] In an interesting turn, the bill defines "unlawful assembly" to mean "*two or more* persons who meet for the purpose of *violating any of the criminal laws of this state or of the United States.*"[74] This definition appears to expand the scope for the crime because Missouri, like other states, criminalizes a wide range of nonviolent action, including disobeying an officer. Its inconsistency with the rest of the criminal code, however, creates ambiguity. Missouri, unlike many states, closely follows the nineteenth-century common law under which the crimes of unlawful assembly and riot were limited to situations of violence or threatened violence.[75] Under Missouri's criminal code, an unlawful assembly is defined as an assembly of "*six* or more other persons," which intends "to violate any of the criminal laws of this state *with force or violence.*"[76] Missouri courts have been clear that this means that an assembly is not unlawful until it undertakes "actions that make it reasonable for rational people in the area 'to believe the assembly will *cause injury to persons or damage to property* and will interfere with the rights of others by committing disorderly acts.'"[77]

The Missouri bill is troubling: It indicates a desire in Missouri to construe the definition of unlawful assembly more broadly to include any assembly engaged in unlawful (as opposed to violent) activity—a move that further narrows constitutional protections for outdoor assemblies.

Beyond these efforts, eight legislatures have considered bills to criminalize the specific tactics undertaken during protests against the North Dakota Access Pipeline. While these bills are likely on reasonably strong constitutional footing insofar as they target assemblies that trespass on private property, they do raise eyebrows insofar as they are clearly motivated by opposition to the views of dissenters.

The first major proposal of this kind emerged in Washington and sought to make a felony of "economic terrorism." Economic terrorism was defined as a crime intended to

> (a) Influence the policy of a government by intimidation or coercion; and
> (b) Obstruct, hinder, or delay the passage of any train, truck, car, ship, boat, aircraft, or other vehicle or vessel engaged in the carriage, hauling, transport, shipment, or delivery of goods, cargo, freight, or other item, in commerce; or
> (c) Interfere with, tamper with, damage, or obstruct any pipeline facility, bulk oil terminal, marine terminal, tank car, waterborne vessel or barge, or power plant.[78]

The bill's sponsor publicly explained that the effort was "prompted by recent illegal actions that have blocked rail and highway transportation" during demonstrations.[79]

A similar bill in North Carolina defined economic terrorism as follows:

> A person is guilty . . . of economic terrorism if the person willfully and maliciously or with reckless disregard commits a criminal offense that impedes or disrupts the regular course of business, the disruption results in damages of more than one thousand dollars ($1,000), and the offense is committed with the intent to do either of the following:
>
> (1) Intimidate the civilian population at large, or an identifiable group of the civilian population.
> (2) Influence, through intimidation, the conduct or activities of the government of the United States, a state, or any unit of local government.[80]

The most distinctive feature of the North Carolina bill was that it entitled individuals "to recover three times the actual damages sustained or fifty thousand dollars ($50,000), whichever is greater, as well as court costs and attorneys' fees in the trial and appellate courts if the person prevails in the claim."[81]

The Arkansas legislature recently passed a milder version only to have it vetoed by Arkansas's Republican governor. The bill that passed would have criminalized "unlawful mass picketing," defined as obstructing the entrance to "a business, school or private facility" subject to up to one year in jail or $2,000 in fines.[82] The term "unlawful" was introduced to account for the law's inapplicability to situations where "a person . . . is validly exercising his or her rights as guaranteed by the US Constitution or the Arkansas Constitution."[83] While the bill was vetoed by Arkansas's governor, the mere fact that it passed the legislature is worrisome.

There is good reason, moreover, to believe these legislative efforts are being spearheaded by the American Legislative Exchange Council (ALEC), a conservative organization with close ties to the Koch network. In fact, in January 2018, ALEC created a template for state legislation to penalize pipeline protesters who have tampered with or damaged oil and gas infrastructure—one that creates civil liability for any damage occurring while trespassing on private property.[84] This legislation prescribes criminal penalties for both individuals and groups that seek to disrupt "critical infrastructure," holding both liable for any damages to personal or real property while trespassing. Louisiana recently passed a version of the model bill after an amendment was added to make clear it would not apply to any "[l]awful assembly and peaceful . . . demonstration for the redress of grievances or to express ideas or views regarding legitimate matters of public interest."[85] That law is likely to be challenged on constitutional grounds.[86]

A final locus of legislative activity has focused on addressing the perceived pathologies of ideological conflict, including protest, on college campuses. While the ostensive purpose of such efforts is to require educational institutions to provide access to all viewpoints on campus, the details reveal a more complicated story.[87] A Wisconsin bill, for example, would have required that disciplinary action be taken against community members "who engage[] in violent, abusive, indecent, profane, *boisterous*, obscene, *unreasonably loud*, or other *disorderly conduct* that interferes with the free expression of others" while forbidding state educational institutions from taking any public stands or actions with respect to public policy controversies—a rather vague prohibition.[88] While this bill failed to pass, the University of Wisconsin adopted a similar policy itself, allowing it to discipline and potentially expel those students who "materially and substantially" disrupt the free speech of others.[89] Arizona, North Carolina, Florida, and Georgia have all passed analogous policies through legislation.[90]

These efforts to target the nonviolent tactics of recent protest movements are particularly concerning when one considers that very few jurisdictions have explored legislative efforts to address one significant problem that has emerged with millennial protest: heightened risks of violence between protesters and counter-protesters in the era of polarized politics. These situations are distinguishable from the core cases of dissent where the object of criticism is the government itself. Instead, the protest/counter-protest scenario most typically involves resistance to the views and actions of other private citizens. Such scenarios are particularly ripe for violence, as the history of nineteenth-century ethnic festive politics demonstrates.[91]

The most salient and extreme recent example took place in Charlottesville, Virginia, when a UNITE the Right rally of white supremacists, who opposed the removal of a confederate statue, clashed with counter-demonstrators. The violence and rioting in Charlottesville, which resulted in the murder of counter-demonstrator Heather Heyer, was preceded the night before with a parade on the University of Virginia grounds, during which the UNITE the Right demonstrators marched with lit torches, shouting slogans such as "Jews will not replace us" and "White lives matter."[92] They were met by counter-protesters, and the scene soon erupted into a physical altercation.

Although Charlottesville was not the only example of violence erupting between demonstrators and counter-demonstrators,[93] only the State of Virginia has enacted regulations to address scenarios like Charlottesville: Crowds around the Robert E. Lee statue in the state's capitol were limited to 500 and required to obtain a permit for a period of eighteen months; the legislation also temporarily prohibited the carrying of guns near the statue.[94] Wisconsin's effort to impose new penalties for participating in a riot or unlawful assembly while carrying a firearm or dangerous weapon was defeated.

Elsewhere, efforts to address the risk of violence from such confrontations have focused on criminalizing the wearing of masks during protests. Unfortunately, it is often only too apparent that such efforts are aimed at a particular group. The recently proposed federal legislation, for example, is entitled the "Unmask Antifa Act of 2018."[95] Finally, there has been no sustained effort to address the fact that violence is most likely to occur after the intervention of law enforcement—as with Occupy Oakland, Ferguson, and North Dakota. These gaps are all the more striking when one considers that the campus speech legislation, previously discussed, is largely superfluous as campuses already have a number of regulations in place to manage the disruption of dissent—most prominently, extremely limited "free speech zones."[96]

These legislative efforts, both successful and unsuccessful, must therefore be recognized for their discursive significance as efforts to delegitimize the disruptive tactics of recent resistance movements. They seek, at bottom, to legitimate a vision of politics as necessarily orderly, deliberative, and electoral—the same vision offered in Ford's chapter for this volume—and to delegitimize nonconforming modes of dissent as un-democratic, possibly even un-American. The irony, of course, is that they evidence an ignorance of both the American constitutional tradition and the value of the right to peaceable assembly. As the history recounted above makes clear, the suggestion that public dissent given its implicit threat of violence poses a threat to legitimate political processes and thus to liberal democracy is a flatly inaccurate portrayal of our American constitutional tradition. Outdoor assembly in both its deliberative and disruptive forms has been a foundational tactic in the repertoire of American politics, and its legitimacy was intentionally institutionalized with the adoption of the First Amendment. Assembly is not, as Ford suggests, "an alternative to,"[97] much less an "assault" on,[98] the normal political process. It is part and parcel of it.

Moves to render assemblies outside of constitutional protection for their passion, inconvenience, or disruptiveness, therefore, constitute a significant step backward in our constitutional tradition.

The fact is that this nation owes a "huge debt . . . to its 'troublemakers.'"[99] As Judge Jed Rakoff recently stated:

> From Thomas Paine to Martin Luther King, Jr., [troublemakers] have forced us to focus on problems we would prefer to downplay or ignore. Yet it is often only with hindsight that we can distinguish those troublemakers who brought us to our senses from those who were simply . . . troublemakers. Prudence, and respect for the constitutional rights to free speech and free association, therefore dictate that the legal system cut all non-violent protesters a fair amount of slack.[100]

The freedom of assembly, like the cognate right to free speech, demands breathing room, including tolerance for the low risk of violence that comes with disruptive outdoor politics.[101] Our law already recognizes that the freedom of speech, which was established to protect civilized discourse in the service of republicanism, requires tolerance for provocative and hateful speech, for pornography, and for advertising.[102] In fact, the general rule is that the freedom of speech protects anything short of incitement and true threat.

How can it possibly make sense that the First Amendment demands less robust protection for gatherings of the people? The Founders understood that public assemblies rarely, if ever, resemble our idealized conceptions of public discourse as reasoned disquisitions on difficult choices of public policy. They understood that sometimes the people would need to gather, and sometimes that would be because they were angry and dissatisfied. And so, they created a political safety valve with the inclusion of a separate clause to protect peaceable assembly. The provision was meant to ensure that citizens would be free to express their collective dissatisfaction—to shout, stomp their feet, and even to throw tea into the Boston Harbor.

Thus, while there is certainly plenty of reason to be concerned that an unchecked tendency toward enthusiasm in contemporary resistance movements will escalate polarization and draw legal backlash, we must avoid accepting, even discursively, a pristine account of nonviolence. It is one thing to worry about the strategic and political costs of the more confrontational tactics of nonviolent politics today. It is quite another to accept a discursive move in which such activities are rendered violent (or at least lose their status as "nonviolent"). The latter plays right into the hands of authorities, who already possess vast discretion to ritualize and sanitize the act of assembling—both by redirecting assemblies to locations distant from their intended audiences[103] and by making questionable arrests for minor public order offenses in their efforts to control protest.[104] The latter decisions largely escape judicial notice, preventing state courts from resolving the modern constitutional constraints on the elements of the crimes of unlawful assembly and riot. This is because most charges are dismissed before trial and those that are not dismissed before trial rarely stick.

We as a scholarly community also cannot afford to forget that cultural attitudes toward dissent influence the scope of First Amendment protection.[105] The suggestion that the uncivil is coercive risks further undermining the precarious constitutional protections for freedom of expression, including assembly, that exist today by reinforcing a false normative vision of democratic politics as orderly, deliberative, and electoral while delegitimizing nonconforming modes of dissent that have long been central to American democracy.

Only a broad public conception of nonviolence will ensure a definition of "peaceable" for constitutional purposes that adequately protects protest and dissent at this critical moment in our democratic politics. Our troublemakers must be entitled to engage in protests, marches, vigils, and sit-ins, and that entitlement must include the legal right to disrupt ordinary routines. The ability to disrupt the ordinary is essential to the political power of dissent—at the very least it indicates a withdrawal of consent to the norms of an existing political order.

Lessons to Be Learned from the History of Nonviolent Protest and Dissent

Beyond questions of the conceptualization of nonviolence, however, there remains the separate strategic question: Would millennial protest movements be more politically successful if they focused on identifying concrete, achievable demands and eschewed tactics that trade on intimidation or coercion?

Millennial resistance movements have tended toward generalized demands for reform of injustice, rather than more concrete, achievable ends. As such, they have been effective at a discursive level, but, to date, have not achieved the momentous political wins of their predecessors—national independence or the Voting Rights Act of 1965.

A recent study demonstrates that Occupy measurably increased media attention to economic inequality and the need to raise the minimum wage in eight major newspapers.[106] It is also probably safe to opine that Occupy helped introduce into public discourse the dichotomy between the 99 percent and the 1 percent—a dichotomy that has shaped major political debates, since that time, from the repeal of the Affordable Care Act to the debate about tax reform.

The BLM movement has been slightly more successful at achieving concrete political change. The initial impact took the form of a slew of civil rights settlement agreements between municipalities and the Obama administration's Department of Justice. Beyond that, the movement has brought national attention to long-standing issues of police behavior. In 2015, President Obama set up a Presidential Task Force on 21st Century Policing and devoted his speech to the NAACP that same year to the need for comprehensive criminal justice reform. Indeed, there are some signs that the protests in Ferguson, St. Louis, New York, Baltimore, and Cleveland may eventually lead to a federal statute to address endemic racism and bias within the American criminal justice system. In January 2018, Congress passed with bipartisan support The First Step Act—the first entry into criminal justice reform at the federal level in decades.[107]

Despite these successes, there is certainly force to invitation to reflect on the political efficacy of coercive protests.[108] For one, some research supports the worry that acts of nonviolence that appear intimidating and coercive breed polarization and backlash, thereby putting political success at risk.[109] This risk is obvious anecdotal as well. For example, there is little question that for a majority of self-identified Republicans, the tactics of a few "Antifa"-ists in Charlottesville excused President Trump's mealymouthed repudiation of the idea of white supremacy.[110]

Nowhere is the cycle of passion, polarization, and resentment more visible—and the strategic risks of being oblivious to it more evident—than on college campuses. A growing number of young progressives express reservations about the freedom of speech and reject the calculus of the previous generation that, on balance, the harms associated with hate speech are outweighed by the benefits of a guarantee of freedom of speech.[111] Instead, they have embraced the view that it is sometimes appropriate to disinvite, shout down, and confront—even physically—those who espouse hateful messages of racism, sexism, and other forms of bias and discrimination.

Public outcry against these tactics of advocates for political equality on college campuses, including among liberals, consistently distracts from the merits of their substantive concerns. Public conversation tends to focus on the inappropriateness of the means chosen by activists—whether at the University of Missouri, Berkeley, or Middlebury—rather than the underlying justice of their complaints about racism or sexual violence on campus and in society writ large. Thus, despite some successes—individual resignations and renamed dorms—college leftists have a deficit of public support, even among liberals, who consistently worry about leftist millennials' apparent repudiation of core liberal democratic values. Yet, campus activists appear willfully oblivious to the "play of unintended consequences" and their long-term political implications.[112]

At the same time, it is unclear whether contemporary protest movements would be any more likely to achieve meaningful political wins if they hewed more closely to a Gandhian practice of nonviolence. Despite the nostalgia of Ford and Mantena for the social movements of yesteryear, the political context has changed so significantly since the mid-twentieth century that it is not evident that the Gandhian practice of nonviolence—with its pristine definition of nonviolence, its hierarchical discipline, and its requirement that political objectives be articulated in advance—remains politically viable.

The sources of injustice today are much more complex—or, perhaps more accurately, their complexity is more evident as the most visible injustices have been peeled back by prior social movements. It was easy to articulate a demand when British imperial forces ruled India and statutes mandated racial segregation. Formulating meaningful and feasible demands to address rising income inequality, the political and economic fallout of deindustrialization, mass incarceration, and the pervasiveness of money in politics, let alone the continued prevalence of racial and gender bias, is much, much harder. To some degree, at least, millennial movements must be forgiven for their failure to articulate specific demands.

The state today is also different in important ways. We should not underestimate the degree to which Gandhi's practice of nonviolence was shaped by the nature of the British colonial state, which had little compunction about using live ammunition and brute force to quell both violent and peaceful protests, as necessary. Gandhi's first major nonviolent campaign followed on the heels of the massacre in Amrisar. The crowd—many of whom were present in the square for a simple celebration of an annual spring festival—was peaceable by all accounts. Nevertheless, a British commander ordered a unit of the British Indian Army to open fire, without warning, on the grounds that the crowd had congregated in violation of an order banning public gatherings. Around four hundred civilians died, and a thousand civilians were injured. Nor was Amrisar the only time the British Raj showed its firepower.[113]

In the mid-twentieth century, state violence was also closer to the surface in the United States—and not only in the South.[114] During the 1950s and 1960s, however dignified, graceful, orderly or silent civil rights protests were, the threat of violence from the state and its allies in the Ku Klux Klan was always on vivid display for the media, the public, and officials in Washington, DC. Moreover, as in India, this proved politically useful to the movement. The United States' federal structure along with outside global forces allowed the movement to harness public outrage at such violence to undercut the stability of Southern regimes.

The contemporary American state is much less prone to maintain order through overt acts of violence.[115] Certainly, it is slower to do so, and when it does, it generally opts for less lethal methods. No doubt this is partly because it has more effective tools for subverting dissent, but it is also the case that it has become more constrained by the rule of law. American courts have established more limits on official discretion and policing since the 1950s, and the public, at least until recently, has come to expect a certain adherence to procedure and respect for due process, although that expectation may be breaking down.

Where the state has become exceedingly good at hiding its underlying monopoly over violence, it is not clear that tempered and disciplined disruption dramatizes political injustices. In his *Letter from Birmingham Jail*, Martin Luther King Jr. explains that "[n]onviolent direct action seeks to create such a crisis and establish such creative tension that a community that has consistently refused to negotiate is forced to confront [an] issue. It seeks to so dramatize the issue that it can no longer be ignored."[116] How newsworthy would large, organized demonstrations in which participants marched slowly in silence, song, or prayer be today? Would the BLM movement have emerged had Michael Brown's death in Ferguson led to a march that comported with strict rules for how to dress, walk, and talk? Certainly, it would not have resulted in the shocking pictures of local police officers in military gear driving tanks and throwing tear gas and pepper spray. Absent those pictures, would anyone have stopped to learn who Michael Brown was, how he died, or that his body was left out on the street for four hours after he did?

My larger point is that the nature of the state must be recognized as a central factor shaping both the opportunities available to shift politics and the tactics of nonviolence that groups choose. As such, any assessment of the efficacy and legitimacy of one iteration of nonviolence over another must account for the state. This includes both the nature of state violence but also the ways that in the United States, governments may be significantly less amenable to change due to legislative gridlock, partisan polarization, and the fact that policymaking increasingly takes place in administrative agencies and courts. Put slightly differently, the question of whether coercion or intimidation is a wise political choice for nonviolent movements must consider the structural constraints within which the movement is operating, not just general human tendencies toward enthusiasm and hubris. Indeed, it is difficult to see either the British Raj or the Southern regimes of the Jim Crow South as liberal except in the most formal ways.

Finally, we must acknowledge a variety of cultural shifts since the mid-twentieth century that may make a disciplined form of nonviolence less tenable today. Both the Indian nationalist and the US Civil Rights movements were importantly defined by the male figures at their helms. It is not at all clear how well that translates to the secular, egalitarian movements of the twenty-first century. In fact, there is some evidence that the decision of BLM to eschew a narrow conception of nonviolence is not unrelated to its embrace of Ella Baker's collective models of leadership over Martin Luther King Jr.'s hierarchical, often patriarchal, organizational model.[117]

Conclusion

To my mind, then, the political task must be to find the appropriate contours of a practice of nonviolence suitable to the unique attributes of our current rough and tumble democratic state. We must acknowledge and appreciate the ways in which the tactics of contemporary nonviolence, like their demands, are in conversation with the successes and failures of the social and political movements that preceded them. And we must defend the constitutional right of social movements to adopt broad conceptions of nonviolence.

The primary strategic lesson to be learned from the history of nonviolent movements is that meaningful political wins are only attainable when nonviolent tactics function as part of a larger political strategy aimed at drawing in established power brokers. Put differently, we must recognize that outdoor assembly—whatever its form—is only ever one element of a larger repertoire of democratic practices that includes political parties, elections, litigation, and lobbying before legislatures and administrative agencies. Material political gains ultimately require a willingness to compromise with established power brokers and to work within a compromised and frequently unjust political system. In that regard, the surge of women entering Congress and state legislatures in the wake of the 2018 midterm election, and the 2017 election of civil rights attorney Larry Krasner, a favorite of local BLM activists, as Philadelphia's new District Attorney, are hopeful signs. Nor are these isolated incidents: St. Louis, Denver, Chicago, Boston, Dallas, and San Antonio have also elected district attorneys committed to criminal justice reforms and to addressing the second-order costs of both incarceration and police bias.[118]

More important, whatever our personal reservations about some of the tactics that millennial groups have adopted, as scholars, we should defend millennial protesters' broad conception of nonviolence if only for the way it has politically energized Americans across the socioeconomic and political spectrum. Initial forays into politics, as is well known, breed deeper political engagement and participation. It is therefore not surprising that in the aftermath of the 2017 Women's March, women across the country buckled down to create and join associations and make political change.[119]

Disruption, even that which is coercive, is the least of our democratic dysfunctions. Executive branch officers routinely engage in what anywhere else in the world would be called kleptocracy. The president routinely attacks the free press and believes that the pardon power extends to pardoning cronies and criminals—far from its original conception. Our legislatures rarely govern but actively seek to disenfranchise voters directly and indirectly through gerrymandering. Meanwhile, attacks on judicial independence are rampant—and not just from the president and his Twitter account. The leaders of our political parties increasingly are willing to break with constitutional norms and practices to hold out for Supreme Court justices more amenable to their ideological views, and calls for judicial impeachment in the face of decisions that are disliked are no longer off the table.

NOTES

1 Sarah Frostenson, "The Women's Marches May Have Been the Largest Demonstration in US History," *Vox*, January 31, 2017.

2 Karuna Mantena, "Competing Theories of Nonviolent Politics," this volume.

3 Richard Ford, "Protest Fatigue," this volume.

4 Ibid.

5 Ibid.

6 Ibid.

7 Ibid.

8 Mantena, "Competing Theories."

9 Ibid.

10 Ibid.

11 Ibid.

12 Ibid.

13 Ford, "Protest Fatigue."

14 Felicia Sonmez, "Trump Suggests that Protesting Should be Illegal," *Washington Post,* September 5, 2018.

15 Paul Krugman, "Why It Can Happen Here," *New York Times,* August 27, 2018; RonNell Anderson Jones and Lisa Grow Sun, "Enemy Construction and the Press," *Arizona State Law Journal* 49, no. 4 (2018): 1303–1368; RonNell Anderson Jones and Sonja R. West, "The Fragility of the Free American Press," *Northwestern University Law Review* 112, no. 3 (2017): 568–595.

16 Mantena, "Competing Theories."

17 Ford, "Protest Fatigue."

18 Tabatha Abu El-Haj, "Changing the People: Legal Regulation and American Democracy," *New York University Law Review* 86, no. 1 (2011): 1–68.

19 This conception of politics is influenced by that of Charles Tilly, who recognized that politics takes place within a repertoire of structured action that changes over time. Charles Tilly, *Contentious Performances* (New York: Cambridge University Press, 2008), 5–7. I, however, exclude violent forms of politics as they are, by definition, illegitimate in our system of government. Tilly does not. Ibid.

20 Abu El-Haj, "Changing the People," 9–15.

21 There are obviously significant philosophical differences between democracies and republics, but both are fundamentally liberal in the sense in which Ford is invoking that term, so the rise of American democracy within the contours of a republican Constitution should not affect the role of dissent in the political order.

22 U.S. Const. amend. I.

23 Tabatha Abu El-Haj, "Defining Peaceably: Policing the Line Between Constitutionally Protected Protest and Unlawful Assembly," *Missouri Law Review* 80, no. 4 (2015): 961–986; Tabatha Abu El-Haj, "The Neglected Right of Assembly," *UCLA Law Review* 56, no. 2 (2009): 543–589. For two different takes on the constitutionally appropriate contours of the crimes of unlawful assembly and riot, see John Inazu, "Unlawful Assembly as Social Control," *UCLA Law Review* 64, no. 1 (2017): 4–52; Margot E. Kaminski, "Incitement to Riot in the Age of Flash Mobs," *University of Cincinnati Law Review* 81, no. 1 (2012): 1–84.

24 Kaminski, "Incitement to Riot," 4; Abu El-Haj, "Neglected Right," 548–552.

25 Abu El-Haj, "Neglected Right," 569–579.

26 Tabatha Abu El-Haj, "All Assemble: Order and Disorder in Law, Politics and Culture," *University of Pennsylvania Journal of Constitutional Law* 16, no. 4 (2014): 949–1040.

27 Abu El-Haj, "Neglected Right," 561–579.

28 Ibid., 561–569.

29 Ibid., 554–561, 578.

30 Abu El-Haj, "All Assemble," 969, 992.

31 Abu El-Haj, "Defining Peaceably," 980–986.

32 For an account of the highly regulated form of protest in the period, see John D. McCarthy and Clark McPhail, "Places of Protest: The Public Forum in Principle and Practice," *Mobilization* 11, no. 2 (2006): 229–247, and more generally Timothy Zick, *Speech Out of Doors: Preserving First Amendment Liberties in Public Places* (New York: Cambridge University Press, 2009).

33 Mark Engler and Paul Engler, "The Recipe for a Successful Protest Movement," *In These Times*, December 11, 2014.

34 Abu El-Haj, "All Assemble," 958.

35 Initially, this may have been because there were few leaders and organizations driving the outpourings.

36 Vince Lattanzio, "Ferguson Die-In Protesters Disrupt Philly Rush Hour, City Hall Tree Lighting," *NBC News*, December 4, 2014.

37 Eric Golden, "Police Made on-the-Spot Decision Not to Arrest Protesters," *Popular Resistance*, December 15, 2014.

38 The two major BLM protest to result in significant rioting took place in Ferguson, Missouri, and Baltimore, Maryland. The latter was precipitated by the death of Freddie Gray, a twenty-five-year-old black man who suffered fatal injuries while in the custody of Baltimore police. The city was put under a curfew for more than a week after the governor of Maryland declared a state of emergency and called out the National Guard in response to riots that convulsed the city for several days.

39 For a tally of cases where a riot conviction was based on the crowd's violent response to efforts by police to contain or disperse an originally peaceful crowd, see Martin J. McMahon, "What Constitutes Sufficiently Violent, Tumultuous, Forceful, Aggressive, or Terrorizing Conduct to Establish Crime of Riot in State Courts," *American Law Reports* 38 (1985): § 20.

40 Justin Worland, "What to Know About the Dakota Access Pipeline Protests," *Time*, October 28, 2016.

41 Rebecca Solnit, "Standing Rock Protests: This Is Only the Beginning," *The Guardian*, September 12, 2016.

42 Jack Healy, "North Dakota Oil Pipeline: Who's Fighting and Why," *New York Times*, August 26, 2016.

43 Sue Skalicky and Monica Davey, "Tension Between Police and Standing Rock Protesters Reaches Boiling Point," *New York Times,* October 28, 2016.

44 Ibid.

45 In November 2016, North Dakota law enforcement engaged in a second effort to dismantle the encampment. This time the police used water cannons, tear gas, and rubber bullets against the protesters. Twenty-six people were hospitalized and upwards of three hundred injured. Julie Carrie Wong, "Dakota Access Pipeline: 300 Protesters Injured After Police Use Water Cannons," *The Guardian,* November 21, 2016.

46 Juliet Eilperin and Brady Dennis, "Trump Administration to Approve Final Permit for Dakota Access Pipeline," *Washington Post,* February 23, 2017; Eric Wolff, "Obama Administration Blocks Dakota Pipeline, Angering Trump Allies," *Politico,* December 4, 2016.

47 Mary Jordan and Scott Clement, "Rallying Nation: In Reaction to Trump, Millions of Americans Are Joining Protests and Getting Political," *Washington Post,* April 6, 2018.

48 Jen Kirby, "The March for Our Lives, Explained," *Vox,* March 24, 2018.

49 Kanisha Bond, Erica Chenoweth, and Jeremy Pressman, "Did You Attend the March for Our Lives? Here's What It Looked Like Nationwide," *Washington Post,* April 13, 2018. March 2018 also saw a campaign to recommit to Martin Luther King Jr.'s Poor People's Campaign through six weeks of nonviolent action in Washington, DC, and in nearly forty state capitals.

50 Erica Chenoweth and Jeremy Pressman, "This Is What We Learned by Counting the Women's Marches," *Washington Post,* February 7, 2017.

51 Ibid. Other cities with large marches (between 100,000 and 250,000) included Oakland, Seattle, San Francisco, Denver, Boston, and Chicago.

52 Emily Stewart, "Poll: More Americans Are Hitting the Streets to Protest in the Era of Trump," *Vox,* April 7, 2018. While participation in the 2018 Women's March was not nearly as large, even the low estimate of 1.6 million is hardly insignificant—making it the second largest in US history. For a more scientific but less precise estimate, see Bond et al., "Did You Attend?"

53 On the ways that the Women's March has bred political activism particularly among women, see Lara Putnam and Theda Skocpol, "Middle America Reboots Democracy," *Democracy,* February 20, 2018.

54 David Chang, Brian X. McCrone, and Vince Lattanzio, "Mayor Kenney, Gov. Wolf, Protesters Gather at Philly International Airport for Detained Immigrants," *NBC News,* January 28, 2017, www.nbcphiladelphia.com.

55 The immigration actions, for instance, bolstered the strength of local groups working to obstruct ICE officials' detainment of undocument-

ed individuals. These groups have since mobilized at various moments—including in response to the administration's policy of separating children from asylum-seeking parents.

56 Sarah Kaplan, "A Scientist Who Studies Protest Says 'The Resistance' Isn't Slowing Down," *Washington Post,* May 3, 2017.

57 Jordan and Clement, "Rallying Nation."

58 Kaplan, "Scientist Who Studies Protest."

59 To be sure, occasionally dissent toward the Trump administration has fallen outside constitutionally protected nonviolent action. Trump's inauguration drew out DistrupJ20, which engaged in vandalism and received press attention as riots. That said, as with Occupy, BLM, and the North Dakota Access Pipeline protests, it is now clear that police engaged in significant overcharging. Although 234 individuals were arrested on Inauguration Day on charges that included unlawful assembly and riot, the charges against all but the 21, who pled guilty early on, have since been thrown out. The six defendants, who went to trial first, were acquitted on all charges—felony and misdemeanor. A second trial also led to acquittals. Ultimately, in July 2018, federal prosecutors announced they were dropping charges against the remaining 39 defendants. Keith L. Alexander, "Federal Prosecutors Abruptly Dismiss All 39 Remaining Inauguration Day Rioting Cases," *Washington Post,* July 7, 2018.

60 David Weigel, "At Raucous Town Halls, Republicans Have Faced Another Round of Anger Over Health Care," *Washington Post,* August 11, 2017; Laurel Raymond, "GOP Representatives Take a Verbal Beating at Town Halls Across America," *Think Progress,* May 12, 2017.

61 Mark Hanrahan, "'Do Your Job!': Rep. Jason Chaffetz Faces Angry Town Hall Crowd in Utah," *NBC News,* February 10, 2017, www.nbcnews.com.

62 Ford, "Protest Fatigue," 4.

63 Paige St. John, "Inside the Black Bloc Militant Protest Movement as It Rises Up Against Trump," *L.A. Times,* February 12, 2017.

64 For a comprehensive analysis of the strategies employed against Occupy protesters in New York City, see generally The Global Justice Clinic (NYU School of Law) & The Walter Leitner Int'l Human Rights Clinic and the Leitner Ctr. For Int'l Law & Justice (Fordham Law School), Protest and Assembly Rights Project, *Suppressing Protest: Human Rights Violations in the U.S. in Response to Occupy Wall Street,* 3–75.

65 To give a tally with respect to the incidents discussed above: In the Mall of America case, all felony charges were dismissed by the district court, although a few organizers were eventually convicted of misdemeanor trespass and obstructing legal process by interfering with police officers. *Order & Mem. Op., State v. Montgomery,* 27-CR-15–1304 (Minn. Dist. Ct., Hennepin Cnty. 4th Div., November 10, 2015); see also Mike Mullen, "Black Lives Mat-

ter Leaders Cleared of Dumb Charges in Mall of America Case," *City Pages*, November 11, 2015, www.citypages.com. Similarly, while around 411 protesters were arrested and charged with crimes, including rioting offenses, as a result of the clearing of the Standing Rock Sioux encampment, only five individuals were ultimately charged with federal crimes, and to date only seventeen have been convicted on state charges. Sue Skalicky and Monica Davey, "Tension Between Police and Standing Rock Protesters Reaches Boiling Point," *New York Times*, October 28, 2016; Water Protector Legal Collective, State and Federal Crimes, https://waterprotectorlegal.org/.

66 "U.S. Protest Law Tracker," International Center for Not-for-Profit Law, last updated July 12, 2018, www.icnl.org; Tracey Yoder, "New Anti-Protesting Legislation: A Deeper Look," *NLG*, March 2, 2017, www.nlg.org.

67 Ford, "Protest Fatigue."

68 Mississippi S.B. 2730 (died in Judiciary Committee on January 31, 2017).

69 Obstruction of Traffic During a Protest or Demonstration, Florida S.B. 1096/HB 1419 (introduced February 21, 2017) ("A person may not obstruct or interfere with the regular flow of vehicular traffic on a public road, street, or highway during a protest or demonstration for which a public assembly permit or other applicable special event permit has not been issued by a county or municipality.").

70 SF 3463, Sess. of 2017–18 (Minnesota, March 15, 2018) (vetoed May 30, 2018); HF 390, Sess. of 2017–18 (Minnesota, January 23, 2017) (vetoed May 19, 2017); SF 803, Sess. of 2017–18 (Minnesota, February 9, 2017), (vetoed May 15, 2017).

71 South Dakota S.B. 176 (signed into law March 14, 2017). Similar legislation was passed in Tennessee.

72 H196, 190th Gen. Court (Massachusetts, January 23, 2017).

73 Missouri H.B. 826 (introduced February 2, 2017).

74 Ibid.

75 Abu El-Haj, "Neglected Right," 561–569.

76 Mo. Rev. Stat. § 574.040 (2000).

77 *Abdullah v. Cnty. of St. Louis*, 52 F. Supp. 3d 936, 953 (E.D. Mo. 2014) (quoting *State v. Mast*, 713 S.W.2d 601, 602, 603–04 (Mo. Ct. App. 1986)) (emphasis added).

78 Washington S.B. 5009 (reintroduced June 21, 2017).

79 "Bill Would Increase Penalties for Those Blocking Roads, Railways as Part of Protests," *Q13 FOX*, February 2, 2017, http://q13fox.com.

80 Ibid.

81 Ibid.

82 Arkansas S.B. 550 (vetoed by governor, April 8, 2017).

83 Ibid.

84 "Critical Infrastructure Protection Act," American Legislative Exchange Council, last visited October 14, 2018, www.alec.org; Steve Horn, "ALEC, Corporate-Funded Bill Mill, Considers Model State Bill Cracking Down on Pipeline Protesters," *DeSmog Blog*, December 11, 2017, www.desmogblog.com.

85 Louisiana, ACT No. 692 (La. 2018). Bills have also passed in North Dakota and Oklahoma. H.B. 1123 56th Leg., 2d Reg. Sess. (Okla. 2018) (enrolled); Natasha Geiling, "These States Want to Make Planning a Pipeline Protest a Crime," *Think Progress*, April 16, 2018, https://thinkprogress.org.

86 Travis Lux, "Tougher Laws on Pipeline Protests Face Test in Louisiana," *NPR*, September 19, 2018, www.npr.org.

87 For a nice overview and analysis of such efforts, see "Legislative Briefer: Campus Speech Bills and the Right to Protest," International Center for Not-For-Profit Law, April 2018, www.icnl.org.

88 Campus Free Speech Act, S.B. 250 (Wisconsin 2017).

89 Debra Cassens Weiss, "New Policy Authorizes University of Wisconsin to Expel Students for Repeatedly Disrupting Speakers," *ABA Journal*, October 12, 2017, www.abajournal.com.

90 Georgia S.B. 339; Arizona H.B. 2563; Campus Free Expression Act, Florida Ch.2018–4, Sect. 1004.097.

91 Abu El-Haj, "All Assemble," 973–975.

92 Joe Helm, "Recounting a Day of Rage, Hate, Violence and Death," *Washington Post*, August 14, 2017, www.washingtonpost.com.

93 So far, such clashes have mostly occurred on college campuses and at Trump campaign rallies. Ben Mathis-Lilley, "A Continually Growing List of Violent Incidents at Trump Events," *Slate*, April 25, 2016, www.slate.com; Katie Reilly, "How Violent Protests at Middlebury and Berkeley Became a Warning for Other Schools," *Time*, March 13, 2017, http://time.com.

94 Matthew Haag, "Virginia Restricts Protests at Lee Monument in Richmond After Clashes," *New York Times*, November 20, 2017, www.nytimes.com.

95 Unmasking Antifa Act of 2018, H.R.6054, 115th Cong. (2018).

96 For a brief overview of the history of managing dissent on college campuses, see Timothy Zick, "Managing Dissent," *Washington University Law Review* 95, no. 5 (2018): 1423–1457.

97 Ford, "Protest Fatigue."

98 Ibid.

99 *Garcia v. Bloomberg*, 865 F. Supp. 2d 478, 482 (S.D.N.Y. 2012).

100 Ibid.

101 Abu El-Haj, "All Assemble," 953–954. In prior work, I have criticized the trajectory in criminal law of removing violence to persons or

property from statutory definitions of the crimes of unlawful assembly and riot, arguing that First Amendment interests demand narrow definitions of the crimes of riot and unlawful assembly and preclude rendering nonviolent, illegal action unpeaceable. I have also criticized the current constitutional order for permitting significant, advanced regulation of outdoor gatherings, absent *significant and genuine* concerns about monopolization of public space, counter-demonstrations, or security, demonstrating that in the past Americans did not have to ask *permission* from the state to assemble outdoors.

102 See, e.g., *Edwards v. South Carolina*, 372 U.S. 229, 237–38 (1963) ("The Fourteenth Amendment does not permit a State to make criminal the peaceful expression of unpopular views. [A] function of free speech under our system of government is to invite dispute. It may indeed best serve its high purpose when it induces a condition of unrest, creates dissatisfaction with conditions as they are, or even stirs people to anger. Speech is often provocative and challenging. . . . That is why freedom of speech . . . is . . . protected against censorship or punishment, unless shown likely to produce a clear and present danger of a serious substantive evil that rises far above public inconvenience, annoyance, or unrest. . . . There is no room under our Constitution for a more restrictive view.") (internal citations and quotations omitted).

103 Timothy Zick, "Speech and Spatial Tactics," *Texas Law Review* 84, no. 3 (2006): 581–651; James J. Knicely and John W. Whitehead, "The Caging of Free Speech in America," *Temple Political and Civil Rights Law Review* 14 (2005): 455–493.

104 *Suppressing Protest*, 73–75.

105 Zick, "Managing Dissent," 1423, 1428–1452 (demonstrating that the tradition of narrowly managing public dissent is deeply rooted and arguing that recent official efforts "to curb, tame and marginalize public dissent" are the newest iteration of that tradition).

106 Sarah Gaby and Neal Caren, "The Rise of Inequality: How Social Movements Shape Discursive Fields," *Mobilization: An International Quarterly* 21, no. 4 (2016): 413–429.

107 The First Step Act, First Step Act of 2018, Pub. L. No. 115–391, 132 Stat. 5194 (2018).

108 Mantena, "Competing Theories."

109 See, e.g., Matthew Feinberg, Robb Willer, and Chloe Kovacheff, "Extreme Protest Tactics Reduce Popular Support for Social Movements" (February 3, 2017). Rotman School of Management Working Paper No. 2911177.

110 Scott Clement and David Nakamura, "Poll Shows Clear Disapproval of How Trump Responded to Charlottesville Violence," *Washington*

Post, August 21, 2017 (reporting 62% of self-identified Republicans supported his response to Charlottesville).

111 The debate between these two sensibilities is nicely on display in the following interview with Erwin Chemerinsky, a leading First Amendment scholar. See "Opinion: The Free Speech-Hate Speech Trade-Off," *New York Times*, September 13, 2017.

112 Mantena, "Competing Theories."

113 Another particularly notable massacre of a largely peaceful crowd took place in 1930, when British soldiers were ordered to open fire on a boisterous, but largely peaceful, crowd, which had gathered to protest the arrest of Khan Abdul Ghaffar Khan and his followers, in Qissa Khawani Bazaar. Vaqas Asghar, "Qissa Khawani Bazaar Massacre: Standing Tall Before a Hail of Gunfire," *Express Tribune*, April 24, 2011.

114 The Report of the Task Force on Violent Aspects of Protest and Confrontation of the National Commission on the Causes and Prevention of Violence, for example, concluded "that the [1968 Democratic] convention violence was unusual more in the fact of its having been documented than in the fact of its having occurred." Jerome H. Skolnick, *The Politics of Protest* (New York: Simon & Schuster, 1969), 248; see generally Clark McPhail et al., "Policing Protest in the United States: 1960–1995," in *Policing Protest: The Control of Mass Demonstrations in Western Democracies*, edited by Donatella della Porta and Herbert Reiter, 49 (Minneapolis: University of Minnesota Press, 1998).

115 Since the protests in Seattle at the World Trade Organization meetings in 1999, police have been more willing to engage in escalation—with the use of so-called less-than-lethal policing tactics. Still, policing remains nowhere near as violent as it was in the 1960s and 1970s. McCarthy & McPhail, "Places of Protest," 232–234.

116 Martin Luther King Jr., "Letter from a Birmingham Jail" (April 16, 1963).

117 Barbara Ransby, "Black Lives Matter Is Democracy in Action," *New York Times*, October 21, 2017.

118 Justin Jouvenal, "From Defendant to Top Prosecutor, This Tattooed Texas DA Represents a New Wave in Criminal Justice Reform," *Washington Post*, November 19, 2018.

119 Lara Putnam and Theda Skocpol, "Women Are Rebuilding the Democratic Party from the Ground Up," *New Republic*, August 21, 2018.

9

ON THE STRIKE AND DEMOCRATIC PROTEST

JOHN MEDEARIS

As a wave of audacious teachers' strikes spread west across the United States in early 2018, at least one observer was quite certain of the political principle at stake, calling the struggle "a fight over the future of American democracy."[1] After walkouts in West Virginia and Oklahoma had ended, but before new ones had erupted in Colorado and Arizona, the writer attributed a crucial but largely instrumental role for the strikes in supporting democratic life. He argued: Strong public education supported by ample funding is essential for democracy; the strikes were part of a movement to resist austerity budgets that imperil such education; and so the strikes represented a crucial front of democratic struggle. Strikes and other collective action by workers do have profoundly important instrumental or indirect democratic benefits, especially ones resulting from their effect on inequality—economic and political—and on the attitudes and allegiances of workers. For some people, these effects alone would be enough to establish the strike's democratic credentials. But I aim in this chapter to advance two additional and arguably stronger claims: that strikes are in themselves democratically valuable forms of collective action, and that they are illustrative, even exemplary, of important things we should remember about all forms of democratic protest, characteristics integral to how we should assess it.

The remarkable 2018 teachers' walkouts notwithstanding, this is a worrisome, ironic historical moment in which to be making the democratic case for strikes. The strike, long neglected by political theorists, seems in recent years to be getting its due, just as it seems also to be deeply endangered. It is difficult in these circumstances to resist the gloomy attraction of German philosopher G.W.F. Hegel's reflection that, by the time philosophy captures the meaning of some "shape of life," it "cannot be rejuvenated, but only recognized, by the grey in grey of philosophy."[2] And the sobering import of approaching this particular subject matter at this particular time can be framed in another way, as well—by responding to Richard Thompson Ford, who argues elsewhere in this volume that there is too much protest in the United States today, protest that has become too "safe, predictable, and frequent." Strikes, at least, are now anything but "safe" and "frequent." And yet, if the central contention of this chapter is right, they are intimately linked to democratic vitality. So, in addition to reclaiming the democratic credentials of the strike, I shall draw in the concluding section an inference that is in stark contrast to Ford's claim: Far from too much protest in the United States today, we suffer from having far too few of one particular, crucial democratic variety.

In the first part of this chapter, I review the particulars of the drastic reduction in strike activity in the United States since the middle of the twentieth century; then I evaluate the evidence for the positive effects of strikes—and, more broadly, labor movement protest—on the vitality of democratic politics. Next, I set about demonstrating that strikes are distinctly democratic responses to the particular social relations and conditions of employment. I begin with recent republican arguments upholding the right to strike, viewed as the act of quitting work without quitting the job, as a justifiable response to the threat of domination in the workplace and labor market. The democratic case for the strike, I contend, rests on recognizing the strike as more than just cessation or refusal—as a positive statement about the effort, skill, and agency of workers, and as a multifaceted collective action of a particular egalitarian kind.

The next section of the chapter expands the focus from the context of labor and employment. I argue that my analysis of the strike sheds light on democratic protest more broadly—in several ways. Even when we leave the realm of employment behind, we do not leave behind *work*. In fact, I argue that we ought to understand protest as political work and appreciate it as such. A second point concerns the experimental quality of much protest, in which inquiry, communication, and the setting of goals come not from reflection or discussion, per se, but through active, intelligent intervention in the social world. Finally, recognition of protest as political work, and of work's experimental quality, provides another consideration supporting recent important arguments for recognizing the interrelation of means and ends in politics. The conclusion returns to our present predicament, in which the strike, historically a mainstay of democratic vibrancy, is profoundly diminished, but in which there is no obvious way to revive it or to restore the impact it had on the larger polity.

The Decline of Strikes and Labor Activism and of Their Effects on Inequality and Democracy

The collapse of the strike as a form of politically significant collective action must surely be recognized as one of the most notable changes to affect protest in the United States in the last fifty years. During the first decade that the Labor Department collected the data, from 1947 to 1956, there were 3,438 strikes in the United States, involving 1,000 or more workers. For the decade from 2007 to 2016, the number had declined by a startling 96 percent, to a mere 143.[3] In 2016, a total of fifteen such strikes involved 99,000 workers—as compared to 424 strikes involving 1.7 million workers in 1950, a fairly typical year in that first decade of data collection. And, of course, the decline of the strike reflects or tracks the decline of union membership and participation in the United States. About 11 percent of employed people were members of unions in 2016, about half the proportion in 1983, and just a third the proportion in the first postwar decades.

One side of the democratic significance of this decline in strike activity can best be assessed in light of a wealth of empirical evidence about the effect of strikes—and more broadly, collective action by the labor movement—on inequality and the political behavior of workers.

First, organized labor is rightly seen as having been "the core equalization institution" in the United States in the middle of the twentieth century, at exactly the time when strike activity was most robust.[4] Effective unions can improve the earnings of their own members, as well as those of non-members in sectors of the economy that have strong union representation. The equalizing power of unions and union activity can thus be seen in wage benefits to unionized workers, and in the effect that a higher degree of union organization has on wages across an industry, even for the sector's non-unionized workers.[5] The precise role of strikes in raising wages is a complicated question, and one whose answer has probably changed over time. In the golden age of organized labor in the United States, workers often won considerable wage benefits through striking. But since the 1980s, many strikes have ended badly for labor. This is likely because of broad forces that have weakened the position of workers and reduced the effectiveness and incidence of strikes. The decline of the strike may represent in part a calculation by workers and unions that the potency of this form of action has diminished.[6]

Economic inequality, in itself, may constitute an affront to democratic sensibilities—if, for example, disproportion in the distribution of goods that everyone needs does not benefit "the least advantaged."[7] But one can say more about the indirect democratic effects of declining labor activism. Economic inequality and the decline of collective labor activity have troubling effects on representation and policymaking. Above all, they make the state less responsive to large swaths of people and their interests. A great deal of political science research confirms what many might guess: that representatives are far more responsive to richer people.[8] This could be due to a number of factors, but evidence suggests, unsurprisingly, that the greater ability of the rich to donate to election campaigns is crucial.[9] And since the rich tend to be less generous and less empathetic to others,[10] the differential responsiveness of elected officials to their needs, ideas, and preferences tends to pull policymaking away from the interests of poor and average people. As inequality worsens, it is plausible to think that both gaps—between the demands of the rich and of everyone else, and between politicians' levels of responsiveness to them—become more pronounced. Meanwhile, as organized labor gets weaker, it has less ability to serve its traditional role of counteracting this political dominion of wealth.

The decline in unions and the related waning of labor's most significant form of collective action, the strike, also likely represents a weakening of a possible hedge against the attraction of white nationalism, right-wing populism, and authoritarianism—all threats to democratic institutions, norms, and practices. For example, research shows that in Europe, union membership decreases support for radical right parties.[11] There are a number of possible mechanisms involved in this result. Collective organization and the greater economic security that comes with it may make workers feel less vulnerable—and so make them less open to messages that exploit such vulnerability. Unions can also be effective at persuading even those who might otherwise be sympathetic to racist or xenophobic messages to vote their economic interests instead.[12]

Because of the marked focus in US media in recent years on those working-class voters who are white, it may seem that the way in which labor's activism affects the attitudes and participation of this particular demographic is all that is relevant for us. But this is not at all the case. While a strong majority of union members in the United States are still white, the numbers of African American, Asian, and Latino unionists are nevertheless quite significant. And this matters, inter alia, because union membership may have the salutary effect of increasing underrepresented workers' political participation, again with benefits for democratic health. A recent study estimates, for example, that union membership increases Latino voter registration by 7 percentage points and turnout by about 5 percentage points.[13]

All of this might be true, yet one could wonder if strikes are in themselves democratic. Perhaps strikes are only instrumentally valuable for democratic life, having effects like these that only in turn benefit democracy. Perhaps the effects discussed above are purely contingent, empirical ones, not to be confused with the intrinsic character of striking as a form of collective action. In the next section, I seek to respond to these concerns—to argue for the democratic value and significance of the strike.

From the Republican to the Democratic Case for the Strike

A recent growing body of scholarship explores labor relations—including strikes—from the standpoint of a contemporary republican concern about domination and the standing of citizens.[14] This work claims inheritance of an old tradition of labor republicanism dating to the early nineteenth century, a central tenet of which is that "free labor" is "a requirement for republican self-government."[15] A leading example of this contemporary work is found in an article by Alex Gourevitch that refocuses serious political inquiry on the strike. The piece makes a vigorous republican case for the right to strike, showing how this form of protest, viewed especially as a cessation of labor, resists two forms of domination—one characteristic of labor markets and the other characteristic of workplaces and firms.[16]

The argument I develop in this section shares referents and important commitments with this republican work but is nevertheless distinct from it and adds to it, strengthening the case for the strike by demonstrating its specifically *democratic* value.

It is possible to grasp something of the novelty of the strike by recognizing that it involves a "suspension of the employment contract" while also positing a "just expectation that strikers may return to their jobs after the resolution of a labor dispute."[17] As Gourevitch sums it up pithily, striking workers claim that they should be able to *quit working without quitting their jobs.*[18] Contemporary labor republicans seek to demonstrate how workers come to think they have such a seemingly peculiar right. And they show how the strike is a particularly apt response to the deepest of republican concerns, the threat of domination, as the phenomenon arises in labor relations. Certainly the claim in question—to be able to quit working even while retaining one's job—warrants examination. It seems contradictory, even paradoxical, from the familiar standpoint of the commercial, transactional norms and assumptions that animate much of what we all do, so much of the time, in market societies. It challenges the roughly libertarian[19] view that we should see social life primarily through the lens of our transitory market interactions with others to buy and to sell—and that such exchanges fully express our freedom and equality. And it would seem to be in tension with individual rights to freedoms of contract, property, and association.[20]

Gourevitch's republican explication and justification of this rights claim focuses on detailing two forms of domination faced by workers that can scarcely be recognized from such a generally libertarian viewpoint. The libertarian view would hold, after all, that regardless of what happens at work, freedom of labor is fully guaranteed by one's ability to quit a job, to stop selling one's labor to one employer and start selling it to another. And such an account of free labor might be plausible if labor were like many things individuals can buy and sell each other—items such as books, coffee tables, or shoes—items one can part with easily, at no cost to one's essential interests. There is no problem thinking of such things as commodities, as goods that can be unproblematically exchanged in markets.

But transferring one's labor to another person, alienating one's labor, is not unproblematic in the same way. Gourevitch quotes an American labor journal articulating the familiar and well-founded claim that "labor is intrinsically bound up with the laborer."[21] Many scholars would associate the exploration of the economic and social implications of this fact most closely with Karl Polanyi, who in reflecting on the rise and near-ubiquity of markets in modern liberal capitalist societies called labor a "fictitious" commodity—"only another name for human activity which goes with life itself," something that cannot be "detached from the rest of life" or from oneself.[22] Since labor cannot be separated from life and self, "there is no way for the boss to enjoy his property right in the purchased labor-power without also exercising . . . arbitrary power over the person of the laborer."[23]

Gourevitch introduces this inseparability-of-labor consideration to secure his second argument about labor and domination—his case that workers are subject to the personal domination of the boss in the workplace.[24] But in fact this characteristic of labor underlies both forms of domination he describes. The inseparability of labor from the person explains, of course, why the sale of labor power leads to personal subordination in the workplace, in the course of making good on the sale of labor power. But insofar as it underscores the significance, the oddity of commodifying labor—the counter-intuitiveness of selling labor—it also highlights the peculiar character of a society in which such sales are ubiquitous, in which most people *must* sell their labor (or really, their labor power) to others in order to survive. And this necessity is at the root of what Gourevitch calls structural domination.

And so a crucial point, for both republican and democratic accounts, is really the deep interest any person has in protecting and managing the conditions under which she labors. The realm of labor is a realm in which questions of autonomy are deeply implicated. Historically, many republicans have been keen to argue that threats to autonomy in employment also amount to threats to "full standing in the polity."[25] And some democrats have contended that issues of autonomy and authority in employment point to the need for workplace democracy.[26] With hardly anything more than an appreciation of this crucial interest of workers and the threats to it that are built into employment, one can quickly grasp a central, almost primal, and basically negative element of the strike—the refusal to work, the refusal to accept domination. As Gourevitch puts it: "The typical worker can quit the job, but she cannot quit work. To avoid being exploited, she turns the table: she quits working without quitting the job."[27] So he sums up elegantly a republican case for the necessity of the right to strike.

Here and elsewhere, Gourevitch strongly stresses the negative dimension of striking, using cognates of "quit," "refuse," and "stop" over and again in his account. This is not an unusual way to understand strikes.[28] And, to be sure, stopping is a crucial feature of the strike—and a distinctive if not a unique one as well.[29] But in order to arrive at the democratic significance of the strike, it is necessary first to ask: What else do strikers do, besides refusing and stopping? We need to explore the strike as an ensemble of activities, and not just as an interlude of inactivity. We need, relatedly, a more specific sense of exactly how strikes respond to oppression and domination. And we need to view strikes not as inactive breaks—moments out of time—but as phases of action, of processes thoroughly situated in the flow of time.

As a first step in this direction, it is useful to remember that labor is always expended, work always done, within social relations or institutions of some kind, relations or institutions that condition and shape labor. Marx is perhaps most associated with the argument that capital should not be seen only as a sum of money or a set of things—and that wage labor, similarly, should not be seen simply as workers acting on material nature. Both capital and wage labor, he argues, should be viewed as social relations. And this is because, in laboring, workers "not only act on nature but also on one another. They produce only by co-operating in a certain way and mutually exchanging their activities."[30] To be clear, Marx's argument does not just show that labor is expended *within* social relations; it shows that labor and activity are intimately connected with such relations, constitutive of them, and cannot be understood in isolation from them. The ongoing activity in and of a workplace does not just produce cars or microchips or burgers—or instruct children, or clean hotel rooms—it also reproduces social relations, maintains them over time: wage labor as a system, most broadly, but closer to home, and more concretely, the workplace, the company, the school, the union, and so on.[31]

This is not especially controversial. The reason to dwell on what might seem like a familiar point of social ontology is this: In considering strikes, democratic theory should focus on not one, but two questions. We should indeed ask: What happens, during a strike, to labor in the most familiar sense—the making of things, the working-on-nature, or the service-providing activity of workers? But we should also ask: And what happens to the other dimension of worker activity, to the acting on one another, the various forms of social cooperation, the production and reproduction of social relations?

Insofar as the strike is a success, labor in the familiar sense—the working-on-materials or service-providing—stops for a period of time. That much is clear. As we have seen, at a crucial point, Gourevitch describes this from the standpoint of the "typical" individual worker: "She quits working without quitting the job."[32] The worker's deed is premised on the idea that she can claim a right to her job, a claim that Gourevitch sees as rooted in a justifiable response to the danger of domination.[33] Describing the strike in this way explains how it can be defended as a matter of right, alongside, though in tension with, various liberal rights, such as contract, property, and association—and how it can be justified as a response to domination.

But in order to highlight the democratic significance of the strike, it is necessary to emphasize that a strike is not merely a cessation of work—and it can never be just an individual act. To be sure, a strike might be experienced as nothing more than *not-working* by a worker who participates only by staying home on strike days. But a work stoppage by an individual worker would not be a strike. To be potent and meaningful, a strike must be collective.[34] And for this reason it must also be more than just a collective cessation. For even the cessation of labor necessarily entails collective action: an ongoing ensemble of reflexive activities directed toward coordination among many agents. Examples of this coordinating activity include designing and carrying out a program of face-to-face mobilizing, planning, and holding mass meetings, and related organization-building. The nine-day West Virginia teacher walkout in 2018 took place only as the culmination of a long process needed to achieve such coordination, an active process whose incidents included the organization and use of a Facebook group for dissenting public employees in late 2017; teachers' meetings in many counties beginning in January 2018; informational "walk-ins" beginning at about the same time; smaller daylong walkouts in February; and finally, strike votes in counties across the state.[35]

There is a further sense in which a strike intrinsically is a collective action, and not just an individual act or a collective cessation. A strike is an action of a collective that constitutes and posits the collective. The few political theorists who write about strikes often emphasize that they are coercive, but it is important to recognize one of the specific kinds of coercion involved. Many movements adopt strategies that restructure power relations, strategies that forcefully shift contention between challengers and more powerful elites from one arena to another.[36] Strikes fit this mold, reshaping power relations by combining the power of employees, forming them into a collective for dealing with an employer, forcefully insisting that the boss cannot bypass collective demands and impose terms of employment on isolated workers, in a series of one-on-one negotiations.

In fact, strikes, as autonomy-seeking exercises of collective power, cannot be summoned without workers cooperating with each other on terms that recognize equal voice. Under most established labor law regimes, strikes must be authorized by a democratic vote. And this democratic requirement is more than a contingent imposition by the state on workers' range of action—a democratic principle imposed, extraneously, on the nature of the strike.[37] For one thing, strikes by minorities of workers generally cannot succeed. And the idea of democratic authorization is arguably inscribed in the purpose of strikes: supporting the autonomy of otherwise isolated, individual workers vis-à-vis the market and employers. Two relevant and interrelated forms of autonomy can be distinguished here: private autonomy—the autonomy protected by individual liberties, and public autonomy—the collective autonomy of democratic agents.[38] Strikes, we have seen, are often necessary to counteract domination and oppression faced by isolated workers, to support their autonomy. But, again, there can be no such thing as an individual strike, and so no way for an isolated individual to support just her private autonomy through an individual suspension of labor. An exercise of workers' public autonomy is required to protect both public and private autonomy in this instance. If the goal is to protect autonomy, in other words, workers' only choice is to act collectively and democratically. Neither inaction nor undemocratic combined action will do.[39] Some recognition of considerations like these probably explain why West Virginia teachers held strike votes, sought democratic authorization, even though this procedure was not mandated by law—even though, in fact, it was probably illegal under state law for the teachers to strike at all. So, to sum up: Even the apparently simple collective stoppage of work usually seen to characterize a strike is never just a cessation. It is also an active phase, a culmination of a process of coordination and cooperation among equal workers, part of an extended democratic collective action.[40] And in any case, as we shall soon see, there is generally more to a strike than stoppage and the degree of active coordination needed to initiate it.

Republican theorists make a strong case for understanding strikes as statements about domination. But in addition to a statement about domination, a strike can also justly be interpreted as a positive statement, or a reminder, about the agency, power, and skill of rank-and-file actors, and the way the exercise of these capacities or qualities shapes firms and organizations—as well as their ability to achieve their recognized goals. Jane McAlevey notes that "the ability of workers" to strike—"to withdraw their cooperation from interdependent relationships of power"–such as workplaces, firms, schools, governments—depends on their already "understanding their contribution" to those institutions and social relations.[41] Indeed, it is not uncommon for workers, even those planning to strike, not just to recognize but to be positively disposed toward some of the purposes of their workplaces, firms, and organizations—and to be proud of their contributions to fulfilling those purposes.[42] Citing the Chicago school strike of 2012, McAlevey argues that even as teachers withdrew their labor, they were conscious that they "labor[ed] for something deeply purposeful," that they valued, and were fully aware of "their contribution to the education and development" of children, and regarded this as their mission even as they geared up to walk out.[43]

Here it is worth acknowledging that, as crucial as it is to recognize the potential for oppression and domination in employment, it is also essential to recognize the need and potential for satisfaction and fulfillment through work. Robert Kuttner observes that much orthodox economic analysis assumes workers see work only as "a burden and something to be avoided."[44] Work does entail effort, exertion, and the overcoming of difficulty. But this is not necessarily negative. For work is also "a source of self-esteem and mastery; an engagement with the social world; a basis for positive or negative self-identity."[45] G.W.F. Hegel's account of the lord and bondsman—one of the best known treatments in canonical political theory of the ethical significance and characteristics of labor—rests on the related idea that labor is valuable to workers as an externalization of their will, and a demonstration of their skill, agency, and potency, one they can see reflected, sometimes in the material results of their work, but more generally in the constructed social world around them.[46]

With all this in mind, it is appropriate, first, to regard a strike as a living counterfactual that demonstrates the efforts and contributions—as well as the agency and skill—of workers to the organization for which they work, and at least some of the organization's goals. A variety of university, school, and public employee unions deploy variants of the slogan: *The university (school, city) works because we do.*[47] The slogan is of course in part a warning about the possible impact of a strike—of a work stoppage—but it also reminds us, more generally, that even institutions that are often identified with their most visible leaders—entrepreneurs, CEOs, presidents, superintendents—are made what they are, substantially, by the many, by the active contributions of ordinary actors. This could fairly be described as the *democratic* truth of any organization, the fact that it is made what it is substantially by its rank and file.[48]

In addition to adding a layer to the potential meaning of strikes, the positive consciousness of workers of their own agency, potency, and skill likely helps explain the sense of roughly *political* attachment of many employees to their organizations—their sense of durable membership in the firms or schools or governments of which they are a part in consequence of their work. It explains something additional, that is, about why workers claim to be entitled *to quit working without quitting their jobs*: because they claim a kind of membership that is not cancelled by striking, and that cannot simply be revoked purely on the discretion of management.[49] And this, too, makes strikes more politically, ethically, and expressively more complex than they might seem—at least to some people. Joseph Schumpeter focused on entrepreneurial potency, was contemptuous of workers who also saw factories and firms as in some sense "theirs."[50] But a sense that their effort, skill, agency, and contributions make them legitimate members of their firms and organizations gives workers as well a reason to choose "voice" over "exit"—protest, even deeply contentious protest, over mere quitting.[51] Even as workers stop working, their strike is often in part an expression of this political, incipiently democratic sense of commitment and earned belonging to an organization or association. And although this chapter is not really about workplace democracy, it is worth noting that insofar as workers seek to democratize a workplace, they are attempting to democratize an institution that they understand already to be, in substantial part, the result of their work—an association of which they already consider themselves members.

If labor in the most obvious or familiar sense relevant here—making things, or performing services—ceases during a strike, other generative activity, of a different kind, by the same people—cooperating with and acting on other agents—does not end but is instead significantly redirected. Ordinarily, the activity of obeying superiors, following work rules and procedures, and so on, maintains or *reproduces* the hierarchical relationships and lines of authority that to some extent characterize almost every workplace. But during strikes, this activity is redirected toward more horizontal ties and relations between workers cooperating for a common purpose.[52] From beginning to end, a strike is in yet another sense not only a suspension of one kind of activity, but also a robust collective action that has to be planned and actively maintained. In most contemporary instances, as I have already shown, simply to coordinate the work stoppage itself, there must first be a long process of discussion, advocacy, and persuasion between workers—and then, often, a strike vote. And once a strike of any length begins, more egalitarian collective action, more horizontal relation-building, is needed. Workers must organize picket lines, rallies, and similar protests that call attention to and support their efforts. They must engage in bargaining that involves and ultimately wins the support of most employees. They must create and sustain the mechanisms for communicating, sharing information, calling and running meetings, issuing public statements, and so on. The particular work involved varies according to the nature and duration of the strike and the kind of organization struck. Sit-down strikes, ones involving an occupation of the workplace, were perhaps at the far end of the spectrum in the variety and intensity of both the work strikers were called upon to perform, and the social ties and relationships they found it necessary to build in so doing. A description of the 1936–37 sit-down strike at the Fisher One and Two General Motors plants in Flint, Michigan is instructive:

> The strike, which was to continue for six weeks, was a large organizational undertaking. A committee of seventeen was in charge and reported daily to membership meetings. The sit-downers, organized into squads of fifteen under a captain, lived together in these groups in sections of the plant. Strike duty was six hours a day, three on and nine off, consisting of picketing at the gates, patrolling, health and sanitary inspection, [and] K.P.[53]

The teachers' strikes that spread across the United States in 2018 also required many different kinds of work and collective effort. While the West Virginia strike was on, thousands of teachers protested daily in the state capitol building in Charleston.[54] Other strikers collected and distributed food for poor students who normally rely on school breakfasts and lunches.[55] And still others, of course, continued bargaining with political leaders and communicating with and canvassing members. Later, while on strike in Oklahoma, teachers organized a 110-mile march.[56] There is a lot more going on in these instances, obviously, than cessation, than *not-working*.

And these directly-strike-related activities do not exhaust the list of egalitarian, horizontal relationships and institutions that strikes may enact or reproduce. Consider, for example, the matter of labor rights, or what we might call a regime of labor rights: the right to strike itself, of course, but also the right to engage in a whole range of what American labor law calls "concerted activities," the right to form and take part in unions and other worker associations, the right ultimately to engage in collective bargaining over wages, benefits, and working conditions, and the related association and speech rights needed for this. Even labor rights that are well defined in law and policy and not presently a matter of public debate are only really enjoyed to the degree they are enacted and supported by many people. If, as J. S. Mill argues, to "have" a right is to "have something which society ought to defend [a person] in the possession of," then to *enjoy* and *experience* a right requires both enactment on one person's part and the active support and defense of the enactment by others.[57]

Some relatively well-institutionalized exercises of rights, like voting or publishing an article, mainly require the fairly impersonal, routinized action of many people, such as editors, election officials, poll workers, or advertising salespeople. Other, more extra-institutional rights exercises, such as marching or speaking at a demonstration, are enabled by more consciously enabling activities undertaken by people playing different roles for a shared aim. In either case, one person's exercise of a right—whether a more institutionalized exercise or a more extra-institutional one—may also be made possible by many other people simultaneously exercising the same right. All this analysis applies to strikes. Those engaged in strikes together provide each other the active support that the exercise of any right always requires. And in so doing, they are building horizontal, participation-supportive social relations and ties. They are producing and reproducing, for themselves and each other, an actual labor rights regime—bringing it out of the pages of law books and into lived experience, so to speak.

And this horizontal relation-building in support of labor rights is even more significant, more needed, in the many actual instances where labor rights are controversial, resisted, and contested—where it is an open question what rights workers will have and enjoy. Strikes, as opportunities actively and forcefully to enact and experience labor rights, have sometimes been at least as important to determining what labor rights ultimately are as simple legislation, litigation, and debate. Even after the US National Labor Relations Act (or Wagner Act) was passed, Ahmed White notes, its meaning "remained in doubt for months after its passage."[58] In fact, many employers simply assumed the Supreme Court would annul Wagner, since the Court had so often overturned labor rights legislation.[59] As White adds: "until this contest was settled there was, as the history of the strikes shows, no real labor law."[60] Under such conditions, "the process of forging the Act's meaning was accomplished not only by the courts, the Board, and other elite institutions, but by labor itself—and, in this respect, not only by the movement's top leaders, but by rank-and-file workers and shop-floor activists."[61]

Something similar could be said about an earlier era, when the question was not so much actively establishing the meaning of new labor legislation, but rather actively overturning established labor law practice and precedent. The scourge of labor then, as it had been for decades, was the court injunction forbidding a strike. James Gray Pope argues that it is the long history of strikes carried out in defiance of injunctions that more than anything else discredited and forced an end to the court orders.[62]

Finally, even if the legislature and courts have determined the legal extent and definition of some labor right, employers may still often attempt to deny workers the enjoyment of that right. If it is true that strikes and other concerted labor actions can contest and determine the content of actual labor rights as against the state and political resistance, the same is surely true as against employer resistance in the economy and workplace.

To take stock, then, the case so far for the strike as a democratic response to the character of labor and employment encompasses: the proposition that even the cessation of labor is a collective action that requires, if it is to serve its purpose, active coordination among workers on equal terms; the proposition that strikes can be seen as positive expressions or reminders of the agency and skill of workers; the related proposition that recognition of how their, effort, skill, and agency help make their firms or organizations what they are provides the basis for a claim to membership in them and so to collective influence in them, a claim that adds to our understanding of why workers strike rather than quit; and the proposition that in a strike, workers redirect some of their activity from reproducing workplace hierarchy to producing and reproducing horizontal, egalitarian ties with other workers, and toward reproducing or practically enacting a regime of democratic labor rights.

These claims take on even greater importance when read in conjunction with the vital republican case for strikes as responses to forms of domination characteristic of employment. Too much democratic theory neglects domination, or ignores the central place of resisting domination and oppression in democratic practice.[63] But contemporary republicanism's characteristic concern for identifying and resisting domination readily complements an approach to democratic theory that understands democratic movements and institutions always emerge in a social world that has already taken shape—a social world, parts of which strongly resists efforts at common egalitarian management, and that provides some groups and individuals the means to oppress or dominate others.[64] With domination and oppression in view, it is possible to distinguish the entire comprehensive argument for viewing strikes as democratic: They consist of workers striving to act together, on equal terms, building horizontal relations with each other, to resist economic domination and to achieve some rough sort of collective management of the terms of labor.

From the Strike to Democratic Protest

What does this exploration of the strike tell us about democratic protest and collective action, generally? One rendering of the question would be: What does the strike tell us about when we are justified in saying that a protest or collective action has democratic value—in characterizing the protest or collective action as democratic? And it is not too difficult to see that the desiderata that make strikes democratically valuable should qualify other protests as democratic as well. In short, then, protests and collective actions that are coordinated on equal terms by their participants; collective actions that are exercises and expressions of the effort, agency, and skill of ordinary people; protests that build, maintain, or reproduce horizontal, egalitarian ties and relations among participants; protests that enact and give life to a scheme of democratic rights; and protests that counter oppression and domination are in this measure democratic. But I think it is possible to learn more than this about protest—especially democratic protest—from the analysis of the strike.

To this point, my case for the democratic value and significance of the strike has rested in part on recognition of a number of claims. It has rested on appreciation of the uniqueness of labor—or labor power—as compared to other purported commodities, and the resultant, troubling potential in employment for oppression and domination.[65] It has rested as well on recognizing that strikes involve a cessation of labor—but also much more. For human activity, of which labor is just one variety, does not just make commodities and services, it also reproduces relations of employment and other social relations. And the socially reproductive activity of workers does not cease in a strike, but instead is redirected democratically. My argument so far has also rested on the related recognition of the effort, agency, and skill of workers, on their recognition of this effort, agency, and skill, and on the claim of membership in workplaces, firms, and organizations to which this recognition may give rise.

So the question about the broader implications of what we have learned about the strike cashes out, in part, as a question about the generalizability of these claims about labor, domination, activity, agency, and skill. As we move away from the sphere of employment, which of these assumptions still pertain? To answer, we must expand the scope of attention from labor (and labor power), narrowly, to activity, generally—or at least the kinds of activity that characterize politics. And we must broaden the scope of attention from protest or collective action within relations of employment and within the political economy to protest or collective action in virtually any social domain.

It seems clear that the particular concerns associated with selling labor power, while essential in the domain of employment, are not necessarily relevant outside of it. Other forms of protest are focused on domination and oppression, but they are not necessarily focused on the particular forms of these phenomena that can arise from selling one's labor power. Similarly, the fundamental relation between cessation or withdrawal and the strike does not necessarily pertain to other forms of democratic protest—though it is crucial to some, such as boycotts.

But many of the crucial assumptions or claims from the previous section are still relevant when we turn our attention away from employment and employees to protesters and political actors, generally. More specifically: their effort, agency, and skill; the consciousness they often have of this agency and skill and of their importance for their campaigns, movements, or organizations; the sense in which their protest activity builds and reproduces horizontal ties and social relations among participants—these all apply to activity other than labor, as well, and so are quite relevant outside of the realm of employment. And I want to suggest now that these pertinent assumptions—these facts about protesters or participants in collective action—jointly support a claim that democratic protest should be understood as *work*.

By calling a variety of political action *work*, by calling attention to *political work*, I seek to accentuate activity that is purposive, that involves exertion and effort, and that both requires and develops, in varying measure, know-how and skill. We are very conscious of work as a feature of employment—of work as something that goes on in the political economy—but my point is that work is a crucial feature of political life as well. Yet the importance of political work is not well recognized in either of the two reigning approaches to democratic theory today. Elite approaches have typically seen voting—or some other relatively untaxing form of participation—as the activity characteristic of democracy, and have doubted the ability of citizens to do much more than vote.[66] And although one recent trend in deliberative theory de-emphasizes the need for any particular individuals to engage in principled deliberation, it still emphasizes discourse over other forms of participation.[67] Work as democratic participation tends not to get its due.

The concrete types of activities indicated by "political work" are fairly clear in the case both of strikes and other non-strike collective actions. Just as (potential) strikers must persuade other workers to join them on strike, both strikers and other protesters and activists must often work to gain the support of other similarly situated or like-minded people, or to persuade them to join them in some other form of protest, such as a rally, march, or picket. But it is not easy to organize such a campaign of agitation, to canvass others to participate politically. (This is especially true of canvassing that aims to get a majority of some group of people—not just the "usual suspects"—to engage in a costly or risky effort.) Such an endeavor involves assessing the target group, deciding who among them is to actually to be contacted and recruited, creating a system or organization for reaching those people and recording the interactions; learning through trial and error how to communicate with them persuasively and effectively. Similarly, organizing the rally or march itself also requires work. Someone has to choose and scout the location; some participants must obtain permission or permits and deal with the police (or plan for the consequences of not doing so); some participants must serve as leaders or monitors, to make sure more casual participants understand and abide by decisions about the nature of the protest; someone has to train those leaders and monitors; and so on. Meetings to decide on the goals and parameters of the protest—sometimes smaller leadership meetings and sometimes larger mass-membership ones—are inevitably involved, as well. And planning and organizing meetings is another sort of skill or art. Almost all of these efforts involve using and developing what we tend to call *social* skills: listening and responding to frustrated people, defusing conflicts, making people feel welcome and appreciated. And, of course, situated within these broader tactical and strategic efforts are smaller practical tasks, from making signs to feeding, hydrating, and caffeinating marchers or canvassers.

Some democrats, convinced that all this *is* work, still may not be sure they should pay attention or pay heed to such run-of-the mill effort and skill. Surely keeping lists, designing posters, or making coffee are beneath the interest of democratic theory. But it is telling that democracy's skeptics and critics have always doubted the ability and proficiency of ordinary people to participate significantly in politics—that this doubt has been part of their case against democracy, or at least against enthusiasm for democracy. Schumpeter is not alone in having concluded that "the electoral mass is incapable of action other than a stampede."[68] By contrast, theorists favorable toward democracy have tended to evince an appreciation of the capacities to act of ordinary people, even if this appreciation has usually taken the form of appreciation of lay capacities to engage in a fairly narrow range of specific activities they have considered to be truly democratic, like voting and deliberating. Surely this appreciation of lay capacities (even when applied only to a narrow range of capacities) makes sense for democrats. If an "ought" implies a "can," then democratic theorists have reason to find evidence for and grounds to appreciate the relevant capacities of ordinary people. And so, if I am right that democratic protest requires ordinary people to engage in political work—that ordinary people *ought to* do such work for the vitality of democracy—then it behooves us to find evidence for and the grounds to appreciate the capacities of ordinary people for such work. Democratic theory should explore and recognize the value of what Mary Dietz calls "sustained, purposeful activity that meets obstacles and undertakes acts of transformation in the world"; democratic theory needs "an action-coordinating concept that appreciates the purposeful nature of human struggle as politics."[69]

Democratic theorists might offer another objection to recognizing the centrality of political work. Surely, some might say, it is possible to distinguish the reflection, deliberation, and judgment that go into planning such work from the subsequent drudgery of actually carrying it out. And surely, the critics might say, it is the deliberation—the distinctly discursive, thoughtful phase leading to a decision—that, once distinguished from the phase of action, should be carefully studied and democratically appreciated or critiqued. I have argued elsewhere that this sort of objection stems, in part, from a mistaken view that takes action to be divisible into a series of discrete acts, each preceded by a distinct decision.[70] Action is better seen as a continual, reflexive process, ongoing in time.

But rather than deducing a response to this objection from a relatively abstract theory of action, it is better to notice the way that a little concrete familiarity with actual cases of "political work" furnishes a response to the idea that we should distinguish and valorize the reflection, deliberation, and judgment involved in protest. The teachers who went on statewide strike in West Virginia in 2018 did not arrive at that point through completion of a distinct phase of pure reflection and deliberation. Rather, they got to the point of mounting a lengthy statewide strike by series of active interventions—and learning from them. They had tried lobbying the state government and learned from the failure of that effort. They tried smaller walkouts and informational walk-ins and learned from the meager results of those actions. And as the movement grew, other teachers were drawn to join those first to act, not through deliberative persuasion alone, but through active example. And strikes themselves are always active tests of hypotheses. Workers do not know if they will succeed. They are trying their powers and testing the intentions and strength of their opponents.

In general, then, strikers, activists, and other participants in political work usually do not engage in a distinct and prior process of study, discussion, deliberation, and judgment all before engaging in any action. Rather, they learn, communicate, and even formulate goals through engagement in a continual active process. The activity itself is infused with inquiry, thought, and communication. They start acting, and their action elicits or provokes responses that have to be considered—exposes them and others to experiences and information that would never have been available to them had they opted for a distinct a priori discursive process. Another clear example of this, one not tied to labor and employment, is the lunch counter protests that spread across the American South in 1960.[71] The upsurge did not begin with a full plan, or even a clear policy demand or singular message. In initiating the sit-ins, protesters, in effect, were poking a stick at a complex system of institutions, laws, and disparate groups all sustaining—or at least not yet undermining—the racial caste system. Unpredictably, businesses and officials in Greensboro, North Carolina, hesitated to crack down harshly on the early sit-ins. Crucial allies had previously disapproved of sit-ins, but now new ones stepped in to help. Protesters learned, reacted, and formulated new tactics, and revised goals in response to these countermoves, growing more ambitious all the time. What mushroomed in spring 1960, it is important to emphasize, was a novel form of action, not so much any new contribution to discourse—a new argument or policy proposal. And it is not just the activists who learned from this tactical intervention. So did other lay actors. And they learned from watching an active intervention playing out—not, primarily, from listening to or taking part in an exchange of reasons.

Drawing on John Dewey, it is appropriate to call this sort of active political process *experimental*. Dewey stressed scientific practice of experiment as a model for political action and social inquiry because experimentation always involves active intervention, rather than mere passive observation and reflection—a continual process of thoroughly entwined action and thought, rather than just "comparison of ideas already current" or "elaboration of ideas and policies after ideas are once put forth" as a prelude to a distinct phase that puts those ideas into action.[72] In such a process, thought and deliberation cannot be seen as purely prior to action. Nor can ends or goals—since these are likely to change as active experience spurs reconsideration.

This understanding of political work as experimental and continually ongoing provides, I think, a valuable perspective from which to consider recent work on *means and ends* in politics. The critique of political theory that is overly focused on ends—to the exclusion or derogation of means—is a growing genre.[73] Ends-centered political thought often assumes that it is possible to posit ideal ends, goals that are valuable in themselves, and then later devise means capable of achieving them. Karuna Mantena shows how M. K. Gandhi perceived the dangers of this approach and transcended it. Gandhi, according to Mantena, was deeply concerned with "cycles of violence" and the "inherent tendency towards escalation in conflict."[74] He believed that those who unduly elevated their ideal ends would be prone to choose means that would lead toward violent escalation. The alternative was to understand that means and ends are not categorically distinct, but are "convertible terms"—and to select means that would minimize the likelihood of resistance and violent escalation.[75] Alexander Livingston has made the case for a remarkably analogous reading of Dewey, one focused on the unpredictability and contingency of action. Livingston's Dewey argues that once we recognize that action is unpredictable in outcome; that it is an always ongoing, endlessly iterative process; and that ends are never more fallible projections from our current situation, rather than fixed, certain beacons, guiding our action from beyond its native realm, then we recognize that means and ends are interdependent. Today's ends are always tomorrow's means.[76] Interestingly, Livingston shows how this approach leads Dewey to justify strikes, despite the fact that they are coercive. Strikes can be a "democratic means" when they serve "as a tool of provoking public inquiry," where inquiry means "the practice of creatively responding to problematic situations that arise when the means of action escape their anticipated ends."[77]

Mantena's Gandhi, then, demonstrates how potential destructive cycles of violence should lead us to see means and ends as interrelated. And Livingston's Dewey should prompt us to recognize that action's contingency—and the revisability of ends—establish the same. I would add: Recognition of the chief claims of this chapter—the significance of the agency and skill of workers and activists, their participation in political *work*, the experimental quality of much of that work—provides a complementary but distinct justification for viewing means and ends as interdependent.

The interrelation of means and ends—indeed the difficulty of making a sharp distinction between means and ends—is quite clear with respect to strikes. Strikes are intended to protect and achieve worker autonomy, but they are also active exercises of it. They are intended to establish a democratic regime of labor rights, but they attempt to establish such rights through collectively putting them into action. The point, I think, is quite generalizable. Mantena, for example, argues that "Gandhi's understanding of *swaraj* or self-rule may be the clearest instance of an end that is constitutive of the act itself."[78] Citizens and activists often understand their participation not as a one-off tactic chosen to accomplish an end and then abandoned, but as a long-lasting process, in the course of which they seek to become more effective. They obtain satisfaction now in exercising their skills, agency, and their power—individual and collective—and they also understand that the present exercise can help lead to greater future efficacy as citizens. Experimental action, then, should not be seen just as a means to democratic ends: first because, like other kinds of political action, it may be one form of a never-ending process of growth in citizen efficacy and power.

It should not be seen just as a means, additionally, because in fact it often entails a process of clarifying and choosing purposes and values and understandings that are not determined ahead of time or externally from the activity itself. Interviews suggest, for example, that Occupy Wall Street activists saw their varied activities neither just as fulfillments in themselves nor merely as means to some ideal democratic future, but as part of an ongoing process of developing their political capacities for future democratic involvement. Participants celebrated the fact that movement activity "unleash[ed] all these sorts of talents and energies," that it "politicized" people, enhancing their understanding of the world; gave them opportunities to "learn the right skills" and become "really good leaders and good organizers"; engendered pride at having "transformed" the Occupy encampment to make it a better site for democratic activity; and fostered a "sense of community."[79]

Conclusion

Strikes and other concerted activities by workers are, even in the best times we have ever known, crucial for what we could fairly call democratic equality—for combating the forms of economic inequality that are so dangerous to political equality and in turn to the health of democratic politics. Strikes are also important democratic collective actions that address the deep interest workers have in exercising control over how they labor, in influencing the structure of employment. And strikes are vivid exemplars of two things we should remember about all democratic protest: its character as political work, purposive, strenuous, and skillful; and its status as neither means nor end, but both.

It remains then only to link these claims to the task of assessing of the health of democratic protest in the United States, generally. A simple approach to such an assessment would be to set forth one or more conditions for the health of democratic protest—states of affairs that are conducive to healthy democratic protest—and then to assess whether these conditions in fact pertain. The preceding sections of this chapter establish that robust strike activity is one such condition. But a portion of the first section also establishes that the strike activity in the United States is anything but robust, that the strike is a deeply imperiled form of protest in the United States today. And so we come to the long-foreshadowed conclusion: rather than too much protest, generically, we have far too few strikes.

This is an even more disheartening conclusion than it may seem. Because it is unlikely that it is enough simply to declare that there are too few strikes, hoping workers will respond with greater efforts. The problem is not just that we do not have the kind of robust strike activity that could effectively check corporate policies that produce income and wealth inequality—and so, in turn, reduce the undemocratic power of money in politics. Nor is it just that we lack a labor movement sufficiently visible and activist to turn voters from right-wing populism toward democratic alternatives. Nor is it simply that we do not have the tactical repertoire to resist autonomy-threatening forms of labor organization—from familiar workplace domination to new practices found in the gig economy.[80] The problem is not even just that episodes in which workers connect with each other to experience democratic life, as in the teachers' strikes in 2018, while inspiring, are now too rare. The difficulty is that it is by no means clear how, in the contemporary political economy, to reclaim the benefits of vibrant strike activity. There is no reason to believe that the reduction in strikes is simply due to oversight or choice—that workers simply forgot or lost the courage to strike. The long decline of the strike is likely due to structural changes that have made striking a less attractive option for workers and have also directly acted on and through some of the other phenomena discussed here, such as greater economic disparities and the power of money in politics.

One reaction might be to search for government policies that could reverse or counteract the trends leading to fewer strikes. And such policies may in fact be a part of an appropriate response, if they can be legislated. But if my portrayal of democratic action and the strike is right—especially if I am right that we should see democratic protest as both end and means—then a more fruitful approach will be for workers and activists to try—and for democratically inclined thinkers to reflect upon—new approaches to striking, new forms of protest to supersede or restore traditional strikes. What is needed are new or revitalized forms of democratic protest that aim to achieve worker autonomy and a robust regime of democratic labor rights, and that are also at once immediate exercises or embodiments of them.

Notes

1 Pedro Noguera, "What's at Stake in the Teachers' Strikes?" *The Nation,* April 19, 2018, www.thenation.com.

2 G.W.F. Hegel, *Elements of the Philosophy of Right,* edited by A. W. Wood (Cambridge: Cambridge University Press, [1820] 1991), 23.

3 Data on strikes and union membership are derived from: Bureau of Labor Statistics 2017, "Work Stoppages Summary [press release], Table 1. Work Stoppages Involving 1,000 or More Workers, 1947–2016," www.bls.gov; Bureau of Labor Statistics 2017, "Union Members Summary [press release]. Table 1. Union Affiliation of Employed Wage and Salary Workers by Selected Characteristics," www.bls.gov.

4 Jake Rosenfeld, *What Unions No Longer Do* (Cambridge, MA: Harvard University Press, 2014), 2.

5 Rosenfeld, *What Unions No Longer Do,* 68–73, 74–79.

6 Rosenfeld, *What Unions No Longer Do,* 84–99.

7 John Rawls, *A Theory of Justice,* Revised Edition (Cambridge, MA: Harvard University Press, 1991), 72.

8 Larry M. Bartels, *Unequal Democracy: The Political Economy of the New Gilded Age* (Princeton, NJ: Princeton University Press, 2007); Martin Gilens and Benjamin Page, "Testing Theories of American Politics: Elites, Interest Groups, and Average Citizens," *Perspectives on Politics* 12, no. 3 (September 2014): 564–581.

9 Bartels, *Unequal Democracy,* 275–282.

10 Jennifer E. Stellar, Vida M. Manzo, Michael W. Kraus, and Dacher Keltner, "Class and Compassion: Socioeconomic Factors Predict Responses to Suffering," *Emotion* 12, no. 3 (April 2012): 449–459.

11 Christoph Arndt and Line Rennwald, "Union Members at the Polls in Diverse Trade Union Landscapes," *European Journal of Political Research* 55, no. 4 (November 2016): 702–722.

12 Timothy J. Minchin, "A Pivotal Role? The AFL-CIO and the 2008 Presidential Election," *Labor History* 57, no. 3 (September 2016): 299–322.

13 Peter L. Francia and Susan Orr, "Labor Unions and the Mobilization of Latino Voters: Can the Dinosaur Awaken the Sleeping Giant?" *Political Research Quarterly* 67, no. 4 (December 2014): 943–956.

14 Alex Gourevitch, "Quitting Work but Not the Job: Liberty and the Right to Strike," *Perspectives on Politics* 14, no. 2 (June 2016): 307–317; Alex Gourevitch, "Labor Republicanism and the Transformation of Work," *Political Theory* 41, no. 4 (August 2013): 591–617; Josiah Bartlett Lambert, *"If the Workers Took a Notion": The Right to Strike and American Political Development* (Ithaca, NY and London: Cornell University Press, 2005); Brishen

Rogers, "Employment Rights in the Platform Economy: Getting Back to Basics," *Harvard Law & Policy Review* 10, no. 2 (Summer 2016): 479–520.

15 Lambert, *The Right to Strike*, 23.

16 Gourevitch, "Quitting Work."

17 Lambert, *The Right to Strike*, 191.

18 Gourevitch, "Quitting Work."

19 I am using "libertarian" stipulatively here, not claiming to offer a definitive interpretation of any libertarian author.

20 Gourevitch, "Quitting Work," 310.

21 Gourevitch, "Quitting Work," 316.

22 Karl Polanyi, *The Great Transformation: The Political and Economic Origins of Our Times* (Boston: Beacon, [1944] 2001), 75.

23 Gourevitch, "Quitting Work," 316. Carole Pateman likewise pointed out some years ago that not just the employment contract, but all "contracts about property in the person"—the traditional marriage contract as well—are peculiar and troubling in that they "place right of command in the hands of one party to the contract." See *The Sexual Contract* (Stanford, CA: Stanford University Press, 1988), 8.

24 Gourevitch, "Quitting Work," 315–317.

25 Lambert, *The Right to Strike*, 33.

26 Robert Dahl, *Preface to Economic Democracy* (Berkeley and Los Angeles: University of California Press, 1985); Carole Pateman, *Participation and Democratic Theory* (Cambridge: Cambridge University Press, 1970).

27 Gourevitch, "Quitting Work," 314.

28 As we have seen, Lambert understands a strike to be "a temporary collective cessation of work." See *The Right to Strike*, 191. Michael Walzer writes that under most circumstances a strike is "the simple withdrawal of workers from their routine activities." See Michael Walzer, *Obligations: Essays on Disobedience, War and Citizenship* (Cambridge, MA: Harvard University Press, 1970), 31. And a standard labor relations textbook defines the strike as "a withholding of effort by employees." See John A. Fossum, *Labor Relations: Development, Structure, Process*, 5th ed. (Homewood, IL and Boston, MA: Richard D. Irwin, 1992), 352.

29 It's not a unique feature because boycotts, noncooperation, and various forms of disobedience also emphasize refusal and cessation in a similar sense.

30 Karl Marx, "Wage-Labour and Capital," in *Karl Marx, Selected Writings*, edited by D. McLellan (Oxford: Oxford University Press, [1849] 2000), 281.

31 For more on this general principle of structuration, see John Medearis, *Why Democracy Is Oppositional* (Cambridge, MA: Harvard University Press, 2015), 99–102.

32 Gourevitch, "Quitting Work," 314.

33 Gourevitch, "Quitting Work," 309, 310.

34 Republican proponents of the strike unquestionably recognize that strikes must be collective to be effective. See Gourevitch, "Quitting Work," 311, 314; Lambert, *The Right to Strike*, 190. But it is beyond their remit to explore the positive significance of this fact, significance that points in the direction of the democratic value of the strike.

35 See Adam Gabbatt and Mike Elk, "Teachers' Strikes: Meet the Leaders of the Movement Marching Across America," *The Guardian*, April 16, 2018, www.theguardian.com; Dave Jamieson, "West Virginia Teachers Plan Statewide Strike," *Huffington Post*, February 21, 2018, www.huffingtonpost.com; Campbell Robertson and Jess Bidgood, "'All-In or Nothing': West Virginia's Teacher Strike Was Months in the Making," *New York Times*, March 2, 2018, www.nytimes.com.

36 John Medearis, "Social Movements and Deliberative Democratic Theory," *British Journal of Political Science*, 35 (April 2005), 53–75, 66–67.

37 Walzer argues that certain kinds of strikes, like sit-downs—under certain kinds of conditions, especially the absence of recognized labor rights—may be undertaken without majority participation; but this is only feasible where organizers have attempted to gain majority support and have a reasonable expectation of obtaining it. See *Obligations*, 37–39.

38 Jürgen Habermas, "On the Internal Relation between the Rule of Law and Democracy," in *The Inclusion of the Other, Studies in Political Theory*, edited by C. Cronin and P. de Greiff (Cambridge, MA: MIT Press, 1998). Habermas argues that public and private autonomy are mutually constitutive. The argument here is an illustration of this.

39 In principle, workers could also subject themselves to an agent empowered to initiate collective actions without the democratic approval of workers. Corrupt or authoritarian labor organizations that can ignore what most workers want do exist—especially in illiberal, undemocratic polities, where unions serve mainly to disguise the exercise of others', especially employers', power—but they simply replace one form of domination or oppression with another. And in fact such labor organizations rarely strike. Witness the fact that strikes were illegal in the Soviet Union, communist Poland, and apartheid South Africa. See Lambert, *The Right to Strike*, 7.

40 Democratic authorization of the strike does not mean that strikes are not coercive toward some workers. They do coerce employees who do not want to strike, and other workers who would be willing to be hired to replace strikers. See Gourevitch, "Quitting Work," 310–311.

41 Jane McAlevey, *No Shortcuts: Organizing for Power in the New Age* (Oxford: Oxford University Press, 2016), 102.

42 There are really several distinguishable claims at work in this condensed one. (1) Workers' activity reproduces the institutions in which they work—workplace, firm, organization, school, government, or agency. (On this general principle of structuration and its relation to democratic theory, see Medearis, *Why Democracy Is Oppositional*, 99–102. I return to this point below.) (2) Workers' skill and knowledge of how their institutions function contribute crucially to the ability of the institution to achieve recognized goals. (3) Workers often recognize (1) and (2). (4) Workers often share or sympathize with at least some of the purposes of the institutions for which they work and take some pleasure and pride in their contributions to achieving them.

43 McAlevey, *No Shortcuts*, 102.

44 Robert Kuttner, *Everything for Sale: The Virtues and Limits of Markets* (Chicago: University of Chicago Press, 1996), 84.

45 Kuttner, *Everything for Sale*, 1984.

46 G.W.F. Hegel, *Phenomenology of Spirit*, trans. A.V. Miller (Oxford: Oxford University Press, [1807] 1977), 117–119.

47 For an example, see Gregory Halpern, *Harvard Works because We Do* (New York: Quantuck Lane Press, 2003). A Google search readily confirms the broader point. Nationwide "Day without Immigrants" protests reflect a similar counterfactual claim.

48 Here I am echoing Marx's claim that "democracy is the truth of monarchy"—in fact, the "resolved mystery of all constitutions." See Karl Marx, *Critique of Hegel's "Philosophy of Right"* (Cambridge: Cambridge University Press, [1843] 1967), 29, 29–30. Even monarchy, as a political form, is reproduced by the people, and this is fundamental to understanding what democratic movements are and try to accomplish. For a longer discussion of this element of Marx's democratic theory, see Medearis, *Why Democracy Is Oppositional*, 63–64.

49 In general, Gourevitch emphasizes the idea that the claim to be able to quit work without quitting the job is based on a claim to have a right to the job. But he also writes that republicans can view the strike as similar to the ancient plebeian secessions in Rome, whose participants insisted on "continued membership" in the polity, even as they withdrew from it ("Quitting Work," 307).

50 See Joseph Schumpeter, "Sozialistische Möglichkeiten von heute," *Archiv für Sozialwissenschaft und Sozialpolitik*, 48 (1920–21): 305–360, 336.

51 Albert O. Hirschman, *Exit, Voice, and Loyalty: Responses to Decline in Firms, Organizations, and States* (Cambridge, MA: Harvard University Press, 1970).

52 I have in mind here a distinction analogous to the one Carole Pateman makes between political theories of vertical obligation—obedience of

citizens to the state—and political theories of horizontal obligation between citizens. See Carole Pateman, *The Problem of Political Obligation: A Critique of Liberal Theory* (Berkeley and Los Angeles: University of California Press, 1985). Of course, I do not mean that strikes, in themselves, decisively or permanently challenge vertical, hierarchical obedience in the workplace, or that the horizontal bonds among workers organizing strikes are a comprehensive answer to the need for horizontal, democratic arrangements there.

53 Irving Bernstein, *Turbulent Years, A History of the American Worker, 1933–1941* (New York: Houghton Mifflin, 1970), 526.

54 Robertson and Bidgood, "All-in or Nothing."

55 Valerie Strauss, "Why the Remarkable West Virginia Teachers Strike Is Not Over after Eight Days," *Washington Post*, March 5, 2018, www.washingtonpost.com.

56 Gabbatt and Elk, "Teachers' Strikes."

57 John Stuart Mill, "Utilitarianism," in *Collected Works*, edited by J. M. Robson. Vol. 10. (Toronto: University of Toronto Press, 1969), 251.

58 Ahmed White, "The Depression Era Sit-Down Strikes and the Limits of Liberal Labor Law," *Seton Hall Law Review* 40 no. 1 (2010): 24–25.

59 White, "Sit-Down Strikes," 27.

60 White, "Sit-Down Strikes," 24.

61 White, "Sit-Down Strikes," 24–25.

62 James Gray Pope, "The Thirteenth Amendment Versus the Commerce Clause: Labor and the Shaping of the Post-New Deal Constitutional Order, 1921–1957," *Columbia Law Review* 102, no. 1 (January 2002): 15–16.

63 For two exceptions, see Sabeel K. Rahman, *Democracy against Domination* (Oxford: Oxford University Press, 2016) and Ian Shapiro, *Politics against Domination* (Cambridge, MA: Harvard Belknap Press, 2016).

64 Medearis, *Why Democracy Is Oppositional*.

65 I understand labor to be the particular variety of human activity that produces or helps produce commodities, and labor power as the capacity to produce or help produce such commodities.

66 Joseph A. Schumpeter, *Capitalism, Socialism and Democracy* (New York: HarperPerennial, [1942] 2008); Christopher H. Aachen and Larry M. Bartels, *Democracy for Realists: Why Elections Do Not Produce Responsive Government* (Princeton, NJ: Princeton University Press, 2016).

67 Jane Mansbridge et al., "A Systematic Approach to Deliberative Democracy," in *Deliberative Systems: Deliberative Democracy at the Large Scale*, edited by J. Parkinson and J. Mansbridge (Cambridge: Cambridge University Press, 2012); David Owen and Graham Smith, "Survey Article: Deliberation, Democracy and the Systemic Turn," *Journal of Political Philosophy* 23, no. 2 (June 2015): 213–234.

68 Schumpeter, *Capitalism, Socialism and Democracy*, 285.

69 Mary G. Dietz, "'The Slow Boring of Hard Boards': Methodical Thinking and the Work of Politics, *American Political Science Review* 88, no. 4 (December 1994): 873–886, 874.

70 Once we see action as a continuous flow of conduct that is always already ongoing, it becomes clear that reflection and decision are not separable from and regnant over action in this way. See Medearis, *Why Democracy Is Oppositional*, 26–27, 96–99.

71 Taylor Branch, *Parting the Waters: America in the King Years, 1954–63* (New York: Touchstone, 1988), 272–311.

72 John Dewey, *Liberalism and Social Action* (Amherst, NY: Prometheus Books, [1935] 2000), 73.

73 Alexander Livingston, "Between Means and Ends: Reconstructing Coercion in Dewey's Democratic Theory," *American Political Science Review* 111, no. 3 (August 2017), 522–534; Karuna Mantena, "Another Realism: The Politics of Gandhian Nonviolence," *American Political Science Review* 106, no. 2 (May 2012): 455–470; Medearis, *Why Democracy Is Oppositional*, 34, 44, 48, 71–72, 78, 148–149.

74 Mantena, "Another Realism," 459, 461.

75 Mantena, "Another Realism," 462.

76 For a somewhat different but largely comparable account, see Medearis, *Why Democracy Is Oppositional*, 71–72, 78.

77 Livingston, "Between Means and Ends," 530, 527.

78 Mantena, "Another Realism," 462.

79 Ruth Milkman, Penny Lewis, and Stephanie Luce, "The Genie's Out of the Bottle: Insiders' Perspectives on Occupy Wall Street," *Sociological Quarterly* 54, no. 2 (Spring 2013): 194–198, 196–197.

80 Rogers, "Employment Rights."

10

ARE PROTESTS GOOD OR BAD FOR DEMOCRACY?

SUSAN STOKES

Democratic theorists are not sure what to make of protests. Many embrace them, seeing them as offering voice to individuals and groups that are far from the centers of power. These theorists point out that protest movements have helped bring about crucial extensions of rights to marginalized groups. Some democratic theorists, though eschewing violence, want to challenge the boundary of what is considered unacceptable or "uncivil" in protests.[1] In the face of elected leaders intent on eroding democracy, as in Hungary, Poland, Turkey, and Nicaragua in recent years, demonstrators have been lonely defenders of democratic governance.

Other theorists see in protests threats to liberal institutions. Far from deliberative, protests are expressions of raw numeric power. On this view, protesters do not attempt to persuade but instead chant slogans in unison with like-minded individuals. Protest movements sometimes allow minorities to override the will of majorities, blocking legislation enacted by the people's representatives. They can even topple elected governments. More common and less dramatic is the inconvenience that protesters impose on the public, inconvenience that is not incidental but a key element of their strategy.

In this chapter I begin by identifying ways in which protests can improve on electoral democracy, by correcting for inequalities in political resources, offering a voice to those who are kept from the polls, and strengthening mechanisms of accountability. That said, in the second part of the chapter I point to shortcomings and risks that protests represent for democracies. We cannot imagine a free society banning protests; but organizers should consider ways of improving the deliberative quality of demonstrations and refrain from interrupting what may be delicate electoral equilibria.

Protests as Democracy-Improving

Inclusiveness and Equality

In several ways, protests correct for inequalities that make their ways into democracies. Indeed, a powerful justification of electoral democracy is that it is unique among political systems in instantiating equality.[2] In well-functioning democracies, nearly every adult citizen has the right to vote and votes are counted equally, independent of who casts them. Robert Dahl goes further, in his "Principle of Equal Consideration of Interests."[3] He says that nearly *everyone who is affected by public policies* should have a right to vote and have their votes count equally.

But democratic polities include many noncitizens, who are influenced by public policy and cannot vote for those who devise it. Many other people fall into a category that Cohen calls "semi-citizens": minors, prisoners, and former felons who have lost their voting rights.[4] All of these people are excluded from voting. But they can, and do, join protests.[5] What's more, voting and demonstrating are not substitutes. The electoral turnout rates of demonstrators tend to be higher than that of those who stay off the streets.[6] The availability of protests and other forms of voice to these excluded groups makes the promise of political equality more real in democracies.

Elections fall short of the ideal of equality in other ways, as well. Even among citizens, if we zoom out from a narrow focus on the ballot box to the broader range of forces that shape election outcomes and public policy, inequalities reassert themselves. Crucial political resources are unequally distributed: campaign contributions, lobbying, social connections with officeholders and their staffs, media access, and so on. The implication is not that the democratic promise of equality is hollow but that it can be better fulfilled in the presence of an active civil society. By contrast with elections, the key resources required for protesters are time and passion. Protest movements are one of a menu of stratagems available to citizens who lack money, power, and connections.

Communications, Information, and Accountability

Positive democratic theorists have uncovered a number of factors that weaken elections as mechanisms of accountability and representation.[7] In the textbook model, office-seekers advertise popular policies to get elected and then pursue these policies once in office, to get reelected. But problems arise because voters have to cast judgments over many kinds of issues, because they are often ill-informed and pay attention to irrelevant events, and because they weigh recent events too heavily, more time-remote ones not heavily enough.

On the multidimensionality of the issue space, voters cast one ballot for a party or individual, but that party or individual represents a package of policy proposals. Once in power, the office-holder may deviate from some promised policies and conform to others. The voter then must decide whether to support the incumbent for reelection. How do voters weigh the promises kept against the promises broken? What metric do they use to assess incumbent performance?[8] The problem is made worse by severe information asymmetries between the governors and the governed. Unpopular policies will be explained away, but the voter doesn't know, and may have little incentive to find out, whether the deviation from her preferences was justified.[9]

Ill-informed voters, likewise, undercut accountability. Scholars who have measured degrees of ideological cogency or political knowledge in US public opinion have come away unimpressed.[10] Quite apart from the challenges represented by a multidimensional issue space, if we are not paying attention, change our criteria of choice from one election to the next, or only pay attention to events taking place soon before elections, we undermine our ability to hold politicians to account. A recent literature documents the role of irrelevant events in voting behavior[11]—not just irrelevant, but beyond the control of politicians (the performance of local sports teams, bouts of bad weather, shark attacks).

Another problem is voter myopia. There is evidence that voters tend to pay attention to outcomes that take place soon before elections and discount ones that happen early in the term. For instance, Americans focus on the state of the economy in the final six months before presidential elections.[12] In non-US democracies, symptoms of myopia can be found, as well.[13] Voters' forgetfulness gives public-oriented politicians a window for introducing policies they view as painful but necessary. But it also allows politicians to pack self-serving, ideologically self-indulgent, or special-interest-pleasing policies into the first months of the term, soon—they hope—to be forgotten.

Protests circumvent some of these information problems. Though they are not necessarily unidimensional, they are low-dimensional, and often feature one main issue or cause (reversing a fuel tax or bus fare hike; protecting an urban park; securing voting rights for subjugated citizens). Protesters frequently are, and are able to be, more single-minded than voters. This low dimensionality can be helpful to organizers, who can keep the people and their leaders focused on issues before they fade. The low dimensionality can also be helpful to politicians. They publicly construct mandates out of election results: "I was elected to lower taxes" or "to defend healthcare." But the reality of public opinion as expressed in an election is murky and can shift over an officeholder's term. When faced with protests, the officeholder has an easier time assessing the political benefits and risks in the nature of his response.[14]

Protest dynamics mitigate the time or myopia problem. They unfold in real time. They are often sparked quickly in response to an action of government (or of some other actor). This rapid-response quality means that governments have less freedom to bury an unpopular policy—one that, say, caters to a special interest or offers paybacks to major donors—in the early months of the term. Of course, the rapid-response dynamic can be a burdensome constraint on public-spirited politicians. The remedy for the latter is officeholders capable of clearly communicating the benefits of their actions to the public at large. They may win some recruits, or at least buy time, from would-be protesters.

Protests as Democracy-Detracting

Protesters Espouse Repugnant Goals

One argument against protests is that they sometimes promote goals that are repugnant. Arguing that democracies should not be responsive to people who have especially intense preferences—intensity that can bring them onto the streets—Ian Shapiro notes that it was deference to intense preferences of Southern whites that kept Jim Crow alive until the 1960s.[15] Indeed, there is nothing inherent in protests that guarantees their use as a means toward enlightened policy. Protesters mobilize in favor of Nazism, racism, and many other abhorrent "isms." But neither do voters always use their votes to elect enlightened leaders; nor do duly elected legislators necessarily pass enlightened public policies; and nor do presidents and prime ministers always pursue the public good. But these are not reasons to look askance at the institutions of elections, legislatures, or heads of state. And they are not reasons to look askance at the phenomenon of protests.

Protests Provoke Authoritarian Backlashes

A more serious claim is that street mobilizations undermine support for democracy. This is Adam Przeworski's fear: "when conflicts spill to the streets, public support for authoritarian measures designed to maintain public order tends to increase, even if street protests are targeted precisely against authoritarian tendencies of governments."[16] It is unclear, from the context, which protest experiences Przeworski has in mind. Certainly the risk is greater in new and fragile democracies than in established ones. His words bring to mind protests like the "banging of the pots" in Santiago, Chile, in late 1973—a country and period Przeworski knows well—when the wives of military officers objected volubly to policies of the Allende government. (Though in this case many of the protesters themselves hankered for a military intervention against the democratically elected government.)

Protests in advanced democracies, as well, sometimes provoke authoritarian sentiments. In the United States, in the tumultuous early days of the (ever-tumultuous) Trump administration, people took to the streets in the Women's March but also in smaller ones throughout the country. State representatives, in states like Indiana, proposed legislation that would have exposed these demonstrators to heightened risk. One proposal was that drivers who ran into protesters on public highways would be shielded from prosecution.

We can assume that these state legislators reflected some of their constituents in their support for "authoritarian measures" like protecting those who use cars as weapons against demonstrators. If so, this scenario conforms to Przeworski's fears. Yet in the United States, these authoritarian sentiments have not, for the most part, prevailed. State legislative efforts to shield offending motorists went nowhere. When a counter-protester, Heather Heyer, was mowed down by a white nationalist in Charlottesville, Virginia in August 2017, the general public recoiled from this act of brutality. The criminal justice system proved resilient in this instance, despite the president's view that there were "good people" among the UNITE the Right protests. The motorist was found guilty of first-degree murder and sentenced to life in prison.

In new democracies, as well, demonstrations sometimes provoke humane and anti-authoritarian sentiments in the broader public. Consider this common scenario: Protesters impose inconveniences—they close roads, occupy parks, block entrances to businesses. The police respond by subjecting them to harsh treatment. Any prior support for authoritarian measures fizzles and is replaced by a public outcry for humane treatment of demonstrators. The list of places that have experienced this dynamic is very long, and includes Turkey (2013), Hong Kong (2014), and Selma, Alabama (1965).

It also includes Brazil. In São Paulo, in June 2013, demonstrators opposed to bus fare hikes blocked the Avenida Paulista, a major artery in the center of the city. The press and public figures, from both the left and the right, decried the demonstrators' "hooliganism" and disdain for democratic decorum. For instance, São Paulo Mayor Fernando Haddad, from the leftist Workers Party (PT), declared on June 18 that the demonstrators "rejected the democratic rule of law."[17]

Then, on June 13, the police cracked down. Images of injured demonstrators and journalists went viral on the Internet and looped endlessly on the TV news. Support for the protests shot up to 77 percent, and the press and politicians did abrupt about-faces.[18] Dilma Rousseff, the PT leader and president of Brazil, found a new respect for the protesters, declaring on June 18 that the demonstrations "prove the energy of our democracy, the strength of the voice from the street, the civility of our population."[19] Under the directives of a chastened state governor and his security chief, the Shock Troops who had brutalized the protesters returned to their barracks. Crowd control now featured communications between protest leaders and the police, with prior agreements about where the marchers would go and how the police would behave.[20] Eventually Mayor Haddad retreated on the bus fare hike, as did the mayors of Rio de Janeiro and other cities.

If, *pace* Przeworski, protests do not always evoke authoritarian sentiments but sometimes quite the opposite, the question is, What explains this variation in the public's response? One answer is that, when mobilization involves violence, the public tends to condemn the aggressor and sympathize with the victims. Hence the well-worn strategy, among both the authorities and activists, to tolerate or provoke acts of aggression on the other side while maintaining nonviolence on one's own side.[21] When movements are able to remain nonviolent, they may forestall the emergence of authoritarian sentiments in the general public.

Protests Are Anti-Deliberative

Another knock against protests, one echoed by some contributors to this volume, is that they are anti-deliberative. People who already agree with one another (or who don't bother to probe their disagreements) shout slogans, which simplify the issues at hand and villainize their opponents. There is some truth to this depiction. Demonstrations are not mainly about deliberation and persuasion. They are more about illustrating the power in numbers behind a point of view. They can also be about giving a symbolic shot in the arm to like-minded people. Still, as Medearis argues in his chapter of this volume, the background work of organizers can be quite democratic and deliberative.[22] Of course, the power dynamics behind the scene can reflect those of the society and networks from which activists emerge. How many second-wave feminists emerged in reaction to being told by their male co-organizers to sew banners or stuff envelopes? But again, this is a general fact about the organization of collective life under democracy, not a special problem of protests and their leaders.

And still, there are moments when movements forge broader understandings and challenge the assumptions of their participants. If we pull our focus on more broadly from short-lived street marches to movements that must be planned and organized and that may last over longer periods of time, space opens up for intra-protester communications that more closely approximate deliberation. An exciting instance, reflected in the testimonials of several participants, came during the Gezi Park Uprising in Turkey in 2013.[23] Protesters occupied the park in central Istanbul for more than two weeks, breathing in tons of tear gas and enduring soakings from police water cannons. They were motley crowds, ranging from Kurdish activists to LGBTQ communities to feminists to soccer fan clubs. Members of the latter are typically burly young men not known for their support of women's rights. (But the soccer clubs have extensive experience in dealing with the crowd-control tactics of the Turkish police; for this reason, the less-seasoned protesters already occupying GeziPark greeted their arrival with euphoria.) A gay rights activist recalled seeing a woman from a feminist group saunter over to a soccer fan and ask, politely, if they could tone down their references to people's "mothers." Likewise, secular Turks engaged in discussions with progressive Kurds, the likes of whom they had not met before.

Protests Are Destructive, Not Constructive

This is another criticism of protests. Pierre Rosanvallon sees them as an ingredient in what he calls *counter-democracy*, a political mood that features intense skepticism of institutions and an instinct to block public policy rather than to propose or craft it.[24] Where voters choose governments and legislators craft public policy, demonstrators voice opposition. The characterization may be overdrawn—see Philippe Schmitter's trenchant commentary—but Rosanvallon is not wrong.[25] We look to politics "outdoors"—to borrow Abu El-Haj's s phrase, in this volume—more to put brakes on bad policies and actions than to construct new alternatives and forge coalitions around them.

That said, there are heroic instances of demonstrators ushering in important changes: democracy in Tunisia and, for a brief time, in Egypt; civil rights in the United States and several other countries. Street demonstrations have also emerged as a robust form of resistance in the face of would-be autocrats, in instances of democratic erosions in countries like Poland, Hungary, and Venezuela.

The application of brakes, what's more, is sometimes important. Whatever else one can say about the course of Turkish politics since 2013, Gezi Park is still a park. Even when they block what might be good policies, protesters can shine a light on urgent problems and apply pressure on governments to solve them. Public transit policymakers in Brazil were not happy to see governments rescinding fare increases in the wake of the protests. The increases would have generated revenue for the creation of dedicated bus lanes. This, in the experts' view, was the best way to improve public transit in that gridlocked country. But the protests also pressured the national and state governments to reallocate funds from other sources. In the end, funding for bus lanes increased, despite the stagnation of fares.

Protests Subvert Representation and Majority Rule

Perhaps the greatest fear about protests is that they allow minorities to undermine majorities. At the extreme, they can topple elected governments.

Is democracy diminished when protesters change the course of public policy, enacted by the people's representatives? The answer depends on how well representation and accountability are functioning in the current order. If elections in Country A function to select wise and public-spirited leaders, we want to give these leaders room to govern as they see fit. If elections bring to office leaders who represent majority opinion, and who want to cater to this opinion with their eyes on the next election, there are still good reasons to let them devise popular public policies (with constitutional protections for minorities). But if elections bring to office elites who are unaware of the plights of marginalized citizens, we want to inform them of these plights and pressure them to govern well. Protest is one mechanism for such communication and pressure. Protests are, in this regard, like lobbies, though they are "lobbies" whose currencies are time and passion, rather than money.

The problem of representative government straying far from the people's needs and interests was understood by early theorists of representative government, among them John Stuart Mill. Mill's general stance was that voters should stand back and allow their representatives to exercise their own judgment. On the other hand, Mill observed in mid-nineteenth-century Britain that working-class voters could not rely on wealthy MPs to adequately represent them. He wrote that in some cases the representative would need to "have his hands tied" so that he might be kept true to his constituents' interests, "or rather to the public interest" as his constituents "conceived it."

> This would not be needful under a political system which assured [the electors] an indefinite choice of honest and unprejudiced candidates; but by the expenses of election and the general circumstances of society, to select their representative from persons of a station in life widely different from theirs, and having different class-interest, who will affirm that they ought to abandon themselves to his discretion?[26]

The method for tying the MPs' hands that Mill considered was the pledge or written agreement. Candidates signed the pledge, committing themselves to vote as their constituents indicated. Closer still to our contemporary street protest was the popular petition, such as the People's Charter of the 1830s, signed by 1.3 million Britons (but which Parliament declined to have read in the House of Commons). The general point, just as relevant today as in nineteenth-century Britain, is that when elected officials are unrepresentative of their constituents or unresponsive to them, constituents will seek other means to make their views known.

Unresponsiveness of government as a cause of popular uprisings is on vivid display in France, as of this writing. In late 2018, the Yellow Vests street protests presented an existential crisis to the government of Emmanuel Macron. Macron ran for the presidency in 2017 on a program of economic liberalization combined with a strengthened social safety net. He moved more quickly on the former than the latter and adopted a governing style that communicated a striking aloofness. His early reforms made the French tax structure more regressive, so that when he later announced a new tax on gasoline, the fury of low- and middle-income citizens boiled over.

Are the Yellow Vests a prelude to a France governed by authoritarians, as Przeworski warns? The French historian David Bell observes that past popular uprisings have led the country down distinct paths:

> Sometimes they have blown up into a destructive firestorm that left the country scorched for years to come. And sometimes they have burned more constructively, casting a light that led the country to abolish harmful privileges and to move toward greater equality and human dignity. The real danger today is that the protests might, in the end, clear the way for a reactionary populist to take power.[27]

In the unlikely, though not impossible, event that Macron were to resign (as the Yellow Vests demand), his experience would not be unique. The new millennium has seen other elected governments fall in such circumstances. When demonstrations topple some of these elected leaders, the temptation is to say, Good riddance. Especially when the toppled leadership evinced extremes of incompetence or bad behavior.

Incompetence was the key ingredient in Argentina in 2001, when president Fernando de la Rúa escaped by helicopter from the roof of the presidential palace, with angry mobs shouting slogans from the adjoining square. When de la Rúa came to power, in 1999, his economic policy team ignored signs of an emerging recession and introduced pro-cyclical austerity measures. Two years later the economy fell into a devastating crisis, and the government seemed paralyzed. Popular anger was such that the president simply could not continue to govern.

Another government toppled by a wave of protests was Ukraine's Viktor Yanukovych. The demonstrations began in late 2013. On November 29, Yanukovych backed away from an association agreement with the European Union. That same day, modest-sized crowds of demonstrators rallied against him in Kiev's Maidan Square. Early in the morning of November 30, the government sent a special police force, the Berkut, into the square. The Berkut attacked stragglers from the earlier demonstration with batons. Images of bloodied young people being dragged into custody led to widespread anger. On December 1, an estimated 800,000 protesters packed into central Kiev. Protests persisted weekend after weekend, until on February 22, 2014, Yanukovych resigned. He fled to Moscow, leaving behind evidence of appalling levels of venality. Had the government resisted its early brutality toward demonstrators, and had it turned out to be clean rather than massively corrupt, its movement-induced demise would have been judged more harshly.

As justified as the anger of protesters like those in Argentina or Ukraine might be, there will always be risks when demonstrators force elected governments from office. The democratic equilibrium is frequently better served when even a flawed government hangs on, to face the voters in the next election. Or completes its term and declines to seek another one. Again, the French crisis looms large. Even despite Macron's many missteps, it's hard to believe that French democracy would not be better served by his soldiering on, and responding as appropriate to popular demands, until the end of the presidential term.

The answer to the question this chapter poses, then, is that protests are neither simply "good" nor "bad" for democracy. They can detract from democracy in several ways. They can inconvenience the public. They are often about demonstrating strength in numbers rather than persuasion—they involve chanting among people who agree, not deliberating among those who do not. They are better at blocking policies and actions than at devising them, and they can keep duly elected leaders from leading or even from staying in office. The ultimate risk is that they might destabilize democratically elected governments and, in the process, disturb a democratic equilibrium—one that, in developing democracies in particular, may be fragile.

But I have argued for stronger, positive roles of protests movements. They can enhance political equality, overcome obstacles to accountability and representation such as voter myopia and the multidimensionality of the issue space in elections. They have proved a resilient instrument for citizens who seek to resist democratic backsliding.

Even those who remain unpersuaded that the benefits of protests outweigh their risks should be cautious about concluding that protests should be proscribed. In *Federalist 10*, James Madison wrote about faction—which he detested—that curing it would require curtailing liberty, a cure "worse than the disease."[28] The same is true of protests: They are a natural by-product of freedoms of expression and association which, if curtailed, would threaten democracy itself.

Notes

1 See Candice Delmas, "Uncivil Disobedience," this volume.

2 This moral justification is distinct from the consequentialist ones that empirical and positive democratic theorists emphasize. For important discussions, see Niko Kolodny, "Rule Over None I: What Justifies Democracy?" *Philosophy and Public Affairs* 42, no. 3 (2014): 195–229; and James Wilson, *Democratic Equality* (Princeton, NJ: Princeton University Press, forthcoming in 2019).

3 Robert Dahl, *Democracy and Its Critics* (New Haven, CT: Yale University Press, 1989), 283.

4 On the limited rights of "semi-citizens," see Elizabeth F. Cohen, *Semi-Citizenship in Democratic Polities* (New York: Cambridge University Press, 2009). Exceptions are when residents can vote, usually in local elections. But these votes are extended only to documented residents, never to undocumented ones.

5 In hostile environments, immigrants weigh their desire to join protests with their fears of detection and dire consequences. In pro-immigrant rallies held in the United States in 2006, many immigrants were observed to attend. It is likely that their sense of safety would have deteriorated in more recent, hostile environments.

6 This is true even though protesters tend to be young and young people vote at lower rates. In *Why Bother? Rethinking Participation in Elections and Protests* (New York: Cambridge University Press, 2019), Erdem Aytaç and Susan Stokes place both actions (voting and protesting) in a single explanatory framework, which makes clear that the same factors that drive people to one form of participation also drive them to the other.

7 For a powerful recent statement, see Christopher H. Achen and Larry M. Bartels, *Democracy for Realists: Why Elections Do Not Produce Responsive Government* (Princeton, NJ: Princeton University Press, 2016).

8 An answer, in the abstract, is offered by John Ferejohn, "Incumbent Performance and Electoral Control," *Public Choice* 30 (1986): 5–25.

9 In *Mandates and Democracy: Neoliberalism by Surprise in Latin America* (New York: Cambridge University Press, 2001), I explored real-life instances of baiting-and-switching and the difficulties they pose for the voting public.

10 For classic statements, see Angus Campbell, Philip E. Converse, Warren E. Miller, and Donald E. Stokes, *The American Voter* (New York: Wiley, 1960), and John Zaller, *The Nature and Origins of Mass Opinion* (New York: Cambridge University Press, 1992). Other scholars have found voters to be more adequately informed; see, e.g., Samuel L. Popkin, *The Reasoning Voter: Communication and Persuasion* (Chicago: University of Chicago Press, 1991), and Arthur Lupia and Matthew D. McCubbins, *The Democratic Dilemma: Can Citizens Learn What They Need to Know?* (New York: Cambridge University Press, 1998). More recently, scholars have found citizens to be not so much lacking in the right kind of information but motivated to see political facts in partisan ways. See Charles S. Taber and Milton Lodge, *The Rationalizing Voter* (New York: Cambridge University Press, 2013).

11 See Achen and Bartels, *Democracy for Realists*, ch. 5; and Andre J. Healy, Neil Malhotra, and Cecilia Hyunjung Mo, "Irrelevant Events Affect Voters' Evaluations of Government Performance," *Proceedings of the National Academy of Sciences* 107, no. 29 (2010): 12,804–12,809. This line of research has been hotly contested; see, e.g., Anthony Fowler and Andrew B. Hall, "Do Shark Attacks Influence Presidential Elections? Reassessing a Prominent Finding on Voter Competence," *Journal of Politics* 80, no. 4 (2018): 1423–1437.

12 See, e.g., Mark Andreas Kayser and Michael Peress, "Benchmarking Across Borders: Electoral Accountability and the Necessity of Comparison," *American Political Science Review*, 106, no. 3 (2012): 661–684, and the citations therein. For a contrary view, see Timothy Hellwig and Dani M. Marinova, "More Misinformed Than Myopic: Economic Retrospections and Voters' Time Horizons," *Political Behavior* 37, no. 4 (2015): 865–887; and Christopher Wlezien, "The Myopic Voter? The Economy and U.S. Presidential Elections," *Electoral Studies* 39 (2015): 195–204.

13 For evidence from Brazil, see Germán Feierherd, *The Politics of Informality in the Developing World*, PhD dissertation, Yale University, 2017.

14 It is tempting to equate protesters to "single-issue voters," ones who use the issue they care about most, or exclusively, as a litmus test among candidates. If the electorate were uniformly composed of such voters and they all voted on the same issue, some hurdles that positive theorists identify in the way of accountability could be cleared. An electorate comprised of single-issue voters who care about different issues would not clear

these hurdles. Neither situation is approximated in the world of protesters. First, the number of issues they care about may well go beyond the one or set that got them out onto the streets. Second, demonstrators are demanding attention to a single or small-dimensional set of issues at a given time, but they often place before governments a series of demands or complaints, over time.

15 Ian Shapiro, *Politics Against Domination* (Cambridge, MA: Harvard University Press, 2016).

16 Adam Przeworski, *What's Happening?* (Unpublished typescript, NYU, 2017), 31–32.

17 Cited in Piero Locatelli, *Vem Pra Rua: As Revoltas de Junho Contadas pelo Jovem Reporter que Recebeu Passe Livre para Contar a Historia do Movimento.* São Paulo: Companhia Das Letras, 2014, 10.

18 For details, see S. Erdem Aytaç, Luis Schiumerini, and Susan C. Stokes, "Protests and Repression in New Democracies," *Perspectives on Politics* 15, no. 1 (March 2017): 62–82.

19 Quoted in *Estadão,* June 18, 2013, http://politica.estadao.com.br.

20 These more humane practices, and a more pro-democratic public opinion, did not become permanent in Brazil. Just one year after the bus fare protests, during the soccer World Cup which Brazil hosted, officials, anxious about disruptions in the presence of the international press, reverted to more abusive tactics. Fifteen months after that, in December 2015, the country's president was impeached, on questionable grounds, and street protesters played a part—both in favor and against impeachment.

21 An excellent analytical account, with evidence from the US Civil Rights Movement, can be found in Dennis Chong, *Collective Action and the Civil Rights Movement* (Chicago: University of Chicago Press, 1991).

22 See also Jane Mansbridge et al., "The Place of Self-Interest and the Role of Power in Deliberative Democracy," *Journal of Political Philosophy* 18, no. 1 (2010): 64–100.

23 See Aytaç et al., "Protests and Repression."

24 Pierre Rosanvallon, *Counter-Democracy: Politics in an Age of Distrust,* trans. Arthur Goldhammer (New York: Cambridge University Press, 2008).

25 Philippe C. Schmitter, "Democracy and Distrust: A Discussion of Counter-Democracy: Politics in an Age of Distrust," *Perspectives on Politics* 8, no. 3 (2010): 887–889.

26 John Stuart Mill, *Considerations on Representative Government* (Chicago: Regnery, 1962 [1861]), 237.

27 David A. Bell, "For Emmanuel Macron, How Did Things Get So Bad, So Fast?" *The Nation* online, 2018. www.thenation.com.

28 James Madison, *The Federalist Papers,* Introduction by Gary Wills (New York: Bantam Books 1982 [1787–1788]), 43.

INDEX

1968 Olympic Games: Tommie Smith and John Carlos's black power salute, 130, 141
1995 Million Man March, 168, 170

Accountability, 271; through uncivil disobedience, 27
Ackerman, Bruce, 176
Affirmative action, 72
African American political thought, treatment by liberal political theory, 50, 53
AIDS Coalition to Unleash Power (ACT UP), 27, 36, 140; and confrontational protest, 138; die-ins, 142; and epistemic violence, 126
American Legislative Exchange Council (ALEC), 218
Animal Liberation Front (ALF), 9, 17
Anonymous: and hacking during the Arab Spring, 9; and vigilantism, 23
Arendt, Hannah, 24, 25, 108; and anti-absolutism, 33; on action, 96, 97
Aristotle, 34
Army of God, 30
Authority, and hierarchical relationships, 249
Autonomy: in employment, 244, 262; private and collective, 247

Baker, Ella, collective model of leadership, 227
Baldwin, James, on black anger, 57, 58
Banging of the pots protest, 273
Bell, David, 279
Bell, Derrick, 62n19
Bilgrami, Akeel, 120n66
Black Lives Matter, 16, 18, 34, 36; achievements, 155, 156, 159n28, 223; criticism and delegitimization, 54, 146, 150; focus on violence against black men, 198n15; growth of, 70; Mall of America die-in, 144, 208; mobilization, 208; and police violence, 56, 58; rioting, 230n38; within the wider Movement for Black Lives, 73
Black Panther Party, 68, 74; violation of the Mulford Act, 30; "cop-watching," 34
Boxill, Bernard, 49
Brownlee, Kimberley, 14
Brown, Michael, death of, and Ferguson protest response, 64, 208–209, 226
Bundy, Ammon, 172

Celikates, Robin, 14
Chabot, Sean, 112n1
Chaffetz, Jason E., Utah Congressman, shouted down at town hall, 213
Charlottesville, Virginia, "Unite the Right" rally, 60, 219
Chenoweth, Erica, 28, 108
Citizenship: and available forms of political participation, 270
Civility, 17, 27, 47, 48; and credibility, 207; excusing complicity, 140; and the liberal view of protest, 123; as a moral duty, 34; and opposition to black protest, 45, 46; as a tactic, 106
Civil Rights Movement, 32; and direct action, 138; and female leadership, 191; Gandhian influences, 91; misrepresentation of, 13, 50, 53; the Montgomery bus boycott, 141
Coercion, 93
Colvin, Claudette, 124
Community organizing, 70

Conscientious objection, 19, 44n65
Consent, in the labor market, 176
Coulter, Ann, 177, 178, 183
Counter-protests, 147, 163; and violence, 219
Critical Mass cyclist protests, in San Francisco, 173
Critical Resistance, 76
Cycle of violence, 98, 259

Dahl, Robert, 270
Davis, Angela: on violent resistance, 33; abolition democracy, 76
Day Without Immigrants, 180
Deacons for Defense and Justice, 29, 30
De la Rua, Fernando, fall from power, 279
Democracy: alternative forms of engagement, 68, 206; defended by protest, 269; and the duty to obey the law, 20, 25–27; economic and political inequality, 261; hostility to non-violence, 111; instantiating equality, 270; protest as democratic practice, 204; and racism in the US, 54, 57; shared commitment to, 51; in the workplace, 244, 249
Depoliticization, and a conservative view of protest, 128
Dery, Mark, 16
Dewey, John, experimental politics of, 258
Dietz, Mary, 257
Domination: in labor relations, 242; in democratic theory, 253
Douglass, Frederick, 51, 52, 188
Dostoyevsky, Fyodor, 37
Du Bois, W. E. B., 74
Dworkin, Ronald, 25

Ellsberg, Daniel, and leaking of the Pentagon Papers, 25
Ely, John Hart, 175
Epistemic activism, 125, 158n7; and athletes, 133; through destruction of property, 149; and uncivil acts, 143
Epistemic violence, 125, 148, 158n6; role in die-in protests, 143

Fanon, Franz, 32
Farrakhan, Louis, 170
Femen collective, 36; and *sextremism*, 16
Ferguson, Mo., 36, 58, 64, 67–68, 69, 70, 72, 208, 209, 220, 223, 226, 230. *See also* Brown, Michael
Fiene, Hans, 167
Fight for $15, 194
First Amendment: demands on government, 178; right of assembly, 205, 220
Freedom of speech, 147; and abuse of the First Amendment, 177; young people's reservations about, 224. *See also* First Amendment
Free riding, 22
Friedan, Betty, 172

Gandhi, Mahatma, 18, 33, 53; on action, 97; and British colonial rule, 225; campaigns for Hindu-Muslim unity and against caste oppression, 110; on collaboration with English rule, 88; and dirty hands, 119n50; and *satyagraha*, 83, 90, 112n1, 149, 157n2, 160n29, 209; strategic versus principled nonviolence 85
Garner, Eric, 209
Gezi Park Uprising, 276
Gould, Deborah, 139, 155. *See also* AIDS Coalition to Unleash Power
Gourevitch, Alex, 242
Grab Your Wallet campaign, 186
Gray, Freddie, death of, followed by Baltimore protest, 58, 67–70, 223, 230n38
Gregg, Richard, 91
Guillaume, James, 31

Harris, Deandre, 60
Hegel, G.W.F., and ethical significance of labor, 248
Heyer, Heather, 60, 219, 274
Higginbotham, Evelyn Brooks, 159n20

Identity: construction of, 132; and persuasion, 101
Immigrants' participation in protest, 281n5

Jena Six, 168
Johnk, Zach, 130

Kaepernick, Colin, and protesting the national anthem, 18, 45, 130
King, Martin Luther, Jr., 18, 22, 50; "Letter from Birmingham Jail," 91, 118n29, 134, 150, 226; minority versus anti-regime movements, 11; on responsibility, 136; and submission to punishment, 13; suffering as a transformative force, 102; on the stages of nonviolent resistance, 158n12; strategic versus principled nonviolence, 85
King, Rodney, and LA protests, 9, 46
Ku Klux Klan, 30; as an ally of the state, 225
Kuttner, Robert, on work as a source of self-esteem, 248

Labor strikes and picketing, 179, 244; building social relations, 251–254; decline, 239, 261; democratic benefits, 237; establishing and affirming rights, 245; similarity to boycotts, 254
Lefkowitz, David, 21
Legitimacy: of the government, 166; of protest, 167, 174, 175
Livingston, Alexander, 49, 53, 259
Locke, John, and rebellion, 21
Lyons, David, 12

Macron, Emanuel: and the Yellow Vests (*gilet jaunes*) protests, 1, 278–280
Madison, James: opposition to factions, 281
March for Our Lives, 211
Marx, Karl, 169; on labor, 244; on monarchy, 266n48
Matsuda, Mari, 192
McAlevey, Jane, 247
Memorialization, 197
Micro-aggressions, 156
Mijente organization, 76
Mill, John Stewart: rights, 251; representative government, 278
Mills, Charles, 56
Minow, Martha, 192
Moral suasion, 92; possibility of, 55, 100
Muslim ban, 52
Minuteman Project, 23

National Rifle Association, and protest as lobbying, 172
Nehru, Jawaharlal, 95. *See also* Gandhi, Mahatma
Niebuhr, Reinhold, on Gandhi, 103
Nielsen, Kirstjen, 138, 139
Nonviolence: against authoritarianism, 275; as collective power, 87, 90; and constitutional protections for protest, 222; as disciplined action, 94, 100; and the liberal view of protest, 144; threat of escalation,182; versus mitigation of violence, 126

Obama, Barack, 211; actions on policing, 223
Occupy Wall Street, 181, 207; legacy, 223; the "town hall" practice, 209
Orleck, Annelise, 193

Paley, Grace, 189–190
Pankhurst, Emmeline, 16
Parks, Rosa, 124
Pateman, Carole: and the marriage contract, 264n23; strikes changing social relations, 266n52
Plaza de Mayo march (Argentina), 192
Polanyi, Karl, on labor as a commodity, 243

Police brutality, 36, 155, 201; in response to protest, 209, 231n45; and white supremacy, 73. *See also* Brown, Michael
Pope, James Gray, 252
Przeworski, Adam, 273
Punishment, and leniency, 37
Pussy Riot, 9, 124

Rakoff, Jed, 221
Rawls, John: and the rule of law, 24; and the standard account of civil disobedience, 11, 12, 65
Rechts Gegen Rechts, anti-Nazi fund-raising strategy, 187
Representation, 271; and protest as lobbying, 278; unequal responsiveness, 240
Resistance, 17; duties of, 61; building through protest, 68
Respectability politics, 145, 159n20
Rights: as appropriate ends of protest, 177; as *status quo* preserving, 71; extended by protest movements, 269
Rosanvallon, Pierre, 276
Rule of Law, 24, 25; applicability to victims of oppression, 52; and "preservation-through-transformation," 72

Sabl, Andrew, 31, 32
Sanctuary movement, 9, 29
Scheuerman, William, 25
Schumpeter, Joseph, 249, 256
Seattle World Trade Organization protests, 236n115
Selma envy, 168. *See also* Fiene, Hans
Sen, Amartya, 196
Sessions, Jeff, and dehumanization of immigrants, 77
Shapiro, Ian, 273
Sharp, Gene, 107; and non-violent technique, 84
Shelby, Tommie, 40n19, 50; and political obligations of the marginalized, 61
Shridharani, Krishnalal, 86, 90; critique of pacifism, 91
Singer, Peter, 23
Snowden, Edward, 9, 25, 37
Socrates, 21
Spivak, Gayatri, 158n6
Sports, and the subordination of athlete protestors, 129–131. *See also* Kaepernick, Colin
Standing Rock Sioux, and Dakota Access Pipeline protests, 210, 217
"Stand in the Gap: A Sacred Assembly of Men," 171
Stephan, Maria, 28, 108
Stop-and-frisk, 181
Suffragist movement, 9, 32. *See also* Pankhurst, Emmeline

Terry, Brandon, 50, 51, 53
Thakkar, Jonny, 41n32
Thompson, Debra, 58
Thompson, Takiya, 61
Tilly, Charles, 229n19
Trump, Donald, 45, 180, 211; character flaws, 162; comments on Charlottesville, 60, 150, 224; comments on John Lewis, 195; human rights violations, 140; opposition to dissent, 203; travel ban, 201, 212
Tufekci, Zeynep, 182–183

Unions: corruption, 265n39; demographics, 241; equalizing power, 240; organizing, 246, 255
Unlawful assembly, legal definitions of, 216, 235n101

Velasquez-Manoff, Moises, on mocking the far-right, 187

Walzer, Michael, 264n28; and level of strike participation, 265n37
Wang, Jackie, 67
Watergate, leaks by Deep Throat, 25
Waters, Maxine, 45, 46
Weber, Max, 96

Wellman, Christopher, and the duty to obey the law, 21
Whistleblowing, 23–25; justification of, 42n37. *See also* Snowden, Edward
White, Ahmed, and the US National Labor Relations Act, 252
Wolfe, Tom, 184
Women's March, 161, 273; and the innovation of satellite marches, 212; as an introduction to protest, 201; and solidarity, 196

X, Malcolm, as a foil to Martin Luther King, Jr., 182

Yanukovych, Viktor, fall from power, 279
Yiannopoulos, Milo, 177, 188, 183
Young, Iris Marion, on violence and oppression, 125

Zimring, Frank, 181
Zinn, Howard, 24

Lightning Source UK Ltd.
Milton Keynes UK
UKHW010210140220
358721UK00004B/394

9 781479 810512